# Herod the Great

e Great

*nary, Tyrant*

Gelb

ROWMAN & LITTLEFIELD PUBLISHERS, INC.
Lanham • Boulder • New York • Toronto • Plymouth, UK

Published by Rowman & Littlefield Publishers, Inc.
A wholly owned subsidary of The Rowman & Littlefield Publishing Group, Inc.
4501 Forbes Boulevard, Suite 200, Lanham, Maryland 20706
www.rowman.com

10 Thornbury Road, Plymouth PL6 7PP, United Kingdom

British Library Cataloguing in Publication Information Available

**Library of Congress Cataloging-in-Publication Data**

Gelb, Norman.
Herod the Great : statesman, visionary, tyrant / Norman Gelb.
pages cm
Includes bibliographical references and index.
TISBN 978-1-4422-1065-3 (cloth : alk. paper)—ISBN 978-1-4422-1067-7 (electronic)
1. Herod I, King of Judea, 73–4 B.C. 2. Jews—Kings and rulers—Biography. 3. Jews—History—168
B.C.–135 A.D. I. Title.
DS122.3.G45 2012
933'.05092—dc23
[B]
2012050655

Printed in the United States of America

# Herod the Great

## Statesman, Visionary, Tyrant

### Norman Gelb

ROWMAN & LITTLEFIELD PUBLISHERS, INC.

Lanham • Boulder • New York • Toronto • Plymouth, UK

Published by Rowman & Littlefield Publishers, Inc.
A wholly owned subsidary of The Rowman & Littlefield Publishing Group, Inc.
4501 Forbes Boulevard, Suite 200, Lanham, Maryland 20706
www.rowman.com

10 Thornbury Road, Plymouth PL6 7PP, United Kingdom

British Library Cataloguing in Publication Information Available

**Library of Congress Cataloging-in-Publication Data**

Gelb, Norman.
Herod the Great : statesman, visionary, tyrant / Norman Gelb.
pages cm
Includes bibliographical references and index.
TISBN 978-1-4422-1065-3 (cloth : alk. paper)—ISBN 978-1-4422-1067-7 (electronic)
1. Herod I, King of Judea, 73–4 B.C. 2. Jews—Kings and rulers—Biography. 3. Jews—History—168
B.C.–135 A.D. I. Title.
DS122.3.G45 2012
933'.05092—dc23
[B]
2012050655

Printed in the United States of America

To
Noa, Eliya, and Mica
with love

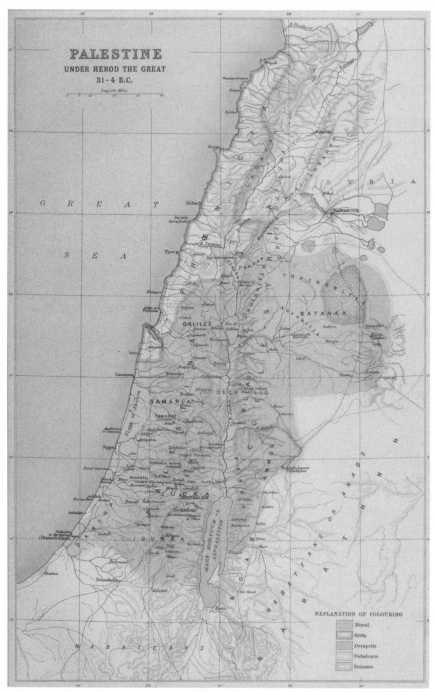

From *Atlas of the Historical Geography of the Holy Land* by George Adam Smith (London, 1915) (http://rbedrosian.com/Maps/)

# Contents

# Principal Characters

Agrippa, Marcus Vipsanius, Augustus Caesar's chief aide, friend of Herod

Agrippa I, Herod's grandson, king of Judaea (41–44 CE)

Agrippa II, Agrippa I's son, king of territories north of Judaea (48–100? CE)

Alexandra, mother of Miriamne, executed by Herod

Alexandra Salome, Queen of Judaea (76–67 BCE), mother of John Hyrcanus II and Aristobulus II

Alexander, oldest son of Herod and Miriamne, executed by his father

Antigonus Mattathias, king of Judaea (40–37 BCE), deposed by Herod and the Romans

Antipas, Herod's Idumaean grandfather, pagan convert to Judaism

Antipas II, son of Herod, tetrarch of Galilee and Peraea after Herod's death

Antipater, Herod's father and counselor to John Hyrcanus II, named procurator of Judaea by Julius Caesar

Antipater II, Herod's firstborn son, executed by his father

Archelaus, king of Cappadocia, friend of Herod, Glaphyra's father

Archelaus, son of Herod and his primary heir, tetrarch of Judaea

Aristobulus I, king of Judaea (104–103 BCE), first monarch of the Hasmonean dynasty

Aristobulus II, younger son of Alexandra Salome, challenged his brother John Hyrcanus II for the throne of Judaea, imprisoned by the Romans

Aristobulus III, younger son of Herod and Miriamne, executed by his father

Aristobulus IV, high priest, Alexandra's son, Miriamne's brother, killed by Herod

Augustus Caesar, first Roman emperor, previously called Octavian

Berenice, Herod's niece, Salome's daughter, wife of Aristobulus III, Agrippa I's mother

Costobarus, Salome's second husband, Idumaean dignitary, executed by Herod

Cyprus, Herod's mother

Cyprus II, wife of Agrippa I

Doris, Herod's first wife, mother of his firstborn son Antipater, estranged from Herod, reprieved then out of favor again

Eurycles, Spartan adventurer and provocateur

Glaphyra, wife of Herod's son Alexander, daughter of King Archelaus of Cappadocia

Herodias, wife of Galilee Tetrarch Antipas, sister of Agrippa I

John Hyrcanus I, warrior–high priest and Jewish national leader (135–104 BCE), converted Idumaeans, including Herod's grandfather, to Judaism

John Hyrcanus II, high priest and sometime king of Judaea, Miriamne's grandfather, executed by Herod

Joseph, Herod's uncle and brother-in-law, Salome's first husband, executed by Herod

Joseph, Herod's younger brother

Malchus, king of Nabataea, enemy of Herod

Malichus, assassin of Herod's father Antipater, his murder arranged by Herod

Malthace, Herod's Samaritan wife, mother of Herod's heirs Archelaus and Antipas

Mark Antony, ruler of the Roman east, Herod's patron until he was defeated by Octavian

Miriamne, Herod's second wife, executed by Herod

Nicolaus of Damascus, Herod's scholarly counselor and tutor

Octavian, Julius Caesar's heir, later called Augustus Caesar

Phaesal, Herod's older brother

Pheroras, Herod's youngest brother

Philip, Herod's son, inherits tetrarchy of northern territories after Herod's death

Quintilius Varus, Roman governor of Syria

Salome, Herod's sister

Syllaeus, prominent Nabataean, enemy of Herod

# Timeline

BCE

| | |
|---|---|
| 134–104 | High priesthood of John Hyrcanus, who conquers Idumaea for Judaea and converts its people, including Herod's grandfather Antipas, to Judaism. |
| 76–67 | Reign of Queen Alexandra Salome during which Herod's father, Antipater, becomes counselor to Hyrcanus II, her son and heir. |
| 73 | Birth of Herod. |
| 63 | Pompey storms Jerusalem. Judaea is absorbed into Roman Empire. Hyrcanus II permitted to remain high priest. Herod's father, Antipater, remains his trusted adviser. |
| 48 | Julius Caesar appoints Antipater procurator of Judaea. |
| 47 | Antipater appoints Herod governor of Galilee. Herod is tried by the Sanhedrin for exceeding his authority. He flees before a verdict is reached. |
| 46 | Sextus Caesar appoints Herod governor of Coele-Syria. |
| 45 | Birth of Herod's firstborn son, Antipater II. |
| 44 | Julius Caesar is assassinated. Octavian is revealed as his primary heir. |
| 43 | Caesar assassin Cassius appoints Herod governor of Syria. Herod's father, Antipater, is assassinated. |
| 42 | Herod is betrothed to Hasmonean princess Miriamne. Octavian and Antony defeat Caesar's assassins at Philippi and divide the Roman Empire between them. Herod vows allegiance to Antony, who appoints him and Phaesal tetrarchs of Jerusalem. |

| | |
|---|---|
| 40 | Parthians capture Jerusalem and install Antigonus as king of Judaea. Taken prisoner, Phaesal commits suicide. Herod flees to Rome where the Senate chooses him to be king of Judaea. |
| 37 | Herod helps Antony overcome military stalemate at the Euphrates. He marries Miriamne. Roman legions help Herod conquer Jerusalem and seize the throne of Judaea. He has Antigonus executed. |
| 35 | Herod appoints Miriamne's young brother Aristobulus high priest, then has him drowned. |
| 32 | Roman civil war between Octavian and Antony. Herod triumphant in war with Nabataea. |
| 31 | Octavian defeats Antony and Cleopatra in battle at Actium and becomes master of the Roman Empire. Herod executes Hyrcanus II. |
| 30 | Herod vows allegiance to Octavian, who confirms him king of Judaea. Antony and Cleopatra commit suicide. |
| 29 | Herod executes Miriamne. |
| 27 | Octavian becomes Emperor Augustus Caesar. |
| 23 | Herod's young sons Alexander and Aristobulus are sent to be educated in Rome. |
| 20 | Herod starts rebuilding the Jerusalem temple. |
| 17 | Alexander and Aristobulus return from Rome. |
| 14 | Herod reconciles himself with his estranged firstborn son, Antipater, who persuades him to suspect Alexander and Aristobulus of disloyalty. |
| 12 | Herod brings Alexander and Aristobulus to Italy to be judged by Augustus. They are reconciled, but Antipater is named Herod's primary heir. |
| 10 | Building of Caesarea completed. Alexander and Aristobulus are imprisoned on suspicion of again plotting against Herod. |
| 9 | Herod invades Nabataea, infuriating Augustus. |
| 8 | Herod is reconciled with Augustus. |

| | |
|---|---|
| 7 | Herod executes Alexander and Aristobulus. |
| 5 | Herod has son Antipater imprisoned. |
| 4 | Antipater is executed. Herod dies. Unrest erupts in the kingdom. Augustus divides Judaea between Herod's heirs. Archelaus is appointed ethnarch of Judaea. |

## CE

| | |
|---|---|
| 6 | Augustus removes Archelaus from office and banishes him. First Roman procurator appointed to administer Judaea from Caesarea. |
| 33 (ca.) | Crucifixion of Jesus. |
| 40 | Claudius appoints Agrippa I king of Judaea. |
| 43 | Agrippa I dies. |
| 48 | Claudius appoints Agrippa II king of Chalcis and custodian of the Jerusalem temple. |
| 53 | Territories northeast of Judaea are added to Agrippa II's kingdom. |
| 66–70 | Jewish war with Rome culminating in Judaea's defeat. The destruction of the temple and the end of the ancient Jewish nation. |
| 100 (ca.) | Agrippa II dies, ending the Herodian dynasty. |

# Preface

The man who came to be known as Herod the Great was a figure of phenomenal achievement. He was an Arab who became king of the Jews. He founded a royal dynasty and transformed his strife-ridden land into an orderly, thriving, modernizing state. He conferred on the kingdom of Judaea an international significance and successfully navigated his way through perilous interactions with superpower luminaries.

He was a builder of new cities for his nation and a promoter of state-of-the-art urban renewal for its existing ones. He magnificently rebuilt the temple in Jerusalem, the long-neglected heart and center of his religion and the religion of his subjects. Its "Wailing Wall" is still an attraction for pilgrims and tourists. Through imaginative agricultural and commercial programs, he strengthened his kingdom's floundering economy. At times of drought and famine that periodically afflicted his realm, he tapped his personal resources to help the needy.

He was also an international philanthropist who undertook public service projects in other countries as well as his own. He had aqueducts, temples, markets, colonnades, theaters, and roads built in cities from Damascus to Athens, enhancing the character of many of them and embellishing their appearance. He rescued the ancient Olympic Games from possibly terminal collapse and was named its president for life.

Herod was greatly valued by the rulers of the vast and powerful Roman Empire of which Judaea was a minute part. He was their instrument for achieving and maintaining peace and order in that strategically important land bridge between Asia and Africa. During power struggles involving such figures as Augustus Caesar, Mark Antony, and Cleopatra, he managed to sustain Judaea's self-rule, self-interest, and security by shifting his allegiance when advisable and making himself useful to the side that came out on top, balancing his service to Rome with his efforts on behalf of his kingdom, his subjects, and himself.

He built a disciplined army and a navy and assisted in ancient Rome's military operations on occasion, once far from Judaea's own shores. He was a skilled military commander and a brave soldier, an excellent horseman and a skilled archer. He was clever, innovative, and accomplished.

Nevertheless, Herod is most known for a totally different aspect of his character and the character of his long reign. He was a brutal, ruthless, vindictive, and dangerously high-strung tyrant. He was ceaselessly convinced conspiracies were being mounted to destroy him and transformed his kingdom into a police state to uncover and crush them. He banned people from meeting in groups, dispatched police spies among them, and required loyalty oaths from them. He had large numbers of his subjects killed for real or imagined disloyalty or dissent or because he feared they might somehow pose a threat to him. Among his victims were three of his own sons, the wife he loved most, and a high priest of the holy temple in Jerusalem. He was said to have ordered the slaughter of all infant boys in Bethlehem when told that a new king of the Jews—Jesus Christ—had been born there. The depth of his morbid insecurity led him finally to the brink of insanity.

From Herod's first appearance as a public figure until his death, he was scorned by the people of Judaea as an interloper, an outsider unwelcome in their midst, though he was as much a Jew as they were. His grandfather, an Arab tribal leader in Idumaea south of Judaea, had been converted to Judaism before Herod was born, and Herod's father became a highly capable administrator of Judaea, the second-most senior figure in the Jewish hierarchy of the land.

Nevertheless, Herod's spectacular rebuilding of their cherished temple, his religious observances, and his beautification of holy Jerusalem failed to convince his subjects that this Arab of pagan ancestry fully shared their religious identity. They had not chosen him to be their king. Nor had he been chosen by the priests of the temple, nor through dynastic succession, nor by God. It was the Romans who had appointed him king of the Jews. Roman legions had been required to help him storm Jerusalem and seize the crown from a popular monarch whom he had then had killed.

Though Herod initially had to struggle to attain and keep his crown, his long reign was never convincingly challenged once he was safely on the throne. However, even after he had grown old and was mortally ill, he feverishly sought to uncover and smash plots against him. He suffered severe physical as well as mental distress during his last days. But agony from a variety of ailments and awareness of the imminence of his death did nothing to moderate his vindictiveness. Knowing his subjects would shed few tears at his demise, he devised a horrific plan to make certain people would mark the occasion in mourning and grief rather than jubilation.

Yet this was a monarch whose reign was marked by bold, original, and laudable insights and perspectives. On a scale of performance by kings and other overlords in the ancient world, his positive achievements may be considered to have outweighed his brutality and tyrannical rule.

When Herod died, his kingdom's lengthy experience of peace and order collapsed into violence and turmoil almost immediately. The ancient nation of the Jews began spiraling toward catastrophe and obliteration. Another two thousand years passed before it would be revived as the modern state of Israel.

This study is meant not only to tell the story of Herod but also to modify the persisting one-dimensional negative image of a monarch who, despite his failings, was a constructive and fascinating historical figure.

\* \* \*

The writings of a number of ancient historians provide insight into the world in which Herod lived and functioned. Among them are Plutarch, Strabo, Suetonius, and Cassius Dio. But the writings of historian Flavius Josephus, who was born some forty years after Herod died, are the indispensable source for understanding Herod's life and times.

# Introduction

## The Making of Herod the Great

*Two nations are in your womb. Two separate peoples shall issue from your body.*

—Genesis 25:23

As foretold, Rebekah, the pregnant wife of the biblical patriarch Isaac and daughter-in-law of the arch-patriarch Abraham, gave birth to twins, Jacob and Esau. The twins grew up together in the land of Canaan but later led lives remote from each other.

In due course, Jacob had twelve sons who became the founders of the twelve ancient tribes of the Jews. Over time, those tribes coalesced into the nation of Israel, precursor of its present-day namesake.

When fully grown, Jacob's brother Esau migrated southward with a large family of his own and settled in the land of Edom between the Dead Sea and the Gulf of Aqaba. It was the place where Herod the Great would be born some two thousand years later.

The Bible says Edom was already a nation when the Jews were still only a cluster of tribes fleeing oppression in Egypt. The king of the Edomites denied those tribes—Jacob's descendants—passage across his territory to their divinely promised land. They had to go roundabout in search of their destiny. That act of obstruction would prove characteristic of the strained dealings between the Jews and Edomites during the long span of time in which their nations existed side by side.

The ethnic identity of the ancient Edomites is hard to pin down. If the Bible account of the twin brothers is true, they and the Jews could not have been more closely linked genetically at first. But successive migrations of peoples—because of famine, war, or invasion—were part of the history and changing demography of the region. Migrating tribes from Arabia and from Nabataea, the ancient Arab kingdom east and south of the Dead Sea, had begun establishing a significant presence in Edom at least five hundred years before Herod appeared on the scene. Over time, their influence on the ethnic makeup of its inhabitants grew dominant. The well-traveled Greek geographer Strabo, a contemporary of Herod, observed, "[t]he Idumaeans are Nabataeans" who had split off from Nabataea.

A succession of superpowers—including the Assyrians, Babylonians, and Persians—dominated the Middle East in ancient times. Sometimes, their rulers involved themselves directly in the affairs of the lands of the Jews and the Edomites. At other times, they required only tacit submission from them.

Alexander the Great of Macedon conquered the Middle East from the Persians in the fourth century BCE and, like his predecessors, changed the course of its history. He and his Macedonian cohorts brought with them the Hellenic ways and influences of their homeland's Greek culture. The Persians had called the land of the Jews Yahud, a shortened form of the ancient Jewish tribal name Yahudah (Judah). The region's new Hellenic masters called it Judaea, the Greek transliteration of Yahud.

After Alexander died, two of his senior officers eventually emerged as his heirs in the Middle East, dividing the region between them. Seleucus Nicator ruled Syria and lands to the east while Ptolemy Soter (the ancestor of the famous Cleopatra) was ruler of Egypt. Judaea became a contested province in the borderland between them, eventually ruled by descendants of Seleucus.

In 168 BCE, Antiochus Epiphanes, Seleucid king of Syria, reacted angrily to a revolt by traditionalist Jews in Judaea who objected to the spread of Hellenization in their land. Deciding he'd had enough of what he considered the primitive ways and beliefs of his non-Hellenized Jewish subjects, Antiochus launched a campaign to fully Hellenize Judaea. Circumcision was outlawed, as were other Jewish rituals and observances. Many Jews clinging to their faith were killed. The Jerusalem temple was rededicated to Zeus.

In the town of Modin, not far from Jerusalem, the draconian clampdown sparked a violent act of resistance. Mattathias, a local priest, ordered by a Syrian officer to make an animal sacrifice to a pagan deity, refused and killed the officer. He then fled into the nearby hills and urged others to join him in resisting the Syrians.

The elderly Mattathias soon died, but his defiance was the catalyst for a Jewish national liberation movement. Led by Mattathias's son Judah and Judah's four brothers, who came to be known as the Maccabees, the uprising against Syrian rule was as much a cultural as a religious struggle—traditional Judaism versus the pagan Hellenism to which Antiochus had been trying to force the Jews to conform. Three years after the incident in Modin, after a sequence of ups and downs, a Maccabee-led guerrilla army entered Jerusalem in triumph. The reconsecration of the temple is still celebrated as the annual Jewish holiday of Chanukah.

But the victory was temporary, and the struggle went on. The Maccabee forces suffered great losses. The Maccabee brothers fell one by one in their struggle for national independence until Simon, the last of them, consolidated victory over the Syrians. By the time he died in 143 BCE—assassinated by his son-in-law in an abortive power grab—Judaea had become a fully independent state where, supposedly, "every man sat under his vine and his fig tree, with no one to disturb him."

Simon's son John Hyrcanus donned his father's mantle as high priest of the Jews and national leader. Hyrcanus was a soldierly figure who took on the reinvigorated Syrians. He ultimately bettered them in battle and, through his conquests, made the Jewish nation almost as large and as formidable as it had been during the days of King Solomon eight centuries earlier. Among Hyrcanus's conquests was Edom, by then commonly known by its Hellenized name Idumaea. Its pagan Arab inhabitants, including Herod the Great's grandfather Antipas, were converted to Judaism.

When Hyrcanus died, his oldest son Aristobulus declared himself king of the Jews, becoming the first to wear their crown since the Babylonians had conquered their land more than five hundred years before. In proclaiming himself king, Aristobulus founded the Hasmonean dynasty of the Jews, named after Hasmon, an otherwise largely forgotten ancestor of the Maccabees. The Hasmoneans would later feature prominently in Herod's rise to power.

Aristobulus reigned only briefly, succumbing to illness after wearing the crown little more than one year. Upon his death, his widow, Alexandra Salome, married one of his brothers, Alexander Jannai, the second Hasmonean to wear the crown of the Jews. When Jannai died after ruling Judaea for twenty-seven years, twice-widowed Queen Alexandra mounted the Hasmonean throne to succeed him.

Fifty-two monarchs ruled the Jews in ancient time, but only two were women who wore the crown in their own right. Alexandra was one of them. The other, Athalia, had been queen seven centuries earlier. But unlike Athalia, who had usurped the throne from her grandson, the rightful heir, and who had been abominated by her subjects, Alexandra was an enormously popular figure. Her achievements as monarch included establishing legal protection for divorced and widowed women in Judaea—the origin of the concept of alimony. During her reign, Judaea was mostly at peace with its neighbors and within itself. But there was conflict within Alexandra's family.

It is with that conflict that the story of Herod the Great begins.

*    *    *

By the time Alexandra had donned the Hasmonean crown, the Jewish nation had become firmly established as a power among the small states of the Middle East. It boasted a strong army and a firmly established monarchy with a large royal court and a privileged aristocracy.

The previous Hasmonean monarchs had also taken on the role of high priest of the Jews. Barred as a woman from doing the same, Alexandra appointed her lackluster older son, John Hyrcanus II, to that position. If he had been a more spirited figure, Hyrcanus probably would have become king when his father, King Jannai, died. But his strong-minded mother had easily upstaged him, though, with the land at peace and Judaea respected by its neighbors, she had no qualms about choosing uninspiring Hyrcanus to be the heir to her throne.

However, Alexandra's younger, more dynamic son, Aristobulus II, had his own eye on the crown. He also had developed a strategy for acquiring it in place of his brother. Aristobulus's plan was based on the rivalry between the major Jewish religious sects, the Pharisees and the Sadducees.

The Sadducees were conservative in their religious beliefs. They held that the rules that governed Jewish religious life were specifically contained in the Torah and only there. Those written rules were not to be open to extraneous interpretation or elaboration or to the influence of oral tradition handed down from times past. The most prominent Sadducees were the elite of Judaean society, the senior priesthood, the wealthy, and the socially prominent. They adjusted most readily to Hellenizing ways, including the use of the Greek language, while most Judaeans clung to Aramaic and/or Hebrew.

Unlike the Sadducees, their Pharisee rivals saw religious belief as an intensely personal and passionate matter for each individual. They, too, considered the Torah central to Jewish life but maintained it did not stand alone in being worthy of reverence. They held that interpretation of holy scriptures by sages and scholars and perceptions handed down orally through the ages were also central to Jewish faith and experience.

Theirs was a response to the vagueness of Torah law on such details as how to observe the Sabbath and what was virtuous and what was not. Unlike the Sadducees, Pharisees believed in an afterlife that featured rewards for virtue and punishment for wickedness, though it was not so defined in the Torah. They believed in angels as God's messengers and allowed that a Messiah would appear among the Jews to prepare the way for God's kingdom on Earth. Considering themselves the guardians of the faith and Jewish heritage, the Pharisees rejected Hellenic influences. Their following among the common people was far greater than that of the Sadducees.

The Essenes composed a third, very much smaller and less influential, religious grouping. They lived in non-Hellenized, all-male monastic communities and devoted themselves almost exclusively to prayer and religious study while awaiting the Messiah whose arrival they believed to be imminent.

The Sadducees and the Pharisees challenged each other in seeking to influence the religious, political, and social leadership of the land, and each sought to eliminate the clout of the other. Famous for her piety, Queen Alexandra strongly favored the Pharisees. Their most senior figure was her brother, recently returned with others from Egypt to which they had fled before Alexandra had become ruling queen to escape Sadducee persecution. With her backing, they removed Sadducees from the positions of authority and sway they had acquired in the land, assumed their place, and avenged themselves for earlier Sadducee ill treatment.

Aristobulus saw the conflict between the two sects as the instrument for his elevation to the throne of the Jews despite Alexandra's preference for his older brother. He became the champion of the ousted and persecuted Sadducees. Annoyed with his contrariness, Alexandra sidelined him at court. But though she favored Hyrcanus, Aristobulus enjoyed the patronage of senior figures who had been intimates of his deceased father, Alexander Jannai. They were dismayed by how the Sadducees, with whom they had been allied when Jannai was king, were being hounded by the Pharisees. With their support, Aristobulus extracted Alexandra's permission to establish sanctuaries in some of Judaea's outlying towns where Sadducee refugees would be safe from harassment by their Pharisee antagonists.

Alarmed, the Pharisees warned Alexandra that Aristobulus was building a sinister power base. Now seventy-three years old and weary, and the nation secure and in good order, she refused to believe the problem was urgent. But when she died, Aristobulus activated the support he had nurtured in Sadducee strongholds and recruited an army of mercenaries to help him win the crown from his newly enthroned older brother.

Hyrcanus fought back against his power grab with the forces that fell under his command when their mother died. But he was not an inspirational leader, nor was he overjoyed being saddled with the burdens of monarchy. After his army suffered an early defeat, he decided the privileged position of brother-of-the-king would serve him well enough in Jerusalem, and he obligingly handed the crown over to forceful Aristobulus.

Much might have turned out differently if the situation had been resolved that way, if Aristobulus, having elbowed the accommodating Hyrcanus aside, had remained unchallenged king of the Jews. But another figure entered the equation and transformed it. His name was Antipater, and his main claim to historical significance was to have been the father of Herod the Great and the one who set him on the road to eminence.

Antipater was a remarkable personality in his own right. He was an Arab from Idumaea, the land south of Judaea that had been conquered and annexed by warrior–high priest Hyrcanus I, under whom its pagan inhabitants had been converted to Judaism. As noted above, among those inhabitants and converts had been Antipater's father, Antipas, Herod's grandfather. Antipas had been an Idumaean tribal leader. In recognition of his rank and influence, and to discourage rebelliousness once Idumaea had become a province of Judaea, Hyrcanus I had appointed him its governor. When Antipas died, young Antipater inherited his father's rank and position, confirmed in them by Queen Alexandra.

The new governor of Idumaea was both ambitious and audacious. His son Herod would learn much from him. Antipater was also very rich. His wealth was based on extensive inherited and acquired property holdings, the huge herds of livestock he owned, and revenue from the caravan trade routes running through Idumaea to and from Arabia. The role of mere provincial administrator was not enough to satisfy his aspirations.

Charming and lavish with his gifts and attentions, he cultivated the friendship of rulers and other notables of the small nations and city-states of the region. He chose his wife, Cyprus, Herod's mother, from a distinguished family in Nabataea, boosting his already influential Arab connections.

Antipater was so highly regarded in the region that he was trusted to negotiate disputes between its prominent figures. Most significantly, he inserted himself into the quarrels, conspiracies, and power struggles that characterized the jockeying for position among the aristocrats and hangers-on at the Hasmonean royal court of Queen Alexandra in Jerusalem.

In particular, he befriended Hyrcanus II and maneuvered himself into being his adviser and confidant when the docile young prince appeared destined to succeed his mother as ruler of Judaea. Having attained that promising position, Antipater was appalled when, having been crowned king of Judaea upon his mother's death, Hyrcanus blithely surrendered the crown to his assertive younger brother. He had imagined himself about to become the gray eminence behind the throne of the malleable figure whose friendship and trust he had cultivated. He had pictured himself enjoying considerable influence at a time when Judaea was a force to be reckoned with in the region.

But there was no future in being attached to someone who was fundamentally uninterested in even the semblance of power. Besides, Antipater realized that having been closely identified with the downgraded ex-king, he was dangerously exposed. He had to do something to protect himself and restore his prospects. The backbone of the weak-willed abdicator had to be stiffened.

It was not easy to achieve. By nature, Hyrcanus shied away from conflict. He rejected Antipater's urgings that he fight to reclaim his royal birthright. The only resolve he displayed was in his refusal to do so. He was roused to action, finally, only when Antipater convinced him his abdication was tantamount to suicide. He explained to him that as his mother's ousted but legitimate successor, his usurping brother would see his very existence as a threat. It would be an ongoing potential challenge that Aristobulus would feel compelled to extinguish. Fratricide in ruling families was not uncommon in the region. Even King Solomon had considered it prudent to kill his half brother Adonijah, who, instead of himself, had earlier been regarded as heir to the throne of their father, David.

Finally accepting that his life could really be on the line, Hyrcanus bowed to Antipater's urgings that he flee from Jerusalem to Petra, the capital of neighboring Nabataea. Antipater had already made the necessary arrangements for his safety with Nabataean king Aretas III, with whom he had good relations, and also for safety there for himself, his wife, and his five children—his sons Phaesal, Herod, Joseph, and Pheroras and his daughter Salome.

But finding a permanent refuge in another land for the wimpish ex-king was hardly the adroit Antipater's end goal. Despite Hyrcanus's wish for a quiet life, he coaxed him back into the fight for his lost crown, assuring him that an irresistible force would pave his path back to power. For a suitable gratuity arranged by Antipater—including the promise of the return of twelve border towns that Hyrcanus's Hasmonean forbears had taken from the Nabataeans—King Aretas provided an army of fifty thousand Arab fighters to help Hyrcanus retrieve his crown from Aristobulus.

It crossed into Judaea where it was reinforced by Jewish units loyal to Queen Alexandra's chosen heir. This combined force outmatched the army Aristobulus was able to field, and he was driven back to Jerusalem and put under siege. Guided by Antipater, Hyrcanus now was set to regain the crown he had timorously relinquished, and he would have done so if a formidable external force had not thrust itself into the situation.

The Romans had arrived with their battle-hardened legions and changed everything, as they often did. The legions of this latest in the succession of devouring superpowers to dominate the ancient Middle East was about to turn Judaea into one of its client states. The Romans would decide who would rule it on their behalf.

The Roman commander Pompey the Great (Gnaeus Pompeius Magnus) was already a celebrated figure. He had obliterated what had remained of the Spartacus slave uprising in Italy, he had eradicated a plague of pirates in the eastern Mediterranean, and he had just finished crushing resistance to Rome's supremacy in Asia Minor. He was on his way to becoming the most commanding figure in Roman affairs.

If, before the Romans became involved, Hyrcanus had ignored Antipater's urgings and persisted in his willingness to surrender his crown to

Aristobulus, Pompey might well have permitted the grasping younger brother to remain king of Judaea, with his client kingdom enjoying a measure of self-rule. The Romans tended to allow existing leaders of the lands they absorbed into their empire to remain in place if they bowed to Rome's supreme authority and paid the required taxes on time. Such local luminaries were normally retained either as subservient rulers with some leeway for independent action in domestic affairs or as figureheads for direct Roman rule. It was less complicated than putting someone unfamiliar with local conditions in charge and caused less upheaval.

But the mighty Romans appeared on the scene when the crown of the Jews seemed up for grabs. Both Hyrcanus, again egged on by Antipater, and Aristobulus appealed to Pompey to back their claims to the throne. But strong-willed Aristobulus stood no chance. Pompey quickly recognized him as unlikely to be as submissive to Rome as he would like. But Hyrcanus was also denied the crown. Pompey let him retain only the position of high priest of a land reduced in size. Judaea was stripped of much of the territory the Hasmonean forebears of the feuding brothers had conquered and annexed. Gaza, Joppa (Jaffa), and other cities were made free again, subject to the guardianship of the Damascus-based Roman governor of Syria. So recently a power in the region, Judaea was effectively reduced to the status of a province of Roman Syria. The rivalry between Queen Alexandra's sons had been a disaster for the land of the Jews.

Aristobulus was arrested for his defiant stance and would soon be shipped off to Rome as a prisoner. But supporters of his entrenched in Jerusalem refused to accept the way things had worked out, and Pompey was compelled to take the city by force. It proved a long and bloody operation; the completion of which, in 63 BCE, marked the end of independence for the Jewish nation in ancient times. From then on, its fate would be influenced by whatever transpired in the leadership of the Roman Empire.

Pompey crowned his victory in Jerusalem with a visit to the temple. He expected to find its most sacred chamber, the Holy of Holies, to which only the high priest was permitted access once a year, on the Day of Atonement (Yom Kippur), lined with treasure. Instead, he found the Holy of Holies to be devoid of riches and virtually empty aside from a Torah. The Ark of the Covenant, that had once been housed there, was believed to have disappeared when the Babylonians had leveled Jerusalem centuries earlier. The Jews considered Pompey's incursion on such hallowed ground to be a scandalous violation. But it was also proof of how profoundly Judaea had been humbled.

Antipater was sorely disappointed by Hyrcanus's failure to emerge as king from the events he had so assiduously tried to manipulate. He also regretted the loss of Judaea's independence and its demotion from ranking position in the region. But he grasped instinctively that it was unwise and futile to challenge the might of Rome. He understood and accepted that the power game in the region had undergone fundamental transformation.

Despite the changed circumstances, he reckoned his personal standing in the region continued to reside with his association with Hyrcanus, who, as high priest and senior Hasmonean figure, was still highly respected by the people of Judaea and was, at least nominally, their leader. Remaining Hyrcanus's trusted adviser, he figured it was best to settle for what little was on offer for the moment and hope for advantageous opportunities to emerge as things worked themselves out. Meanwhile, he looked for ways the altered situation could best be exploited. Herod, ten years old at the time of the arrival of the Romans, would fail to inherit from his father that capacity for patience and self-control.

In the following years, Antipater maintained close contact with the officials of the Roman governor in Damascus and did what he could to make himself useful. The Romans may have sidelined Hyrcanus, but his sharp-witted majordomo gradually evolved into the figure who could make things happen for them in Judaea and elsewhere in the region.

When Roman units ran short of supplies while stumbling across an Arabian desert wasteland in one of their exploratory operations, he arranged for them to be supplied with food and water from Judaea and facilitated their unruffled passage through Judaean border positions. To their mutual advantage, he smoothly negotiated the settlement of a dispute between Rome and the Nabataean Arabs that could have led to a costly war. Enormously wealthy, he personally guaranteed the huge bribe the Nabataeans promised the Romans not to be overrun.

Antipater was a pragmatist first and foremost. The situation being what it was, his prime loyalty was to the Romans rather than to his fellow Jews. When Alexander Maccabeus, the son of exiled and imprisoned failed usurper Aristobulus, stirred a major Jewish uprising against Roman rule, he arranged for Judaean troops to assist the Romans in crushing it. During that affair, he cultivated the friendship of young Roman officer Mark Antony, who later would play an important role in his son Herod's rise to power.

The Romans never greatly prized High Priest Hyrcanus, their supposed instrument for dutifully administering Judaea. But as the years passed, the services performed for them by his adviser and confidant helped the land rebound from the diminished circumstances to which Pompey had reduced it. A Roman governor of Syria was said to have "settled the government [of Judaea] as Antipater would have it." Gradually, the domestic self-rule that the Jewish nation had been denied since the days of Queen Alexandra was restored.

In the meantime, things were developing across the Mediterranean that would have a profound bearing on Judaea, on Antipater's personal fortunes, and on those of his family. Rome had been suffering unsettling bouts of political intrigue in which rival figures competed bitterly while their partisans clashed bloodily in the streets of the city. Celebrated for his military achievements in outposts of the empire, Pompey had become a central actor on the stormy stage at home. But Gaius Julius Caesar had also been growing in fame and popularity through his military triumphs, notably in Gaul, and through his crowd-pleasing activities in the capital. In time, circumstances made it appear advisable for Caesar and Pompey to become allies rather than remain rivals in the leadership of the Roman Republic. Their partnership was seemingly sealed when Pompey married Caesar's daughter, Julia.

But the alliance between those two towering egos was destined to be ephemeral. It collapsed when Julia died and Pompey received almost dictatorial powers from the Roman Senate because of its concern about Caesar's growing popularity. The alliance between the two collapsed altogether when the Senate, dominated by Pompey's supporters, moved to rein in the assertive Caesar by declaring him a public enemy and ordering him removed from command of his legions.

Caesar defiantly responded to this challenge by crossing the Rubicon River dividing Cisalpine Gaul from Italy proper with a legion of his troops. In doing so, he seriously exceeded his authority and was, in effect, threatening to march on Rome. Pompey called it treason. Civil war became inevitable.

Pompey was at a disadvantage. Most of the legions loyal to him were on duty in Spain or in the east. He had no option but to abandon the capital where the reduced Senate—its Pompey-backing senators having fled—granted Caesar dictatorial powers as he advanced on the city. Pompey would have to regroup his legions elsewhere to take on his relentless rival. He ultimately concentrated the bulk of his forces in Greece and prepared for a showdown. Caesar did the same.

The outcome of their looming clash was certain to have momentous consequences throughout the empire and threatened to be a catastrophe for Antipater and Hyrcanus in Jerusalem. They had, in effect, been functioning as administrators of Judaea under the patronage of the Roman governor of Syria, who was a Pompey loyalist. They also came under threat from Hyrcanus's brother and adversary Aristobulus II, who had been wasting away in a Roman prison for having challenged Pompey's decision to deny him the crown of the Jews. Caesar released him from confinement and offered him the support of two legions and logistical backing to seize Judaea for him from Pompey's adherents. Success for Aristobulus would mean doom for Antipater and Hyrcanus. But Pompey supporters managed to poison him before he could get far into his mission.

However the fate of Antipater and Hyrcanus still appeared to depend on the outcome of the face-off between the armies of Caesar and Pompey at Pharsalus in Greece. Though Pompey's army was stronger, Caesar's troops were more battle hardened, and his generalship proved superior. Trounced, Pompey fled to Egypt to seek refuge from Ptolemy XIII, the thirteen-year-old Egyptian king who had been under his protection. Caesar went in hot pursuit to finish him off. But he arrived in Alexandria to discover that the man who had become his mortal enemy had been murdered. Fearing the prospect of ending up on the losing side in this Roman civil war, the advisers of young Ptolemy had obligingly arranged for a boat to be sent to take Pompey ashore from his ship off Alexandria and, less obligingly, for him to be stabbed to death as he stepped onto Egyptian soil.

In Jerusalem, Antipater realized immediately what jeopardy he was in. For almost two decades, he had been a faithful and useful flunky for the Pompey-supporting governors of Syria. It was now possible, even likely, that Caesar, whom the Senate would soon declare dictator for life, would punish him because of the loyalty and service with which he had provided the enemy camp. All he had so diligently achieved for his advancement could be wiped out. Even his personal safety was at risk. He sent his family, including Herod, off to Nabataea to sit out the turn of events in safety. But never resigned to a dismal fate, he quickly found a way not only to salvage his career but also to greatly enhance his prospects.

In Caesar's hurry to reach Egypt to crush whatever remained of the threat Pompey had posed to him, he had impulsively stumbled into a situation that could wreck his rise to supreme power in Rome. It might even cost him his life. He had arrived in Alexandria with only four thousand troops at a time of unrest there. The dead Pompey was no longer a threat, but a smoldering struggle for power was in progress between Queen Cleopatra and King Ptolemy, her boy brother-husband. Caesar's effort to insert himself into the situation aroused bitterness among the Egyptians. So had his triumphant entry into Alexandria, his requisitioning of its royal palace as his command post, and his taking control of its harbor. It was as if he had come to claim Egypt for Rome, which was not far from his thoughts now that his clash with Pompey had brought him to its shores. It was an immensely rich land, and he was very short of funds.

But Alexandria was a huge, proud city and did not readily take this presumptuous swaggerer to its heart. That did not overly bother Caesar. His immediate interests were raising money, facilitating the shipment of grain supplies to Italy to bolster his standing there, and deciding whether to choose Cleopatra or young Ptolemy to rule Rome's Egyptian protectorate on his behalf. Officers who served under young Ptolemy controlled access to the palace, but Caesar wished to see Cleopatra, who was known to be enormously wealthy, before deciding which of the two to favor. She wanted to see him as well and took it upon herself to find a way to evade Ptolemy's guards to do so. She had herself rolled in a length of strong fabric (a rug, according to legend) and delivered secretly into his presence.

The twenty-one-year-old queen quickly captivated the fifty-two-year-old soldier with her youthful vitality and charm, depriving Ptolemy of any chance of winning Caesar's favor. But the officer commanding the boy-king's army refused to accept defeat. He advanced on Alexandria with twenty thousand men to seize command of the situation. The comparatively small Roman contingent with which Caesar had arrived was in danger of being overwhelmed. His troops had to barricade the area around the palace and engage in hand-to-hand fighting to protect him.

They managed to fight off an enemy attempt to cut his supply line by seizing the harbor, but the situation remained perilous for him. He desperately needed help. Antipater in Jerusalem, anxious to find a way into his good graces, hurried to provide it.

Resourceful as always, he arranged to provide the Romans in Egypt with the supplies and funds they desperately needed. At the same time, he facilitated the movement of distant but essential troop reinforcements for Caesar by working through his network of regional contacts. He also personally led three thousand troops from Judaea as part of the rescue-Caesar operation and called upon Hyrcanus's revered status as high priest to persuade communities of Egyptian Jews, especially a long-established Jewish military colony in the Nile delta, not to oppose the embattled Roman leader.

Reinforced and supplied, Caesar emerged from the peril he had muddled into with his position as master of Rome and all its dominions firmly established. Boy-king Ptolemy had drowned while trying to escape capture. Egypt, under Queen Cleopatra, now effectively belonged to Rome, though it would not be officially deemed a Roman client state for more than another decade.

After his triumph, Caesar chose to linger on in Egypt for several months. He and Cleopatra took a leisurely cruise down the Nile as far as Ethiopia, during which he savored her favors and fathered a son by her, a new Ptolemy, nicknamed Caesareon.

Grateful for the help he had received from Antipater, and impressed by the skill with which he had gone about providing it, Caesar was as persuaded as Pompey had earlier been that the Idumaean could be relied upon to serve his and Rome's interests. The physical wounds Antipater personally sustained leading Jewish units that had rushed to Caesar's rescue when he was trapped in Alexandria seemed to testify to that.

He appointed Antipater procurator of Judaea, to serve as the representative of Rome's authority there. He was also awarded Roman citizenship—a treasured prize—as were his son Herod and other members of his family.

Caesar's reward for Hyrcanus was less grand. Since Antipater was now procurator of his land, it would have been a sham for him to be named its king despite the reverence with which this most eminent surviving Hasmonean was popularly held. Instead, he was appointed ethnarch of Judaea (leader of the people), and his status as high priest of the

Jews was confirmed. However, all pretenses that Antipater was Hyrcanus's subordinate had evaporated. The reverse was now manifestly true.

Caesar's appreciation for Antipater's help at a difficult moment also proved a boon for Judaea. He had parts of the territories Pompey had trimmed from it restored, and as a sign of trust, permission was granted for the walls of Jerusalem, which Pompey had torn down, to be rebuilt to protect the city against marauders and invasion.

Jews throughout Rome's empire also benefited from Caesar's gratitude. They were exempted from the ban on exotic religious cults that were deemed by the Senate to be superstitious and potentially troublesome, and their civil rights were recognized by law wherever Roman writ ran. They were permitted to maintain independent judicial councils in their communities, even beyond the borders of Judaea, and were also excused from obligatory military service because it might clash with their observance of their Sabbath. All of this because of Antipater.

Though Caesar chose not to restore the crown of Judaea to Hyrcanus, most Judaeans still considered this descendant of the revered Maccabee brothers to be their king and legitimate successor to the earlier monarchs of the Hasmonean dynasty. He had what passed for a royal court to prove it.

Hasmonean loyalists in Jerusalem resented the procuratorial executive status to which Antipater had been raised, but he remained Hyrcanus's trusted confidant and adviser. Though effectively ruler of Judaea on behalf of Rome, he preferred to govern behind the scenes, shunning public attention and treating Hyrcanus with the respect and consideration due to a king and a Hasmonean blueblood.

That did not prevent Antipater from further upstaging him and additionally offending the Hasmonean loyalists. To the dismay and disquiet of many Judaeans, he proceeded to make the administration of the land a family matter. He named his oldest son, Phaesal, governor of Jerusalem, and he dispatched Phaesal's younger brother Herod to be governor of the often-turbulent northern region of Galilee. It was there, at the age of twenty-five, that Herod started along the path that would lead him to the throne, great achievement, and enduring notoriety.

# ONE
## Beginnings

No warm welcome awaited Herod when he arrived in Galilee to assume command there and start on his rise to power. A prickly, often rebellious people, proud of their upland geographical remoteness, the Galileans had always been wary of outsiders. That this young Idumaean had been made their governor was additionally provocative because it was his father, Antipater, the Roman-appointed procurator of Judaea, who had chosen him to be their overseer. Having been converted to Judaism within the previous four generations, the Galileans retained the zeal of converts and considered both father and son to be little more than Roman lackeys.

Herod further stirred their hostility soon after arriving by showing himself to be a supremely confident, imperious, brutal enforcer despite his youth and lack of previous command responsibility. He chose to demonstrate his freshly acquired authority by dealing firmly with the problem of lawlessness.

A band of Galileans, led by a certain Hezekiah, had been wreaking havoc in neighboring Syrian border towns to the fury of Sextus Caesar, the Roman governor of Syria. Determined to end their raids, Herod hunted Hezekiah down and executed him and some of his followers.

Those raiders had not been without support among their fellow Galileans, who had little sympathy for their victims and besides believed the disputed towns were part of Galilee rather than Roman Syria. But in killing Hezekiah and his men, Herod earned Sextus's gratitude and admiration. It was more valuable to him than the local popularity he was denied, that denial bothering him not at all.

Sextus's approval was no small prize. As governor of Syria, he had substantial gifts at his disposal, and as a cousin and friend of Julius Caesar, who had recently been formally proclaimed dictator of Rome and all its dominions, his patronage could lead to even greater benefits.

Whether Hezekiah and his men had actually been bandits is questionable. Dissidents against the prevailing order, of whom Galilee always boasted its share, were regularly referred to as bandits. Rather than being a criminal, Hezekiah may have been a rebel against Roman rule, agitating for the return to Galilee of Syrian-annexed border territory. A half-century later, his son Judas would lead an attempted uprising against the rule of Herod's son Archelaus and would also be called a bandit.

Though Sextus in Damascus was pleased that Herod had caught and executed Hezekiah, it sparked an angry reaction back in Jerusalem, where prominent figures were already resentful of the rank and power Julius Caesar had conferred on Antipater and of the authority Antipater had conferred on two of his sons. Now the youthful Herod, serving as a Judaean official, had assumed powers well above his station. Executing outlaws was permissible but only when sanctioned by the sages and scholars of the Sanhedrin religious court and council in Jerusalem, an institution held in such reverence by the Jews that Antipater thought it prudent not to risk curtailing its authority. That he was the Roman-appointed procurator of Judaea was already seen as compounding his son's transgression. Herod had ignored legal procedures, violated the law, and offended the guardians of public standards. He was considered defiant, insolent, violent, and excessively bold. He was someone who had to be brought to book. According to the law, what he had done was punishable by execution.

Hasmonean loyalists seized upon the affair with a vengeance. They had been trying, with little success, to drive a wedge between Antipater and High Priest–Ethnarch Hyrcanus, whom they still considered their king despite his having been denied the crown by the Romans. They were exasperated by the authority with which Antipater and his sons had been empowered, apparently without Hyrcanus's objection or concern. They were infuriated by Antipater's assumption of what should have been Hyrcanus's personal link with the Romans. He had, for example, arranged for the tribute due to Rome from Judaea to be passed on through him rather than through the man they considered their king. They now exploited Herod's Galilee executions to exert pressure on Hyrcanus to do something about the brazen Idumaeans.

> How long will you be quiet . . . ? Do you not see that Antipater and his sons have already seized the government, and that it is only the name of a king which is given to you? But do not . . . think to escape danger by being so careless of yourself and your kingdom; for Antipater and his sons are not now your stewards; they are absolute lords; for Herod, Antipater's son, has slain Hezekiah, and those that were with him, and has thereby transgressed our law, which forbids the slaying of any man, even though he is wicked, unless he had been first condemned to suffer death by the Sanhedrin, yet he has been so insolent as to do this, and without any authority from you.

The mothers of the men Herod had slain echoed the call for him to be tried for murder. They converged on the temple to bemoan the killing of their sons and insist that justice be done. Hyrcanus was reluctant to succumb to those demands. He had known Herod since he was a boy. Herod's father, who continued to treat him with the respect due to a king, was still his valued confidant to whom many considered him excessively accommodating. But he found the popular pressure difficult to defy and told Herod to come to Jerusalem to appear before a Sanhedrin court.

The young upstart was not really required to obey. He was a Roman citizen, his family having been awarded the honor by Julius Caesar himself. He could have insisted upon being judged by a Roman court that probably would have ruled he had not acted improperly. But advised by his father, he settled outstanding matters in Galilee, posted garrisons there to deal with any further problems with brigands, and did as told.

He arrived in Jerusalem with an escort of armed guards to protect him from harm in a hostile environment, although Antipater had told him his escort should not be so menacing that it would frighten Hyrcanus and the people into believing a coup was in the making. From Damascus, Sextus sent a more fearsome frightener to Jerusalem. Valuing Herod's ability to crush anti-Roman dissent in Galilee, he commanded Hyrcanus to immediately clear his protégé of all charges without a trial. The timid ethnarch was willing to comply. But having arrived in Jerusalem ready to defend himself, Herod challengingly appeared with his escort before the Sanhedrin.

The presence of his armed bodyguards and Herod's reputation for violence terrified the venerable court members into silence, as did the accused's demeanor. Instead of being attired modestly, as was customary in such circumstances, he had donned an elegant cloak. Nor did he show any sign of being submissive, as was also expected, and he'd had his hair specially trimmed, as if he were attending some sort of celebration.

Not a word was uttered against him by the intimidated members of the Sanhedrin until one of them, Shemaiah, spoke up to rebuke his fellow judges and Hyrcanus for permitting Herod to intimidate them.

> I can recall no previous occasion when an accused person called to stand trial before us has presented himself in such a way. . . . Anyone who comes to be judged by this Sanhedrin presents himself submissively, as a frightened man appealing for your mercy, with hair unkempt and in black attire. But Herod . . . though accused of murder and summoned on no less a charge, stands here clothed in purple, his hair neatly set, and surrounded by soldiers. If we condemn him as the law prescribes, he intends to kill us. This man, who you are now willing to set free to oblige Hyrcanus, will one day certainly punish you.

Hyrcanus was worried that Shemaiah's scolding was emboldening the other members of the court. Chastened, they might well sentence Herod to death. Fearing how Sextus, empowered to exercise jurisdiction over Judaea, would react if that happened, he adjourned the trial before a verdict could be delivered and advised Herod to flee Jerusalem.

He did so and hurried off to Damascus where he was heartily welcomed by Sextus who awarded him authority over Coele-Syria, later to be called the Bekaa Valley, with an army at his disposal. Furious at how he had been treated, Herod turned around and advanced with it on Jerusalem to punish those who had dared to put him on trial.

His father urged him to desist. Antipater realized it would be a humiliation for Hyrcanus and a mistake. The Romans, who frowned on unnecessary wrangling in their client territories, might consider such an assault on the man they had appointed ethnarch of Judaea an act of insubordination. Besides, Antipater could imagine a pro-Hasmonean uprising among the Judaeans if Herod stormed Jerusalem with his Syrian troops. He and Herod's brother Phaesal, governor of Jerusalem, might be condemned as enemies of the people too. Also, Herod had not yet demonstrated skills as a military commander. Antipater feared if it came to a fight, a victory for him over the Judaean army could not be assured. He persuaded his hot-headed son that a show of strength was sufficient to assuage his wounded pride.

In any case, an important matter soon required more immediate attention. Sextus was assassinated in Damascus, an incident in the ongoing struggle between Julius Caesar and his Senate-backed rivals for mastery in Rome. To protect his own position and the careers of his sons, all three of them recipients of Caesar's favor, Antipater sent Judaean troops to neutralize the forces of Sextus's assassins. However, not long afterward, word came that Caesar had also been assassinated, struck down in the Roman Senate by a cabal of senators led by Brutus and Cassius.

Caesar's assassination was a matter of potential disaster for Antipater. Having been a recipient of his patronage, he found himself as dangerously exposed as he had been during the Caesar-Pompey blowup. Herod too. But the assassination was to have momentous consequences far beyond their concerns. It would bring about the final demise of the five-hundred-year-old Roman Republic, its republican character having already been emasculated by Caesar's assumption of dictatorial powers. It set the stage for the emergence within three decades of the first Roman emperor and for the long roll call of emperors who would succeed him.

Caesar's assassins were first granted an amnesty by the Senate for having acted in the name of the republic against tyranny. But their victim had been an enormously popular figure. After Mark Antony revealed that Caesar's will included cash awards for all Romans and the transformation of some of his property into a large public park, angry reaction among the people of Rome forced the assassins to flee for their lives.

Antony had been close to Caesar. They'd had their occasional differences, but he had been his most trusted subordinate in the fighting in Gaul, becoming his second-in-command. He contributed significantly to Caesar's victory over Pompey at Pharsalus, commanding his left flank in the battle. At times during Caesar's dictatorship, he had, in effect, ruled Italy while Caesar was away on military adventures. How close they were was reflected in the emotional eulogy he delivered at Caesar's funeral while others in Rome were suggesting that the assassination of a dictator might not have been all bad. He had reason to believe his legacy from deceased Caesar's estate would not be insignificant. He had, therefore, been surprised and not a little distressed to learn he had been left practically nothing.

Caesar's comparatively obscure eighteen-year-old great-nephew Octavian was the main beneficiary. The youth, whose mother was the niece of Caesar's sister Julia, was bequeathed by far the greatest share of his benefactor's estate. When younger, Octavian had served under Caesar in Spain but was engaged in military training with Roman legions garrisoned in Greece. They were preparing to join Caesar's projected campaign against the Parthians in Mesopotamia when he was informed of his inheritance.

Instead of welcoming the news, Octavian's mother and others close to him were concerned that he too would now be a target of assassins. He was advised that, for his safety, he should flee to the protection of the legions that had been loyal to Caesar or, alternatively, to hurry to Rome and announce that he rejected the awesome legacy he had been surprisingly awarded. He did go to Rome, but it was to claim, rather than reject, his inheritance.

The tall, powerfully built, soldierly Antony was not at all pleased to discover that he had been denied what he considered at least partially his due by a recurrently sickly, occasionally limping, short, slender youth of passable good looks, despite bad teeth, with little in his brief career to justify the prize he had been chosen to receive. Having at times been taunted for effeminacy, Octavian was now subjected to accusations that he had earned adoption by Caesar "through unnatural relations."

Antony chose to ignore him. Not alone in thinking this unexpected newcomer on the scene would prove a nonstarter, he was confident of being able to maneuver Octavian back into obscurity, leaving himself to be a serious contender for the position of Caesar's successor as Rome's dominant figure. He was popular in the streets of Rome, especially after his stirring oration at Caesar's funeral, immortalized by Shakespeare's retelling. He had significant backing in the Senate and was a consul unlike Octavian, who had held no important public office though that was generally a mandatory path to senior advancement. Antony wasted no time in seizing some of Caesar's possessions and documents, purportedly to facilitate any official steps that had to be taken after the assassination, as well as for safekeeping.

But despite his youth, inexperience, and other apparent impediments, Caesar's unlikely heir, arriving quickly in Rome, proved from the start that he was willing and able to fight his corner. Despite the doubters, he was not without support. He appealed for and received the backing of several active service legions as well as that of Italy-based veterans of Caesar's campaigns. Many senators supported him too, suspecting that Antony wished to become as much of a dictator as Caesar had been. Nor did it hurt Octavian's image to have himself officially called by his family name, Gaius Julius Caesar. He well knew that it was a name to be reckoned with. Posthumously adopted as a son in the will of his murdered great-uncle, it was his by right.

To sustain the sense of continuity, he wished to make good Caesar's legacy of cash gifts for all Romans as soon as possible. Denied by Antony access to the resources he inherited, Octavian turned to family connections and to wealthy enemies of Antony to raise the necessary funds and fulfill that obligation. It earned him instant popularity and the wide recognition he needed to climb out of the shadows.

Though Antony remained determined to cut Octavian down to size, his attempts to be dominant in the situation were blocked by the unexpected political astuteness displayed by his youthful, inexperienced rival. In search of support in the Senate and to assist his own rise, Antony favored an amnesty for Caesar's senatorial assassins. But Octavian demanded justice for his murdered benefactor, a view shared by most Romans, forcing Antony to change tack. Other differences between the two were also resolved, and they agreed leadership of the empire would be in the hands of a triumvirate, the third member of which was Marcus Aemilius Lepidus, who had been one of Caesar's most dedicated supporters. They would track down and exterminate the assassins who had fled abroad.

Brutus and Cassius, the leading plotters against Caesar, had plans of their own. They had gone about preparing for a military campaign with the professed objective of restoring the republic Caesar had subverted. They would reclaim Rome and its empire for the Roman people. Brutus remained in Greece, to which they had fled, to organize their forces there. Cassius went to Syria to assume control of the Middle East region and its locally garrisoned legions before Octavian and Mark Antony could take command of them.

All of this had been monitored by Antipater in Jerusalem as best he could. Julius Caesar had treated him with extraordinary generosity, but he recognized that submission to whatever Roman was dominant in the region was of overriding importance to Judaea and crucial to his own survival. That locally dominant Roman was now Caesar-assassin Cassius.

Antipater responded quickly to the transformed situation and adjusted his allegiance accordingly. He made it clear that his loyalty to Caesar had switched to Cassius, just as he had earlier shifted it from murdered Pompey to Caesar. But more was required of him by Cassius than protestations of fidelity. It was customary for Roman officials to get rich from postings abroad. In an earlier role as proconsul of Syria, Cassius's venality had been so outrageous that he had almost been recalled to Rome to be tried for extortion. Now, in addition to his personal cupidity, he needed great sums of money to pay for an army in the struggle for power to be fought against Octavian and Antony.

The amount he demanded of Judaea for funding that army was massive. But the ever-resourceful Antipater, with the assistance of his sons, managed to gather it and hand it over. Cassius was particularly impressed by the thoroughness and dispatch with which Herod, back in charge in Galilee, had extracted the hefty portion required of him from the people there, employing whatever methods were required. As quickly responsive as his father to altered circumstances, he served Caesar's assassin as assiduously and effectively as he had served Caesar's cousin Sextus. The people of four towns in Judaea that failed to raise their quota for Cassius were sold into slavery to make up the required sums.

In recognition of Herod's diligence and reliability, Cassius chose to overlook his earlier association with Sextus and appointed him military commander in southern Lebanon and some nearby areas, with unspecified duties there. To fulfill those duties, he was given command of an army.

It was a significant promotion, but it was more than that. Herod's father had made him governor of Galilee despite his youth and lack of previous administrative experience. Now it was evident that nepotism was no longer required for his career advancement. He had been a favorite of Sextus Caesar and now of Cassius. He had become a trusted Roman minion in his own right. Cassius even promised to make him king of Judaea after his and Brutus's struggle with Octavian and Mark Antony had been won.

In just a few years, Herod had risen from being threatened with execution by the Sanhedrin for exceeding his authority in Galilee to becoming a figure whose rough and ready administrative expertise was greatly valued. He was more highly regarded by the Romans than his older brother, though Phaesal should have been preeminent for having held the more illustrious position of governor of Jerusalem and was probably meant by his father, Antipater, to be destined for greater things than Herod.

The brothers were very different in character and temperament. Phaesal was less brash and brazen. Through efficient, mostly benign governance of the holy city, he strove to overcome the public hostility his Idumaean origins aroused. But he remained in Herod's shadow as a public figure.

Herod's elevation by Cassius was just as well for him because he could no longer count on his father's patronage. Like his own patron, Julius Caesar, Antipater was murdered. He was a victim of the relentless dismay among the Jews over how, through Roman intercession in their affairs, he and his interloping sons had acquired high positions of authority at the expense of members of the Hasmonean royal family descended from the Maccabees. The people were angered also by how willingly they had responded to Cassius's demand for huge sums from them and appalled by word that this new Roman overlord of theirs had promised to make Herod their king.

Malichus, a friend of Hyrcanus and an official at his court, was the instigator of Antipater's assassination. Hoping to launch a Hasmonean revival, he bribed a palace servant to poison him. Hyrcanus may have been aware of the plot. He must have been sensitive to the growing consternation among his fellow Hasmoneans about the authority Antipater and his sons exercised. He certainly had been aware of it at the time of Herod's aborted trial before the Sanhedrin. Though too indecisive to take action himself, he may well have acquiesced to the elimination of the figure who had made his own role as ethnarch largely only symbolic.

Antipater's passing was not mourned by the Jews. He had been the instrument through which they had gained substantial benefits from Rome. Josephus, first-century historian of the Jews in ancient times, describes him as "a man who had distinguished himself for piety, justice and love of his country." But it was not forgotten that he had once helped the governor of Syria crush a popular, Hasmonean-led Jewish independence uprising, and many had never stopped thinking of him as no more than a Roman toady.

Nevertheless, during his long and active career, Antipater had not aroused the bitter public hostility that youthful Herod was already provoking. Recognizing the reality of Rome's might and requirements and overcoming the constraints imposed by his Arab origins, he had orchestrated Judaea's fortunes for two precarious decades. He had done so with considerable shrewdness, expertly shifting his allegiances without hesitation or remorse whenever circumstances advised.

But Antipater's most significant achievement was starting Herod along the path that would lead to his emergence as one of the most memorable kings of the Jews in ancient times. There is no telling how his less demonized, less obsessive older son Phaesal would have ended up if he had not soon met an early death.

* * *

Herod wanted immediate revenge for the murder of his father. He prepared to march on Jerusalem with the army Cassius had put under his command. Phaesal agreed Antipater's killing had to be avenged but dissuaded his brother from precipitous action. A better judge of the public mood than Herod, he feared a general uprising with incalculable consequences if Herod stormed the holy city to exact vengeance. He also warned that if the assassin, Malichus, who insisted he had nothing to do with Antipater's death, were quickly killed, the fury of other Hasmonean loyalists might be aroused. An open confrontation with them might ensue, with an equally unpredictable outcome.

Herod reluctantly bowed to his brother's judgment and held back. Offering the impression that he accepted Malichus's protestations of innocence, he coped with his frustration by trooping in force to Samaria, part of the domain handed him by Cassius, and employed his special talents to extinguish unrest there. But vengeance was not an emotion he was capable of long suppressing, and he soon arranged for his father's assassin to be struck down, organizing it so that the Romans, rather than himself, would be thought to have been responsible.

There were consequences nevertheless. As Phaesal had feared, the killing of Malichus provoked Hasmonean-backed uprisings in Jerusalem and elsewhere in the land. Ethnarch Hyrcanus publicly gave the impression that he accepted the killing of his friend Malichus as appropriate punishment for the assassination of Antipater. But in a rare defiant gesture, he indicated approval of what were, in effect, infectious acts of insurrection against Phaesal and Herod.

Phaesal chastised him for not doing more to help him deal with a situation that could have bloomed into an organized rebellion. It was only a mild scolding, considering it was Hyrcanus's single bid to reclaim authority in Judaea from the Idumaeans. But Phaesal, with the eventual assistance of Herod who had been bogged down in Damascus because of illness, ultimately beat back the challenge to their commanding positions. And Hyrcanus soon reverted to being his old docile self.

Whatever satisfaction Herod derived from having helped prevent matters from spiraling out of control in Jerusalem, he soon had to contend with a greater concern. The world in which he lived and maneuvered was about to undergo another traumatic transformation, and Roman developments would again be the catalyst. Once more, a new master appeared on the scene, and he had to earn his favor.

At Philippi in Greece, the Roman civil war sparked by Julius Caesar's assassination was brought to a violent conclusion. The forces of Octavian and Mark Antony caught up with the legions gathered there by Brutus and Cassius. Poorly led, Octavian's troops were routed by Brutus's, and he was forced to hide in a swamp to avoid capture. But in the fog of battle, Cassius mistakenly believed Brutus's forces had been crushed, dooming their side to defeat. Rather than face certain execution, he committed suicide. When battle was resumed, Antony made good Octavian's earlier setback and went on to rout the remaining forces of Caesar's assassins. Faced with either surrendering or killing himself, Brutus joined Cassius in choosing the latter solution.

Octavian and Antony emerged from Philippi in virtually undisputed command of Rome's empire. Antony's superior generalship in the battle marked him out as more worthy of leadership. But Octavian had by then cemented his position as Julius Caesar's heir. They avoided a renewed struggle for power by agreeing to divide their considerable spoils between them. Octavian would be overlord of Rome's western territories while Antony would rule those in the east. Lepidus, the third member of the triumvirate, was to see to Hispania and Rome's African territories but was soon eased out of the picture.

The partnership was sealed by Antony's marriage to Octavian's sister Octavia. It was received with relief by the people of Rome. They'd had reason to fear the eruption of a new civil war that would have prolonged the uncertainty and upheaval through which they had been living since Caesar's assassination. In assuming command of Rome's eastern territories, Antony became the most powerful figure in the region since Alexander the Great.

In Judaea, Herod fully recognized the significance of what had happened and how he might be affected. He had served Cassius with vigor and diligence, but now Cassius was dead. Another rapid adjustment to his allegiances had become essential, and he rushed to congratulate his former patron's conqueror on his new prominence.

He caught up with Antony at Bithynia in what is now Turkey, where some of his other newly acquired eastern underlings also hurried to report to him and pledge their loyalty. Herod told the new master of the eastern Roman Empire that, despite his previous submission to Cassius, he would now be delighted to be at his service. The gift of a large sum of money he brought along testified as much. In great need of funds to pay his legions and meet his other mounting expenses, Antony was pleased to receive him.

Other Jews also came seeking Antony's approbation. They complained to him that the Idumaeans had improperly become their overlords in place of their legitimate dignitaries. They maintained that only a high priest with suitable credentials should be permitted to preside over Judaea as a servant of God. Hyrcanus fitted that description though the petitioners felt the roles he was permitting the Idumaean brothers to play in Judaea objectionable.

Whatever their arguments, Antony preferred Herod and Phaesal to govern the land for Rome. Accordingly, they were confirmed as joint successors to their assassinated father, who, Antony remembered, had treated him with gracious hospitality when he had been a young Roman officer on duty in the region. It was less messy to choose them and likely to be more monetarily rewarding for him.

Hyrcanus was again sidelined in the process, an act he accepted with equanimity, having spoken with approval of Antipater's sons when asked. Antony did however grant the ethnarch's appeal to free the Jews who had been sold into slavery by Cassius for failing to provide the funds he had demanded of them.

Another visitor Antony received during his travels in the east to establish his command of the region was Julius Caesar's former mistress Cleopatra, queen of Egypt. Egypt was independent of Roman rule but keenly sensitive to Rome's military might. Antony had summoned Cleopatra to explain why she had not done more to help bring about the downfall of Caesar's assassins. But his main purpose was to oblige her to dip into her great wealth to provide funds to help finance his campaign against the Parthians, a people of Iranian origin who were mounting a vigorous challenge to Roman supremacy in the east. The Parthians had become successors in Mesopotamia to the Seleucid Greeks and were pressing westward. Not long before, they had decimated a large Roman army sent to bring them to heel.

Antony had already called on Rome's client states and protectorates in the east to contribute to the sums he needed to take on the threat the Parthians posed. But in many cases, he was too late. Cassius had taxed Judaea heavily when he and Brutus were financing their army in the recently concluded Roman civil war and had gouged out years of advanced taxes wherever he could. The client states Antony wanted to tap for funds had little left in their coffers for him to loot.

But despite his intentions, finances were not what he came to concentrate upon when Cleopatra showed up to meet him at Tarsus. According to Plutarch, her arrival was a triumph of seductive showmanship.

> She came sailing up the river Cydnus in a barge with gilded stern and outspread sails of purple, while oars of silver beat time to the music of flutes and fifes and harps. She herself lay all along under a canopy of cloth of gold, dressed as Venus in a picture, and beautiful young boys, like painted Cupids, stood on each side to fan her. Her maids were dressed like sea nymphs and graces, some steering at the rudder, some working at the ropes. The perfumes diffused themselves from the vessel to the shore.

Instead of calling on Antony, as was to be expected, she presumptuously invited him to attend her on her barge. Amused, Antony did so. Cleopatra is said not to have been a beautiful woman. Images of her on coins of ancient Egypt seem to testify to her plain physical appearance. But from all accounts, she was a woman of great charm and alluring power.

> For her actual beauty . . . was not in itself so remarkable that none could be compared with her, or that no one could see her without being struck by it, but . . . her presence . . . was irresistible; the attraction of her person, joining with the charm of her conversation . . . was bewitching. It was a pleasure merely to hear the sound of her voice, with

which, like an instrument of many strings, she could pass from one language to another.

As she had enchanted Julius Caesar seven years earlier, she now enchanted Antony. That would later prove a problem for Herod who would come to consider Cleopatra a dangerous and vexatious harridan. But for the moment, she did not feature in his thoughts. What mattered most to him was that, despite his previous service to Cassius, he had not been downgraded by Antony or suffered even worse. For the moment, he had the unqualified backing of the new ruler of the Roman east. The impression in Judaea was that he was still an arrogant Roman bootlicker. It did nothing to reduce the level of hostility toward him there. Nevertheless, he now fixed on a new path for personal advancement.

* * *

Miriamne was the young granddaughter of both of Queen Alexandra's sons, Ethnarch-High Priest Hyrcanus and the now deceased Aristobulus. She was thus a Hasmonean twice over, a product of the marriage of Hyrcanus's daughter Alexandra to Aristobulus's oldest son Alexander Maccabeus, who had been killed leading an abortive uprising against Roman rule. If Herod married Miriamne, he would be intimately linked to the Hasmonean aristocracy, which had long tried to bring him down. It would make any future claim by him to be ruler of Judaea closer to legitimacy than it otherwise would be. What was more, Hyrcanus, the most senior surviving Hasmonean, had produced no sons of his own. If Herod became his grandson by marriage, he might even be considered a rightful heir to the throne.

It may have been that Miriamne, probably only eleven or twelve years old, was considered by prevailing standards and tradition too young to wed. But it was permissible for her to be engaged to be married. Accordingly, Herod asked Hyrcanus for permission for them to be betrothed, though he was already married to a woman named Doris. They had produced a son whom he had called Antipater after his father. He had abandoned them both to their own devices as he had gotten on with his public career.

Though Herod was a commoner, Hyrcanus quickly granted his request that he be betrothed to Miriamne. He needed him now. A serious threat to Judaea and himself had developed and had to be met. The

Parthians had pushed deep into Syria. Julius Caesar had planned a campaign to take them on and eliminate the threat they had become, but he had been assassinated before he could organize it. Antony had not yet picked up where Caesar had left off on that undertaking. Now Parthia's intrepid horsemen and feared archers were converging on Judaea with the intention of ousting the Romans and their local figureheads from supremacy. And they had the encouragement and support of the greatest domestic threat Herod, Hyrcanus, and Phaesal could face—the Hasmonean Antigonus Mattathias who was bent on destroying them.

Antigonus was Hyrcanus's nephew and Miriamne's uncle, but he had reason to support the Parthians and their challenge to the existing order in Jerusalem. His late father, Aristobulus, Hyrcanus's younger brother, had been Hyrcanus's adversary when Pompey was deciding which of the two would govern Judaea on behalf of Rome. The Roman Senate had already rejected Antigonus's subsequent petition that it appoint him ruler of Judaea in place of Hyrcanus. It was content to retain the harmless ethnarch in his nominal position, with the reliable Herod and Phaesal looking out for Rome's interests there, as their father Antipater had. Snubbed by Rome, Antigonus had been living in Chalcis north of Galilee under local protection. The arrival of the Parthians in the region, and their advance into Judaea, was the opportunity he sought to acquire the crown the Romans had denied him.

He approached the Parthian commanders and made an arrangement with them to facilitate their conquest of Jerusalem. He would recruit an armed force, invade Judaea, and march on the city. Once he had fought Herod and Phaesal to a standoff within its walls, the Parthians would show up and pretend to offer to mediate between them. They would thereby gain entry to Jerusalem as a prelude to seizing control of it and installing him on the throne. A large bribe from Antigonus, together with his offer of five hundred women from the Herod-Phaesal-Hyrcanus entourage, may have encouraged them to find the plan worth pursuing.

Having the blessings of the Parthian enemies of the Romans was greatly to Antigonus's advantage. As they penetrated Judaea, the Jews welcomed the invaders from the east as liberators from their masters in Rome. The assassination of Caesar four years earlier had deprived them of their Roman champion and benefactor. The extortionist taxes subsequently imposed by Cassius, and then by Mark Antony, and the appointment of the Idumaean father and sons to govern them had revived the anti-Roman sentiments sparked a generation earlier by Pompey when his legions had stormed and ransacked Jerusalem.

Antigonus was seen as someone who not only would rescue them from the recurring Roman shakedowns but also would put the respected but downgraded Hasmonean family back in charge in the land. Hyrcanus was, of course, also a Hasmonean. He had not fallen into disfavor among the people of Judaea, but he was recognized as ineffectual and humblingly subordinate to Herod and Phaesal. It had overshadowed public affection for him.

The people of Jerusalem rallied to Antigonus when he and a troop of his followers forced their way into the city to take a stand and await the arrival of the "peacemaking" Parthians. The plan failed at first. Phaesal and Herod routed Antigonus and his fighters, forcing them to seek sanctuary on holy ground in the temple. But the effort of the brothers to crush this popular challenge to their rule was confounded by thousands of pilgrims arriving in the city to celebrate the annual Shavuot harvest festival.

The brothers did what they could with the resources at their disposal. But they were reduced to control only of the royal palace and the city walls as a small unit of Parthian cavalry made its appearance in Jerusalem at Antigonus's invitation to offer help in resolving the conflict and prevent further bloodshed. By then, Phaesal, understanding the mood of the people, had despaired of victory over Antigonus. Fearing that he and his brother faced doom because of their challenger's popular backing, he decided it was worth determining if a tolerable solution to the standoff could be negotiated, perhaps involving a substantial bribe. He agreed to meet with the Parthians to see what could be done. Also facing personal disaster because of popular support for Antigonus, Hyrcanus concurred.

However Herod was suspicious. Doubting that an agreement could be reached, he wanted to fight on, whatever the odds against them. But ignoring his forebodings, Phaesal and Hyrcanus left their secure positions to meet with the Parthians and were taken prisoner. Believing he would be made a hostage for the surrender of Jerusalem, Phaesal killed himself or was killed trying to escape.

He and their late father had been the only figures able to tame Herod's brash, impulsive reflexes. Phaesal's death deprived him of the only remaining counsel that could later have provided an element of comfort and restraint in his emotionally charged life.

Though having been hoodwinked like Phaesal in seeking to negotiate a settlement with the Parthians, Hyrcanus suffered a less extreme fate. He was handed over by the Parthians to his nephew Antigonus, who now proclaimed himself king in Jerusalem with Parthian blessings. The developments had nullified Hyrcanus's role as ethnarch. Antigonus now also stripped him of the high priesthood by cutting off his ears. By biblical decree, no one with a physical blemish was permitted to hold that sacred office. But his life was spared, and he was sent to live in Parthian-ruled Babylonia where a large, welcoming Jewish community had existed for five hundred years.

Herod now accepted that he would not be able to hold out in Jerusalem against Antigonus and the Parthians. In the confusion of the spirited celebration of the pilgrim-jammed religious festival, he managed to flee the city safely. With him went his mother, his two surviving younger brothers Joseph and Pheroras, his sister Salome, his betrothed Miriamne and her family, and a sizable armed escort. He led them south to Idumaea and then to safety in Masada, the natural rock citadel overlooking the Dead Sea that had been turned into a virtually impregnable fortress during the Maccabee period.

Leaving them there under the leadership of Joseph, he hurried with a small escort on to neighboring Nabataea. Unaware yet that Phaesal was already dead, he hoped to raise money from his father's friends there to ransom him from his Parthian captors. He also planned to recruit an Arab army to recapture Jerusalem from Antigonus.

But the Nabataeans showed him none of the friendship they had offered his father. They said they had no wish to tangle with the Parthians. Herod believed they simply did not want to hand over the wealth his father had kept in reserve among them.

Disappointed, but in no position to do anything about it and word finally having reached him of Phaesal's death, he hurried on to Egypt. He hoped to win military assistance from Cleopatra to seek revenge for his brother's death and to drive Antigonus and the Parthians out of Judaea. She received him cordially but turned him down, drawing up other plans for him involving a command position in her army in which he would help further her expansionist objectives.

With Phaesal gone, Herod had come to think of mastery of Judaea as his personal destiny. He was determined to prevail there. Recoiling from rejection by both the Arabs and Cleopatra, he set sail from Alexandria to

Italy where he hoped to be rewarded by the Romans for his loyal services to them, as he had been by Sextus Caesar, Cassius, and Antony in turn.

He knew the Romans would badly want to regain control of the land bridge between Asia and Africa from their Parthian adversaries. They would want to drive Parthian-backed Antigonus from the throne of Judaea and install an appointee of their own in his place. He believed another Hasmonean, even a Hasmonean nonentity, would be the most likely Roman candidate for the crown of Judaea. When circumstances required the Romans to make changes in the nominal leadership of a client country, they tended to choose from among members of that nation's indigenous aristocracy. It made for continuity and greater stability.

He thought Hyrcanus's grandson Aristobulus IV, the teenage brother of his betrothed Miriamne, would be considered a suitable royal figurehead for them, with himself as the individual in whom Judaea's governance on behalf of Rome could actually reside. He had served the Romans well in the past, and it was the position his father had held.

It was winter, when the seas are notoriously rough. But after surviving a difficult Mediterranean crossing, during which he was almost shipwrecked, he finally reached Italy at Brundisium (Brindisi) and made his way to Rome. There he received a welcome far more hearty than he expected, arriving at a time when the Parthian advances in the Middle East at Rome's expense were under anxious consideration in the Senate. His patron Mark Antony was there as he had hoped, back home to report on his plans for dealing with the Parthians and to refresh his standing at the heart of the empire now that he was spending so much time away.

The Senate well knew there was a task to be performed in Judaea, which had just fallen to their Parthian enemies, and that someone had to be found to take that task on. Herod was invited to attend its consideration of the matter. He listened as his previous services to Rome and his administrative skills were glowingly recounted, as were those of his father. Antigonus, by now comfortably settled on the throne in Jerusalem, was denounced as a dangerous miscreant, shamefully serving the Parthians in their contest with Rome for dominance of the region.

Antony, who had initiated the build-up of support for Herod behind the scenes, effusively added his commendation and proposed that his protégé receive the reward that his fidelity, talents, and achievements deserved. Octavian agreed. He was grateful for the assistance Herod's father had given Julius Caesar, his own adoptive father, when he had run into trouble in Egypt. The Senate also agreed, unanimously, and to his surprise, Herod, the Arab commoner, at the age of thirty-three, was ceremoniously proclaimed king of Judaea, ruler of the Jews.

# TWO
## The Road to Jerusalem

Proclaimed king of Judaea by the Roman Senate, Herod was escorted in proud procession through the streets of Rome with Octavian and Antony, the most celebrated Romans at the time, on either side of him. Lesser dignitaries led the way to the great temple on Capitoline Hill. There, the new king of the Jews made a sacrifice to Jupiter, Rome's paramount deity, as was customary there on special occasions.

A lavish banquet was then held in Herod's honor. But he did not tarry long in Rome. He was not invited to stay on, nor had he any wish to delay his departure. He had work to do in Judaea, which now had one king too many, and he had been assured the Romans would help him get it done.

Though the winter sea was still rough, he set sail from Italy, recrossed the Mediterranean and landed without incident at Ptolemais (Acre) in what is now called the bay of Haifa. His initial task once ashore was to reestablish a respected presence in the region. He recruited "no small army, both of strangers and of his own countrymen" to begin his campaign to remove Antigonus from the throne in Jerusalem and perch upon it himself. He marched his forces into Galilee, not far from where he had made landfall, to recruit more fighters and prepare for his operations. But he immediately had to contend with a preexisting problem.

Under renewed Roman pressure, the Parthian invaders were proving a less formidable adversary in Judaea than they had earlier been. But hostility to Rome's dominance, and to Herod personally, among his prospective subjects remained implacable. Local support he hoped for proved difficult to generate. He found many in Galilee as ill disposed to him as they had been when his father had made him their governor nine years earlier. The Roman presumption in trying to foist him on them as king did nothing to temper their animosity. The resistance he met as he went about trying to establish a base among them had to be crushed.

The Jews preferred Antigonus as their ruler for a variety of reasons. He was favored by them because he was a Hasmonean, a descendant of the idolized Maccabees. Some preferred him because he had relieved them of Roman extortion, and the rapacious Parthians who had installed him on the throne were now on the run, relieving him of having to answer either to or for them. Other Jews opposed Herod because they wanted to be ruled only by God and governed by a high priest. Antigonus's father, Aristobulus, his grandfather Alexander Jannai and his great grandfather John Hyrcanus had all been high priests. Now he was too. That he had been able to occupy that hallowed office only through Parthian backing was not held against him because he boasted the appropriate hereditary credentials.

But whatever public support Antigonus enjoyed, Herod would not be deterred from his campaign to seize the throne of Judaea from him. However, a separate matter required his more urgent attention. There was a tender side to Herod's character that belied the ruthlessness for which he was already notorious. Though his relations with members of his family would cause him much grief, he had deep feelings of love for them and often displayed those feelings in an emotional manner.

Taking Jerusalem was now Herod's paramount objective. But his most pressing concern was the safety of his mother, his surviving younger brothers Joseph and Pheroras, and his sister, Salome, as well as Miriamne, the Hasmonean princess he was betrothed to marry. Members of his family had already played a role in his public, as well as his personal, affairs. Until his death, they would continue to involve themselves in his political and private matters with dramatic consequences affecting his mental balance. Their well-being was now at the top of his agenda. He had already lost his brother Phaesal in his contest with Antigonus. He feared for the safety of his remaining kin.

They were still holed up in the fortress at Masada, under the leadership of his brother Joseph and under siege by Antigonus's soldiers. If captured, they would at best be held hostage. The Romans, quicker to make offers than to follow up with action, were supposed to have sent a rescue force to protect them but had neglected to make the effort.

Before going off to Rome on the journey from which he had emerged king of Judaea, he had made certain Masada was stocked with essential supplies for those who would take refuge there during his absence. But much time had passed, and he knew their situation at the isolated fortress was likely to be dire, and it was.

Some of their supplies were holding up, but rainfall had been sparse, and the water reserves at the fortress were virtually depleted. Joseph had contemplated trying to break through the siege mounted by Antigonus's soldiers to make for Nabataea and return with water. The Nabataeans had cold-shouldered Herod when he had sought their help while on the run from Antigonus and the Parthians. But Joseph thought they might want to make amends. He was saved from risking the desperate breakthrough attempt by a rainstorm that refilled his water cisterns.

Before Herod could mount a Masada rescue operation, he had to make certain of his military footing. He was relieved that his recruitment of fighters gathered pace after the worst of the opposition to him in Galilee had been dealt with. Some Galileans now sensed that Herod was a rising star. Others had grown disenchanted with Antigonus, fed up especially with his Parthian backers from whom they had hoped more than had been delivered and whom, in any case, the beefed-up Romans were now pressing back through the region.

When Herod secured Galilee, or so he thought, he proceeded toward Masada and his marooned family. He chose to advance along an indirect route that took him south down the Mediterranean coast. If he followed the more direct cross-country path, it was likely he would meet greater resistance from Antigonus, take more time, and suffer more casualties than he could afford.

As he stormed ahead, he paused only to capture Joppa, the thriving port on the coast thirty miles from Jerusalem. A hotbed of Hasmonean sentiment, if bypassed, it might pose a threat at his rear when he returned from Masada to lay siege to the holy city.

Joppa taken, he moved on to Idumaea, the homeland of his ancestors, where he recruited more fighters from among its people. They had fond memories of his accomplished father, were impressed by Herod's soldierly bearing, and expected to benefit from the rise to power of one of their own. He then made for Masada where he scattered Antigonus's soldiers who had laid siege to the fortress and rescued his family and Miriamne from their enforced confinement. Dispatching them under guard to Samaria for safety, he headed north to deal finally with Antigonus in Jerusalem.

But the Roman legions Herod had been assured would be at his disposal to assist him in his campaign had still to make an appearance. He had believed that Antony's highly regarded general Publius Ventidius, on the spot, would provide the additional manpower he required to take Jerusalem. It was Ventidius who had driven the Parthians back in Syria. A similar success was hoped for when his legions had laid siege to Antigonus in the holy city before Herod embarked on his Judaea campaign. But Ventidius knew an operation to break through Jerusalem's formidable defenses would be strongly resisted, inflict heavy casualties on his legions, and leave a blot on his unstained reputation as a commander. Rather than preparing his legionnaires to storm the city, his siege tactics outside its walls seemed mostly designed to extort bribes from Antigonus.

Having apparently achieved that objective, Ventidius withdrew to meet a Parthian resurgence in Syria, leaving the siege in command of Silo, his deputy commander. Arriving to join him outside Jerusalem's walls, Herod issued a proclamation to the city's inhabitants announcing that as king he had come for their good. Seeking at least the sufferance of Hasmonean loyalists who supported Antigonus, he declared he bore no grudges and would take no vengeance, even against those who had been his loudest detractors.

Antigonus responded by urging Silo to refrain from supporting Herod's claim to the throne of the Jews because he was only a "half-Jew," a reference to his Idumaean pagan ancestors. What was more, Antigonus said, Roman principles and traditions obliged Silo to favor a member of the Judaean royal family, a Hasmonean like himself, rather than a commoner like Herod. He was prepared to abdicate if his subjects desired it but only in favor of another Hasmonean.

Silo may not have been influenced by Antigonus's argument, but, like Ventidius, he was happy to be put on his payroll. Herod had no choice but to accept the situation as it was. In any case, winter was approaching, and Silo intended to withdraw his troops into winter quarters. He required Herod to call upon his own shrinking available resources to furnish supplies for them. He felt he had no choice but to do so.

In frustration, Herod abandoned his siege of Jerusalem and trekked north again to Galilee where his earlier success in subduing opposition had proved ephemeral. Bands of "brigands," of the kind he had dealt with years before, were again active and were undermining his campaign. They were stubborn fighters. "Their skill was that of warriors but their boldness was the boldness of robbers." His own soldiers showed less pluck. At one point, he had to intercede personally to halt their panic retreat and force the Galilean resisters to scramble for safety across the Jordan River, leaving only a comparative few hiding in caves.

Fearing those holdouts might prove the makings of renewed organized Galilean resistance, Herod went after them too, though winkling them out was not easy. Their caves were in the sides of cliffs reachable only by foot along steep, winding rocky paths dangerous to traverse. Displaying a gift for military engineering, he had a scaffolding pulley erected and winched his men down from above on cage-like platforms from which they could smoke out or cut down the resisters.

As he completed his renewed Galilee operation, the Roman reinforcements he had been promised to help him take Jerusalem finally put in an appearance. But their operational commander, Macheras, was forced to withdraw when Antigonus's archers on the ramparts of the city's well-defended walls targeted him and his legionnaires and he failed to trick his way through. Fearing disgrace because of his setback, Macheras insisted all Jews in sight were Antigonus's supporters, including some of Herod's men, and ordered his soldiers to attack them.

In a rage, Herod fell just short of ordering his soldiers to take on the legionnaires, their supposed allies. But he knew better than to come to blows with the Romans, whatever the provocation. However, he did contemplate sending word to Antony that he could get on well enough without the support of allies who hurt, rather than helped, his cause and that he would deal with Antigonus himself.

It was an idle thought. Antigonus's forces were too strong, and Jerusalem's walls were too well fortified and defended to be easily breached. He needed the Roman legions. Nevertheless, he worried that what had happened with Macheras might have been the prelude to creeping alienation between the Romans and himself. When Macheras pleaded for his forgiveness out of fear of punishment from Antony if he was informed what had happened, Herod agreed not to pursue the matter.

However, time was passing, and Jerusalem remained beyond his reach. His generous rewards to his troops, including half their annual pay to keep them from drifting away, and the requirement that he provide supplies for Roman units, were biting deeply into his resources. Someone had to do something to cut short this agony of delay. That someone could only be Mark Antony.

Antony's reputation was at the time being tarnished by his critics in Rome. They circulated charges that ever since he met Cleopatra and started spending time with her in Alexandria and elsewhere in his domain, he had been living the life of a degenerate eastern potentate rather than that of an upright Roman dignitary. He badly needed a military success in the east to dress up his image and fend off such sniping.

His subordinate Ventidius had done well driving the Parthians out of much of Syria. But he brought his advances against them to a halt for fear that his much-lauded successes would rile Antony. It was just as well for him because Antony had decided it was time for him to take over that campaign. He revived Julius Caesar's aborted plan to deal once and for all with the Parthians.

However, he met stubborn resistance, and his operations had been brought to a standstill at Samosata on the Euphrates River. A decade earlier, not far from where he was now bogged down, Marcus Licinius Crassus, having served as a Roman consul and seeking fame and glory to match his great wealth, had led an expedition to pummel the Parthians. Crassus's legions had been demolished, and he had been killed. A similar outcome for Antony's campaign and for Antony was an alarming possibility.

Herod had been kept informed of his patron's plight. His hopes of having taken Jerusalem by then having been frustrated, he decided his best move was to hurry to Antony's assistance. He would impress him with his fidelity, daring, and dependability and thereby extract from him more reliable military support than he had received in Judaea so far, despite the promises.

En route, he learned that Antony's efforts had been thwarted because his enemies had blocked all attempts to provide him with needed reinforcements and supplies. Thus forewarned, he foiled a potentially disastrous ambush set for him as he and his troops approached Samosata. Breaking through, he provided Antony with the extra might he needed to overcome the resistance that had stalled him on the Euphrates and had prevented him from gaining the battle honors he needed.

Antony was duly grateful. He would be seen to be vigorously meeting the Parthian threat to Roman dominance in the region. It also meant he would be free to hurry off to be with Cleopatra again. Before leaving, he ordered Sosius, his senior general and new Roman governor of Syria, to end the delay in providing Herod with the military support he required to take Jerusalem.

Herod's success in coming to Antony's aid was darkened for him by word of a family tragedy. In his absence from Judaea, he had left his brother Joseph in charge of his interests and remaining forces there, with instructions that he was to mount no offensive operations against Antigonus in his absence or do anything rash. All the resources put under his charge were to be reserved for the assault on Jerusalem when Herod returned.

Joseph disobeyed. To gather food supplies, he had led a raid near Jericho with units of Roman troops. It turned out his soldiers on the operation were barely trained, recent recruits from Syria. They were cut down to a man in an encounter with Antigonus's more seasoned fighters. Joseph was captured and beheaded. A substantial sum offered to Antigonus's men for his mutilated body so he could be properly buried was turned down.

Herod returned to Judaea in distress and fury to find also that while he was away, hostile forces had once again reestablished themselves in Galilee and in other areas he had "pacified," even in Idumaea. Such a situation could not be tolerated or everything would unravel. The attempt to take Jerusalem would again have to wait as he went about reestablishing control as well as undertaking an operation near Jericho where he caught up with and slaughtered Antigonus's soldiers who had killed Joseph. He beheaded their commander and sent his head to Pheroras, his last surviving brother, as proof that Joseph's decapitation had been avenged.

Just after that clash, Herod's life was almost brought to a violent end. He was alone with a servant, naked in a bath, when several of Antigonus's soldiers, who had been cowering in the bathhouse to escape the slaughter of their fellow troops, ventured out, their swords drawn. Instead of running Herod through, as they easily could have, they scampered out and away, relieved they were able to survive.

* * *

It was now time, Herod decided, to secure his royal credentials. Confident that Antony's latest assurances and vow of friendship meant the Roman legions he needed to storm Jerusalem successfully were en route, he made camp outside the walls of the holy city. He fortified his positions, ordered trees to be cut down for building attack platforms, and made other preparations for the assault. Then putting reliable subordinates in charge of completing attack preparations, he turned away from Jerusalem once more and journeyed to Samaria to proceed with his deferred marriage to Miriamne.

Five years had passed since their betrothal, and the Hasmonean princess was now of marriageable age. She had blossomed into a beautiful young woman. Herod was dazzled by the sight of her. He was deeply and genuinely smitten and would remain so for the rest of her brief life. Going through the motions of divorcing his abandoned first wife, Doris, he celebrated and consummated his marriage to Miriamne.

His personal connection to the Hasmonean aristocracy established, he returned to his siege of Jerusalem. The Roman reinforcements had finally arrived in strength outside its walls to join with his own soldiers in taking the city. Together, they far outnumbered Antigonus's fighters, but their assault was fiercely resisted. Defenders atop the walls repeatedly drove off the assault troops trying to break into the city from their attack platforms. Other defenders crawled through mine shafts under the walls to rise in the midst of their attackers and lash out at them. Driven by religious fervor, many in Jerusalem believed God would rescue their city from the Romans and Herod. At one point, temple priests appealed to him to permit animals to be sent through so their regular sacrifices to God at the temple would not be interrupted. Herod let them through, hoping the request signaled a weakening in the defenders' determination to hold out. It did not.

More than four months of fighting and stand-off passed before some of Herod's elite fighters were able to scale the walls successfully, drop to the other side, and open the way for the larger assault force. A hard core of defenders was driven back to the Temple Mount and then into the temple.

Their resistance was finally crushed, but having sustained heavy casualties, the Roman legionnaires were not content simply to hand Herod his victory. Believing any reasonable adversary would have spared them much bloodshed long before by accepting the inevitability of defeat, they embarked on a furious rampage. People of Jerusalem "were cut to pieces by great multitudes as they were crowded together in narrow streets and in houses or were running away to the temple; nor was there any mercy showed." The soldiers "could not be persuaded to withhold their right hand from slaughter, but they slew people of all ages, like madmen." The temple was looted, as were countless homes of the people.

Herod finally ordered his men to end their rampage, and he appealed to Sosius to call a halt to the carnage and destruction of his legionnaires, fearing he would otherwise be left with only a desert for a kingdom. He offered to reward Sosius and the Roman soldiers if they showed restraint. Sosius did especially well from the arrangement. It saved what was now Herod's Jerusalem from even greater destruction, though he had to struggle to save the temple from further devastation by Romans and other foreigners in their ranks, curious to examine sacred areas of the temple from which they were supposed to be barred by the laws of the Jews. Herod personally drove some away.

Antigonus was captured before he could flee. Herod knew that, if permitted to live, he might be taken as a prisoner to Rome where he might attract sympathy from Roman sticklers for propriety. They might be tempted to agree with him that, as a Hasmonean, he, rather than Herod, was the rightful king of the Jews. Even if Antigonus were just imprisoned, it would undermine public recognition in Judaea, however grudging, that Herod was its true monarch.

He was reluctant to kill Antigonus himself. He had no wish to be burdened with being called a killer of a blood descendant of the revered Maccabees, an eminent figure in what little was left of the distinguished Hasmonean family. He already had trouble enough with those who challenged his royal legitimacy and religious identity.

Instead of doing the deed himself, he had Antigonus delivered to Antony to be disposed of. Antony thought of putting him on pre-execution display as one of his victory trophies in the triumphant procession that would await him upon his later return to Rome. But he knew Antigonus had been more acceptable to the Jews than the Idumaean commoner he and the Roman Senate had foisted on them. To avoid the possibility that he would become an enduring source of trouble for him, he had this last of the Hasmonean kings killed.

In his writings, historian Josephus mourns the demise of the Hasmonean dynasty.

> This family was a splendid and an illustrious one, both on account of the nobility of its stock, and of the dignity of the high priesthood, as also for the glorious actions its ancestors had performed for our nation; but these men lost the government by their dissensions one with another, and it came to Herod, the son of Antipater, who was of no more than a vulgar family, and of no eminent extraction, but one that was subject to other kings.

Herod's commoner ancestry was a consideration Antony may have taken into account in choosing the manner of Antigonus's liquidation. He had him beheaded. It was said that never before had the Romans subjected a royal personage to such a squalid form of execution. The Greek historian and geographer Strabo believed Antony dealt with him in such a striking manner to "bend the minds of the Jews so as to receive Herod, . . . for by no torments could they be forced to call him king, so great a fondness they had for their former king. . . . This dishonorable death would diminish the value they had for Antigonus's memory and, at the same time, diminish the hatred they bare to Herod."

If the purpose had been to make Herod more acceptable to the people he was about to rule, it failed. Nevertheless, ten years after Antipater's brash young son had assumed his first official role as governor of Galilee and three years after the Romans had proclaimed him king of Judaea, an Arab was about to found a new Jewish dynasty in Jerusalem in the blood of the old.

# THREE

## Securing the Throne

Herod had taken Jerusalem and disposed of Antigonus, but he still faced great challenges. He had to secure his position as king of Judaea in a hostile domestic environment while administering his often-turbulent land to the satisfaction of the Romans. Rome did not tolerate turmoil and upheaval where its imperial writ ran, certainly not in a territory as strategically significant as the land of the Jews, a gateway to Arabia, Egypt, and East Africa with their fabled riches. Herod's crown could be snatched away as readily as it had been handed to him.

Most of the Roman soldiers who had provided the assistance he had needed to climb the heights he had reached had been withdrawn from Judaea for operations elsewhere. But pockets of armed resistance continued to pose nagging nuisances in corners of his newly acquired kingdom, undeterred by the continuing presence of the single Roman legion garrisoned not far from Jerusalem to assure things did not slip quickly out of control again with Herod at the helm.

Rome may have been pleased with how things had worked out, but the animosity of the people of Judaea toward the king imposed on them remained implacable. Herod received none of the acclaim a newly enthroned monarch might expect from his subjects. The people of Jerusalem had suffered grievously during the siege and conquest of their city, undertaken so he could be their ruler against their wishes. Even among those who had emerged physically unscathed from the fighting and from the subsequent bloodbath Herod had failed to prevent, many were likely to have had relatives and friends who had been killed or injured. Homes

47

had been smashed where the fighting had been intense and plundered where the post-fighting depredations of the soldiers had been heaviest.

The people of Jerusalem were relieved the bloodletting had been brought to an end but could not be convinced that any worthwhile purpose had been served by Herod's triumph. The Torah commands, "Do not abhor an Edomite [the earlier name for an Idumaean], for he is your brother." But the Jews saw Herod not as a brother but as a tool of the Romans who, with the exception of the late, lamented Julius Caesar, had been dogging them with heavy taxes, tribute requirements, and other demands.

Their distress at Herod's victory deepened from foreboding into horror at what their new king got up to in Jerusalem even before settling in. He was ruthless and brutally vindictive in his determination to preempt the reemergence of organized opposition. All who had been publicly critical of him in the past or who he believed might pose a threat were hunted down and butchered. Among those on his list were forty-five of Jerusalem's most prominent figures. All had enjoyed links to Antigonus, or might have, or had suspicious ties to other Hasmoneans.

They included members of the Sanhedrin religious council in front of which young Herod had been made to appear years before to answer for his unauthorized executions of Galileans. He thought it necessary to neuter the Sanhedrin to prevent it from developing into a focus of hostility to him. He made a pointed exception of two of its members, sparing them because, when he was laying siege to Jerusalem, they had argued against resistance, maintaining he had become the instrument by which God was punishing the Jews for their sinfulness.

In addition to having the others killed, he had their homes raided and their wealth confiscated. Even their coffins were searched for valuables their family or friends might have tried to conceal or smuggle away. Guards were posted at the gates of the city walls to prevent anything of value slipping through.

He also took possession of many of the precious gold and silver ornaments in the temple. Three years had passed since he had been proclaimed king by the Senate in Rome and had begun his campaign to seize the throne. During that time, he had dipped deeply into his resources, paying his army, providing for its needs, and rewarding his Roman masters and military allies. He remained wealthy by virtue of the property and related assets he had inherited from his father. But substantial sums were needed to replenish his coffers, pay the tribute Antony expected of him, and fund projects that may already have begun taking shape in his mind.

Highest on his agenda were the means and methods to be employed by the instruments of his administration to guarantee that his hold on power in the land was firmly established. Roots were planted for the police state Judaea would become during his reign. His regional and even local officials were held responsible for winkling out dissenters, brigands, and others who might foment rebellion and disrupt public order.

While disposing of individuals who had stood by Antigonus, he conferred honors and rewards on those in Jerusalem who had previously been linked to himself, his brother Phaesal, and his father. He reshaped the royal court to include only members he believed he could trust.

In contrast to how harshly he dealt with the Sanhedrin and his general clampdown, his treatment of high priest and former ethnarch Hyrcanus seemed an act of particular kindness and civility. He dispatched a gift-bearing emissary to the king of the Parthians asking him to allow Hyrcanus to come home from Babylon where Antigonus had exiled him. No objection being raised, he urged the elderly Hasmonean dignitary to return to Jerusalem.

They'd had occasional differences, but the distinguished exile had known Herod since his childhood, and the new king had reasons to be grateful to him. When Hyrcanus had been the young heir to the throne of Queen Alexandra, he had made Herod's father, Antipater, his trusted counselor. That had eventually fed into the circumstances in which Julius Caesar had appointed Antipater procurator of Judaea, from which position Herod's own climb up the ladder began. When he had been about to be sentenced to death by the Sanhedrin ten years earlier for exceeding his authority in Galilee, it was Hyrcanus who had halted the trial and counseled him to flee Jerusalem before a verdict could be handed down. They had subsequently been allies in the struggle against the invading Parthians. What was more, Herod's new wife, Miriamne, whom he deeply loved, was Hyrcanus's granddaughter.

However, the genuine fondness he might have felt for him would have been tinged with uneasiness because of the suspiciously high regard in which he was held by members of the Jewish community in Babylon among whom he had been exiled. When Herod's father had been procurator of Judaea, he had himself treated Hyrcanus with the deference due to royalty. There was a risk that, once Hyrcanus was back in Jerusalem, the people of Judaea would consider him more legitimately their king than himself, whatever the Romans had decided.

Nevertheless, Herod's invitation for Hyrcanus to come home to Jerusalem was accompanied with words of respect and affection. Though esteemed by Babylon's Jews and though living comfortably among them, he was flattered and pleased by the prospect of going back. He had reason to believe Herod was obliged to him for his having acted to save him from execution by the Sanhedrin so long before and because they had been allies against the Parthians. He had been hoping to return to Jerusalem ever since Herod had taken the crown from Antigonus, by whom he had earlier been disgraced and expelled from Judaea.

Hyrcanus's advisers in Babylon saw the situation differently. Suspicious of Herod's motives and mindful of his chilling conduct since capturing Jerusalem, they pointed out how agreeably he had been living in the Babylonian Diaspora and urged him to stay put. But he rejected their advice and went home to Jerusalem where Herod welcomed him back "with all possible respect." He addressed him as father and placed him in the most prominent and honorable positions at public occasions. The forebodings of Hyrcanus's advisers in Babylon seemed wide of the mark.

But they were not groundless. It soon became obvious that Herod's purpose was to keep this venerable Hasmonean close by in Jerusalem. He had his activities, and the activities of those around him, monitored to stifle any conspiracies to restore Hasmonean eminence in which they might be involved and into which he might be drawn. An analysis of Herod's mental makeup concluded that a "Hasmonean complex" was actually "the dominant feature of Herod's life."

* * *

One of Herod's early tasks as monarch was to choose a high priest of the Jews, if only as a matter of form. The execution of Antigonus, who had assumed the role of high priest when the Parthians had made him king, left the position vacant. The Jews had had high priests as the supreme guardians of their faith, at least nominally, from the time of the Exodus from Egypt. Their first high priest was Moses's brother Aaron. His successors were supposed to be drawn from the tribe of Levi. Originally, the position was handed down from father to son or to another blood relative, but that practice had long since lapsed.

During the four hundred years of foreign domination between the sixth century BCE Babylonian expulsion of the Jews from Judaea and the founding of their Hasmonean dynasty, high priests were meant to have been leaders of the people, empowered to involve themselves in their secular concerns as well as being overseers of their religious standards. But they had not always been up to the task. Some had been ineffectual and others corrupt or not overly committed to performing their sacred duties. But though at times remote from the interests of the main body of the people and often held in low regard by the influential Pharisee sect, they were always part of the elite power structure of the land.

Some had been appointed by foreign rulers of the Jews and often had served the interests of their masters over those of the people. When Hasmonean leaders ruled Judaea, each occupied the high priestly post with the exception of Queen Alexandra Salome, who, as a woman, was barred from holding sacerdotal office. She had instead appointed her son Hyrcanus, now newly back in Jerusalem from exile.

During his reign, Herod would ignore the hereditary principle in choosing high priests. He would appoint and dismiss those eminent figures at will and would strip them of any role in the national leadership. He would keep possession of the biblically ordained ceremonial robes, without which they could not officiate at the temple. He would release those garments to them only for holidays, so they could perform their sacred duties, and reclaim them afterward. At one point well into his reign, he replaced one high priest with another of less exalted priestly rank, bumping him up to the high priesthood only because he wished to marry his new appointee's beautiful daughter, raising her to a social rank suitable for someone he would choose as a wife.

Nothing could have stopped Herod from naming himself high priest when he became king, but he refrained from doing so. It would have caused more bother for him than it was worth at a time when even his identity as truly a Jew was being questioned. But the position had to be filled because only the high priest could perform obligatory ritual duties at the temple.

For Herod to appoint Hyrcanus, newly returned to Judaea, to take on the role again was out of the question. He was the senior remaining male Hasmonean figure. Herod believed that if high priest, he would become too much of a rival focus of national leadership in the minds of the people. Besides, Hyrcanus was made ineligible by religious law because of a physical deformity—his ears having been mutilated by Antigonus. It would have to be someone else. Herod carefully calculated whom to choose.

His most diplomatic choice would have been his brother-in-law, the only eligible surviving Hasmonean person of royal rank. Seventeen-year-old Aristobulus IV was Hyrcanus's grandson and the brother of Herod's wife Miriamne. He was the one Herod had thought the Romans would choose to be king of Judaea rather than himself.

Aristobulus had been too young to have joined those actively involved in publicly challenging Herod's rise to the throne. If Herod chose the youth, it might go some way toward soothing the dismay of his subjects at his having been planted by the Romans among them as their king. But he bristled at the idea of placing a Hasmonean on such a high-profile platform. Instead, he turned to the community of Jews in Babylon to provide the Jews with a high priest with whom he could feel comfortable and who carried no unsettling political baggage.

Ananel was an obscure figure but a friend who had adequate priestly credentials and who would be deemed acceptable by the people. But picking the Babylonian did not prove the uncontroversial decision he had envisaged. It provoked prickly family complaints, with exasperating political and dynastic overtones, and it complicated his life.

His mother-in-law Alexandra—Hyrcanus's daughter and young Queen Miriamne's mother—was a formidable woman. She had always enjoyed the deference and privileges accorded anyone of Hasmonean noble birth. She expected due recognition of, and respect for, her aristocratic standing and that of her family, no matter who was king. Alexandra was outraged that her Idumaean commoner son-in-law, of whom she had always disapproved, had chosen a Babylonian Jew to be high priest rather than her teenage Hasmonean son.

Believing the dignity of her distinguished family was being trifled with, Alexandra refused to let the snub go unchallenged. She doubted whether she could get Herod to change his mind and appoint her son instead of the Babylonian. But she knew people in high places who might, notably her friend Cleopatra of Egypt, Mark Antony's lover and soon to be his wife. She wrote to Cleopatra in Alexandria and asked her to persuade Antony to procure the high priesthood for young Aristobulus. A mere suggestion from him to Herod was certain to be enough.

Cleopatra was a descendant of Ptolemy Soter, founder of Egypt's enduring Ptolemaic dynasty. She was proud of her Ptolemaic origins and aspired to expand her Egyptian realm into the larger Middle East entity her forebears had sometimes ruled. After she and Antony became lovers, she had repeatedly pressed him to help her achieve that objective. But Antony had rejected her request that she be permitted to annex Judaea and Nabataea for Egypt. He had shuddered at the thought of his troops becoming responsible for patrolling Nabataea's desert wastelands on her behalf if there was trouble after she absorbed it into her domain.

As for Judaea, Antony could not ignore the fact that Herod had been chosen to be its king by the Roman Senate. He could not be jettisoned without complications. Besides, he deemed him to be a trustworthy servant of both Rome and himself, capable of maintaining subservience and order in his kingdom, so recently restored as a Roman client state after a disagreeable Parthian interlude under Antigonus. He had no wish to risk renewed unrest in the region by undermining him, particularly at a time when the Parthians still posed a threat in the east. In addition, Antony was a contented recipient of Herod's regular remittances. He had permitted Cleopatra to nibble off bits of Judaea to appease her glory-seeking land hunger. But now she failed to coax him into fulfilling Alexandra's request that he arrange for her son to be made high priest of the Jews in place of the imported Babylonian Ananel.

But then a friend of Antony entered the picture. Quintus Dellius had fought alongside him in the past and was his sometime confidant. Visiting Jerusalem, Dellius was received by Alexandra and was struck by the beauty of her children, Herod's young queen Miriamne and her brother Aristobulus. When Alexandra complained to him about the high priest situation, he suggested how she might have her way, whatever Herod's objections. He urged her to have portraits of her beautiful daughter and son drawn. They should be sent to Antony for him to admire. It might persuade him to act in youthful Aristobulus's favor in the high priest affair. Knowing that Antony had bisexual tastes, Dellius also imagined other possible outcomes.

Alexandra did as he advised, and like him, Antony was struck by the beauty of both of Alexandra's children. Out of decency, or perhaps not to offend Cleopatra, he refrained from asking Herod to send his lovely wife to him. But he did ask that Aristobulus be shipped to Alexandria, provided it would cause him no trouble.

Herod was appalled by that request. He had no wish for Antony to involve himself in his family affairs. Still insecure on the throne, he also feared that striking-looking Aristobulus might replace him in Antony's favor. He had to be tactful in turning down any request from his patron, but he took the risk of warning him of possibly disagreeable consequences if the youth were sent off to Alexandria. He hinted, not without some justification, that it might precipitate Hasmonean-inspired unrest against himself and against Judaea's submission to Rome.

Antony accepted the excuse. Nevertheless, the row over who would be high priest would not die down. Alexandra's campaigning on her son's behalf was unrelenting, and Miriamne joined her mother in pressing her husband to replace the high priest imported from Babylon with her brother. Provoked by their persistence, Herod gathered several members of his royal court to form a tribunal before which he accused his mother-in-law of conspiring to dilute his royal authority and of plotting with Cleopatra to drive him from the throne.

His denunciation terrified Alexandra. She denied she had sought to unseat Herod, something, she said, that would have been foolish for her to attempt because of how safe and secure her family felt with him on the throne. She tearfully admitted she had tried to gain advancement for Aristobulus but only because he was her son as well as a suitable candidate for preferment who might be thought to have been dishonored by being overlooked for the high priesthood.

Herod's appointment of the tribunal to hear his accusations against her had been a warning for his mother-in-law to know her place in his scheme of things. For the moment, it seemed to have served its purpose. He responded to her sniveling apology for offending him by offering to forgive and forget. He would even grant her wish and particularly that of Miriamne. He would appoint Aristobulus high priest after all. Ananel was sent back to Babylon, and the Hasmonean teenager was proclaimed guardian of the faith of the Jews.

It was a prudent move for Herod to make. It would calm family friction that was proving too great a distraction as he went about securing his forceful presence as ruler of the land, and it might tone down some of the pro-Hasmonean hostility to him among the people. It might also pacify Cleopatra with whom Antony was increasingly infatuated. Besides, as high priest, Aristobulus would be unlikely ever to find occasion to leave Judaea and remove himself from where his conduct could be easily monitored. Calm was restored to the royal family.

But not for long. Herod was emotionally incapable of letting matters drop and moving on after feeling obliged to do something he preferred not to do. His grudging appointment of the youth to a high-profile public role haunted him. Rome trusted Herod, but he did not trust Rome. He feared that even if he retained Antony's patronage, as he seemed to be doing, the Senate might be dismayed by continued discontent among his subjects and might think again about its choice of him as Rome's surrogate ruler in Judaea. It might be tempted to seek a more popular and legitimate figure to be its king, perhaps the new high priest Aristobulus.

Nor did Herod remain content with how he had gone about resolving the family row over the high priest appointment. He grew ever more incensed that Alexandra had claimed the right to involve herself in matters of state. Convinced his mother-in-law was bound to cause trouble again, he ordered her confined to her palace quarters where she could be closely watched. She was to do nothing of any significance without his permission.

Mortified by such treatment and worried about her son's safety, Alexandra wrote again to Cleopatra, complaining about being under perpetual guard and other humiliations she was being made to endure. Cleopatra replied quickly to her cry of anguish. She advised her to hurry to Egypt and to bring Aristobulus with her. She would make certain they would come under Antony's protection there.

Certain that Herod would block their departure, Alexandra arranged for two coffins to be made in which she and her son would conceal themselves. Those coffins were to be secreted out of Jerusalem under the cover of darkness and rushed to the coast where a ship would be waiting to carry them to Cleopatra in Alexandria and safety. But a servant who learned what was afoot mentioned it to a friend who was out of favor with Herod. Seeking to gain his gratitude, that friend passed word of the escape plan to the king, and it was foiled.

Herod refrained from making a fuss about the incident. Nor did he inflict further restraints on Alexandra. Not wanting to provoke Cleopatra into moaning about him to Antony again, he made a show of trying to make things up with his mother-in-law. But he could no longer endure the existence of her son, his young brother-in-law, as high priest. Whenever Aristobulus appeared in public, tall for his age, handsome, glowing with youth and looking majestic, crowds formed to cheer and praise him. These were public responses of the kind Herod himself had never experienced. They were made even more galling to him by invoking for the people images of the glory days of the Hasmoneans and the youth's Maccabee forebears. Something would have to be done about him.

The occasion for that something was the celebration of the harvest festival of Sukkoth. Aristobulus, attired in the exquisite robes of his high priestly office, officiated at the temple, offering the customary sacrifice to God. People called out praises of him together with their usual prayers. Herod was in attendance as a worshipper, as was expected of the king on such occasions. Once more, he was stung by the admiration the youth inspired.

But at a royal family feast in Jericho held to celebrate the holiday, he appeared to be in good spirits and paid affectionate attention to Aristobulus. It was a hot day, and some of the male guests went for a dip in a pool to cool off. At Herod's suggestion, Aristobulus joined them and was soon splashing and laughing with the others. Having been previously instructed by Herod, some in the pool playfully dipped him under the water. Then again, and again, holding him under longer each time. It was a game. They continued with it until Aristobulus had drowned.

Everyone there, including his killers, cried out in horror and anguish when they saw that he was dead. His mother, Alexandra, and sister, Miriamne, were devastated. Tears flowing from his eyes, Herod appeared to be as well. As word of Aristobulus's death spread to Jerusalem and the rest of the country, grief among the people was unbounded. The figure many hoped would someday lead a Hasmonean revival was no more.

Herod arranged a lavish funeral for the murdered youth, had a magnificent tomb erected for him, and delayed his plans to recall the Babylonian Ananel to the high priesthood. But Alexandra had no doubt that he'd had her son murdered. For her to make a public accusation would have been suicidal. But she was determined that his death should be avenged. She wrote to Cleopatra in Egypt, recounting her bitterness at Herod's murderous brutality and treachery.

In some ways, Cleopatra and Herod were much alike. Not having her way infuriated her. She had been angry at having been unable to do anything about Herod's earlier treatment of Alexandra. She was now outraged by what had happened to Alexandra's son, whom she had tried but failed to bring under her protection. This time her complaints to Antony about Herod—and how he had murdered Aristobulus who, unlike the instigator of his eradication, had genuinely been of royal blood—were so persistent that he succumbed. He summoned Herod to report to him at Laodicea (Latakia) in northern Syria, to which he had gone to prepare for a new campaign against the Parthians.

Herod feared that Antony's infatuation with Cleopatra had finally brought his own run of good fortune to an end. Believing his visit to Laodicea could turn out seriously disagreeable for him, he instructed Joseph, his sister Salome's second husband, to have Miriamne put to death if he did not return. He was unable to stomach the thought of another man ever enjoying her favors.

But Herod, his incipient paranoia beginning to take firmer hold, had underestimated his favorable standing with Antony, who had no wish to punish him excessively, or at all. The accusation that he had ordered the murder of young Aristobulus did not overly trouble him. As has been written about a later period but had already long been applicable in the Roman Empire, "Neither political expediency nor ruthless efficiency was a vice in Augustan Rome, much less in provincial administration." Antony believed that what happened within one of his client states was of little concern to him, provided it remained orderly, submissive, and reliable and paid the required taxes on time. If a king was compelled to explain everything that happened in his kingdom, what sort of king could he be?

Besides, he was informed that Herod had publicly mourned the youth's death. He knew also that the king's Hasmonean critics continually accused him of all sorts of wickedness, the usual reaction of those removed from power. He still trusted Herod to maintain order in Judaea. If by disciplining him the situation would become unsettled there, it would add to his problems in the region when he still had the Parthians to deal with. It didn't hurt that Herod arrived in answer to his summons bearing his usual extravagant gifts.

But Cleopatra continued to rail against him, and Antony finally gave in. He would mollify her by awarding her Herod's Jericho with its lucrative balsam drug and palm wine industries and bits of other territory Herod dominated, including the Bekaa Valley and parts of the coastal plain.

But Herod escaped with his life, which was more than was achieved by his brother-in-law Joseph, whom he had charged with making certain Miriamne would not outlive him. Loyal, or just terrified of him, Joseph had repeatedly told her what a loving and excellent man he was. He may have been trying to soften the coolness Miriamne felt toward her commoner husband, often openly expressed since the drowning of her high priest brother. To press home his argument, Joseph told Miriamne that her husband loved her so deeply that he could not bear the thought of separation from her, even in death, and revealed she was to be killed if he died while he was away.

When Herod returned to Jerusalem, his sister, Salome, took the opportunity to try to drive a wedge between the king and his beloved wife. The two women despised each other: Salome because of Miriamne's aristocratic airs, Miriamne for Salome's more humble and Idumaean origins. Salome told Herod that Joseph, the husband of whom she had apparently tired and who had been assigned to keep an eye on Miriamne in the king's absence, had lain with the queen while he was away. Enraged by Salome's accusation, Herod thought of killing Miriamne. But while not displaying any greater warmth toward him than she had of late, she managed to convince him she had not been unfaithful.

But then, her fury aroused by his readiness to believe her guilt and counting on his infatuation with her to protect her, she demanded to know why Joseph had been instructed to have her put to death if Herod did not return from his visit to Antony. That this deadly instruction had been disclosed to Miriamne infuriated Herod. Convinced Joseph had revealed it to her as part of a conspiracy against him, Herod had him executed.

As king, he had become a changed man. Over the years, with the guidance of his father and endowed with natural boldness, he had overcome the obstacles and constraints that might have blocked his rise to power in Judaea. But after attaining the crown, he lost the sense of invulnerability that had helped propel him that far. He would rule Judaea for more than three decades but would never fully recover it.

Early in his reign, he enlarged and strengthened a fortress the earlier Hasmoneans had built near the temple in Jerusalem, renaming it the Antonia Tower in honor of Antony. From that citadel, his control of Jerusalem could be maintained if extreme circumstances required. He also began strengthening the fortress at Masada in the south as a place of refuge for himself if things got out of hand. An enduring sense of exposure to regional challenges made him appoint trusted relatives to govern the major regions of his kingdom: Judaea, Samaria, Idumaea, and Galilee, as well as Peraea on the east bank of the Jordan River.

As for Cleopatra, Herod had reason to remain wary. Her best efforts had not yet undermined Antony's trust in his reliability. But after she had accompanied Antony to Syria, where he was preparing to launch a new military campaign, she passed through Judaea on her way home and appeared to make a new attempt to drive a wedge between him and Herod. She gave the latter the impression that she was open to an attempt at seduction by him, any suggestion of which would have enraged Antony if he were informed of it.

Aware of the dangers, and abominating the woman he considered a mortal enemy, Herod resisted her charms. His advisers also talked him out of a potentially dangerous impulse to have her killed while she was at his mercy. Instead, he treated her cordially, heaped gifts on her, and saw her safely on her way back to Egypt. It did not relieve her of the wish to destroy him. Six years into Herod's reign, a new convulsion in the Roman world seemed to provide her with the opportunity to do just that.

\* \* \*

The partnership between Octavian and Mark Antony had been uncomfortable from the start and was now unraveling. Their previously mutually acceptable arrangement on how to rule the Roman Empire had been worked out after the assassination of Julius Caesar. Their partnership had been sealed when they had crushed the army of Caesar's assassins at Philippi. After their triumph in that civil war, they had agreed to divide mastery of the empire between them. But Antony had never abandoned his conviction that Octavian did not deserve to be Caesar's heir. In turn, Octavian had never been reconciled to Antony's refusal to accept that Caesar's will had made him as much of a supreme Roman leader as Caesar had been.

Theirs had been a "doubtful and uncertain" alliance, edging toward break almost from the start, sustained only through "various reconciliation." They had jockeyed for position all along, their relationship barely kept alive by the uncertainty of each about whether he could openly challenge the other without paying too steep a price.

Antony had been a popular figure in the Roman army and in the streets of Rome through his close association with Caesar and because of his own military accomplishments. Though away ruling the Roman east, he had retained strong personal support from old adherents and others who shared his objection to Octavian's sudden rise from comparative obscurity to prominence and authority.

But he and they had underestimated how skillfully Octavian had transformed himself from youthful novice to skilled political infighter and how adept he was in gaining his own crucial backing in the army and the Senate. The Roman historian Dio Cassius writes that he "managed and dealt with [public affairs] more vigorously than any man in his prime, more prudently than any graybeard." In bolstering his position in their rivalry, Octavian was aided by how vulnerable Antony had become because of his sometimes-questionable conduct as custodian of Rome's eastern territories.

He had important responsibilities. He'd had to reorganize the governance of those territories, making certain Roman supremacy and reasonable levels of public order were maintained. He had to protect and further stimulate commerce between Italy and the east to Rome's advantage. He had to oversee the continuing extraction of taxes and tribute for Rome (and himself). Most pressingly, he had to fight off existing or potential territorial encroachments by Rome's adversaries in the region.

In the process of performing those duties, he gradually became something of a stranger in Rome. His visits to the heart of the empire grew increasingly rare. Whatever the rewards of his exalted position away from there, he did not sufficiently appreciate the downside to being a Roman luminary ensconced far from the center of power for extended periods of time. Meanwhile, Octavian, at the heart of the empire, calmly exercised his own complex duties, fought off the declining number of his detractors, and accumulated substantial monetary, military, and political rewards.

Antony's primary military responsibility was to achieve Caesar's aborted objective of finally obliterating the challenge to Roman rule in the east that the Parthians had been mounting from their Iranian heartland. Success for him in that endeavor would be a major achievement, but it was proving a formidable task.

In meeting his own military challenges, Caesar had often personally led his army and always closely superintended the offensive operations of his army commanders until battlefield success was achieved. But Antony was repeatedly distracted by Cleopatra's charms. Spending time with her when he should have been tending to his military obligations contributed to the stalemate into which his Parthian campaign appeared to be developing. It also damaged his image in the eyes of his countrymen.

The Romans were xenophobes. They looked with disdain, or at best with sufferance, on people who were not Romans, or at least inhabitants of the rest of Italy. They thought of the peoples of their eastern territories as exotic but also devious and backward, given to absurd and discreditable conduct and fashions.

Antony had been a model of heroic manhood for them, but many grew to think of him as having gone native in the east. It had, in fact, been difficult for him to resist the temptations on offer there. He was in command of a region "where people accustomed to servility, which carried respect for a master almost to adoration, made the governor the object of the most flattering and impressive demonstrations."

Plutarch writes, "Kings [of the lands of the east] waited at [Antony's] door, and queens were rivaling one another, who should make him the greatest presents or appear most charming in his eyes." It was reported in Rome that while in Alexandria, he had taken to dressing and acting in the manner of Egyptian luminaries. "He posed with [Cleopatra] for portrait paintings and statues, he representing Osiris or Dionysus and she Selene or Isis."

Cleopatra was a great if dangerous comfort for Antony. Whether she loved him as he loved her can only be a matter of speculation. She may have merely seen him as the means for her to reestablish a glorious Egyptian empire, with herself as its empress. She may also have hoped Antony would be the instrument through whom Caesareon, the son she'd had with Julius Caesar, would be recognized one day as Caesar's true heir and for him to become master of a combined Roman and Egyptian empire. (After his birth, Caesareon spent two infant years in Rome with his mother. Their care and accommodations were provided by Caesar, discreetly so as not to offend the people of the city. When he was assassinated, she returned with the boy to Alexandria where he was raised as a future pharaoh.)

Whatever Cleopatra's motives or aspirations, she provided Antony, the hard-pressed warrior and fully stretched administrator, with moral support and endless flattery.

> Were Antony serious or disposed to mirth, she had at any moment some new delight or charm to meet his wishes; at every turn she was upon him, and let him escape her neither by day nor by night. She played at dice with him, drank with him, hunted with him; and when he exercised in arms, she was there to see. At night she would go rambling with him to disturb and torment people at their doors and windows, dressed like a servant woman, for Antony also went in servant's disguise.

She provided him with a magnificent abode at her Alexandrian palace, far more exotic and luxurious than he would have had with his wife Octavia in Rome, and she bore him three children. As queen of Egypt, she was enormously wealthy and relieved him of the financial concerns that would otherwise arise from his military obligations. When she accompanied him on his duty travels, she did what she could to sustain his morale as the pressures on him accumulated. He was happy with her, with himself, and with their relationship.

But to increasing numbers of Romans, Cleopatra was no more than a disreputable seductress who had steered him off course. She was denounced as responsible when he abandoned Octavia, a woman much admired in Rome for her loyalty to him and for her efforts on his behalf in his absence. Antony's treatment of her outraged her loving brother. It deepened Octavian's determination to ruin his brother-in-law.

Antony's marriage to Cleopatra was illegal by Roman law because she was not a Roman citizen and he had not yet formally divorced Octavia. His participation with her in various exotic public ceremonies in Alexandria further tarnished the image his fellow Romans had of him.

Being away from home for an extended period had unbalanced Antony's Roman perspectives. When he conquered Armenia for Rome in 34 BCE (during his campaign against the Parthians, which he had suspended because of enormous troop losses), he held an unwarranted and undeserved triumphal procession. What was more, he held it not in Rome but in Egypt, an act that was both inappropriate in the eyes of his countrymen and of dubious legality.

The event was capped with an exotic extravaganza at the gymnasium in Alexandria in which Antony was dressed as the god Dionysus-Osiris and Cleopatra as Isis-Aphrodite, both of them perched on golden thrones. Their children, also in attendance, were similarly attired as deities. The bizarre nature of the event appalled the Romans but not as much as the liberties Antony took during its proceedings. He took the occasion to make a number of extraordinary announcements that came to be known as the Donations of Alexandria.

He proclaimed Cleopatra to be queen of kings. Ten-year-old Caesareon was to rule conjointly with her as king of kings. Caesareon was also declared to be Julius Caesar's true heir, rather than Octavian. Alexander Helios, the six-year-old son Cleopatra had with Antony, was awarded Armenia, Media, and Parthia. His twin sister, Cleopatra Selene, was awarded Cyrenaica and Libya. The couple's even younger other son Ptolemy Philadelphus was declared master of Phoenicia, Syria, and Cilicia.

This capricious distribution of territories within the Roman realm, or planned for annexation when conquered, did not go down well in Rome when word of it circulated there. Octavian had already been mounting a propaganda campaign demonizing Antony, whose eccentric behavior was said to include plans to make Cleopatra queen of Rome as well as Egypt and shift the capital of the empire to Alexandria. Antony's standing among Romans deteriorated still further while Octavian's rose higher. The narrow possibility that remained for reconciliation between the two beneficiaries of their victory in the civil war completely evaporated when Antony got around to formally divorcing Octavia.

Now bent on finishing him off, Octavian violated religious prohibition to press the Vestal Virgins to permit him access to Antony's will, which had been placed with them for safekeeping and secrecy during his lifetime. As Octavian publicly disclosed, that will provided evidence that Antony's award of Roman territories to his children by Cleopatra had not been meant as just a frivolous gesture without real significance during a fanciful Alexandrian spectacle. It proved he actually intended to bequeath to Cleopatra and their offspring territories that were part of the Roman Empire he did not personally own and which he was not authorized to dole out. Antony's will also repeated his assertion that Caesareon was Julius Caesar's true heir though all Romans knew Caesar's will had named Octavian as such.

Perhaps most disturbing to the people of Rome was the revelation that Antony wished to be buried alongside Cleopatra in Alexandria when he died, even if he happened to be in Rome when his death occurred. It was as if he had chosen not to be Roman any longer. It was alleged that he required that people in the Roman-ruled east salute Cleopatra as their queen though they owed allegiance to Rome rather than Egypt. As well as seeming to be verging on treason, Antony was made to look clownish. He was accused of unseemly displays unworthy of a Roman luminary in a foreign environment, such as rising before assembled dignitaries from his seat at a banquet to remove Cleopatra's shoes and rub her feet and interrupting diplomatic proceedings with distinguished visitors to read aloud "amorous messages" she had delivered to him.

As the popularity and support Antony still enjoyed in Rome frittered away, Octavian became convinced he was in a position to crush him and finally implement that part of Julius Caesar's will that in effect appointed him supreme ruler of all of the Roman Empire. He arranged for the Senate to declare Antony a traitor and an outlaw. Senators and other dignitaries who continued to favor Antony found it prudent to flee Rome.

Armed conflict between the forces each side could command seemed inevitable. But Octavian realized another civil war, just a decade after the last one, would be unpopular among the people and would cause unrest in the army. He had therefore begun focusing his propaganda campaign on Cleopatra rather than on his Roman rival. He promoted the belief that though once honored and respected, Antony had been irredeemably corrupted by this perfidious foreign temptress who wished to rule Rome. Painting her as the primary enemy in an atmosphere of "whipped-up hysterical xenophobia," he manipulated the Senate into declaring war on her and Egypt, rather than on Antony, who would have no choice but to stand with her. As a procedural device, it proved acceptable to the Roman public as both sides gathered their forces for war.

\* \* \*

For Herod in Jerusalem, the deteriorating relations between the two Roman titans were deeply worrying. Through friends in Rome, he had been closely monitoring developments as their rivalry intensified and war became unavoidable. He realized he would not be able to keep from being drawn in. Antony had been the central figure supporting his rise to the throne and was still his master in the Roman east. No matter how greatly Herod abominated Cleopatra, he would be obliged to provide military support for the cause she shared with his patron. He mobilized the Judaean army to do so.

But Cleopatra had other plans for him. She saw the looming Roman civil war as a chance not only to deal terminally with Herod but also to annex Judaea and Nabataea and start reconstructing the Ptolemaic Egyptian empire of her forebears. Convinced the sizable forces at Antony's disposal, combined with hers, would be sufficient to triumph in the war with Octavian, she arranged for Herod to be informed his military support in that conflict would be surplus to requirements. Though preparing to join Antony in the fight against Octavian, he was instructed to lead Judaea instead into a war with Nabataea.

It was ostensibly to settle a local problem. Acting on Antony's authority, Cleopatra had earlier manipulated Herod into the awkward position of being responsible for collecting rents on her behalf from Nabataean King Malchus for property he had leased from her around Jericho. Among the most fertile and lucrative in the region, the property had belonged to Judaea, but Antony had awarded it to her during the uproar over the drowning of teenage High Priest Aristobulus.

At first, Malchus fulfilled his financial obligations in this matter. But later, he grew slow in making the regular payments to Cleopatra that had been agreed. When he did pay up, it was often in sums less than he owed. Then he suspended payments altogether. It was the excuse Cleopatra now used for Herod to be instructed to invade Nabataea to punish Malchus for this malfeasance and collect the missing payments, instead of joining Antony in his war with Octavian.

Though resenting Cleopatra's continuing intrusion in his affairs, Herod had no objections to this assignment. Like her, he had long had his eyes on the land through which a lucrative spice road to Arabia ran. Now the time and occasion had been provided for him to do something about it. Six years had passed since he had conquered Judaea and sat on its throne. His struggle with the Hasmoneans had been won and relegated to history. He was still held in no great esteem by his subjects, but they had been cowed into submission by his draconian rule, and good harvests were bringing his kingdom a measure of prosperity.

In any case, the order for him to attack the Nabataeans had come through Antony, and he was obliged to obey. Cleopatra was pleased, believing herself to be in a position to influence the outcome of the conflict to her own advantage. Herod was to be beaten. She would see to that. At the same time, the Nabataeans were to be weakened and thrown on her mercy. Both would then be hers to command.

Things did not seem to be going her way at first. In their initial encounter, the Judaeans thrashed the Nabataean army. With Herod personally leading his forces, they did so again in the follow-up clash. They might have done so once more and claimed victory in the war if Cleopatra had not intervened, as she had planned to do if circumstances required. To prevent Herod from emerging victorious from the war, she sent army units of her own, held in reserve till then, to stop the Judaean advance.

It performed that task. Herod's army was routed. Now outmatched in numbers, it sustained heavy losses. A Nabataean invasion of Judaea appeared to be in the offing. Herod was forced to resort to guerrilla warfare to retrieve the situation. Rallying his demoralized fighters, he tried to inspire them with eloquence, confidence, and praise and told them God was on their side. But divine support proved not as readily forthcoming as he hoped. The situation he faced in the field remained dismal. What was more, he was confronted with the consequences of a severe earthquake that struck the Judaean heartland. Thousands were killed, and enormous damage was done. Reports of the catastrophe spread quickly, disheartening his troops worried about their families and emboldening the Nabataeans to greater offensive activity.

So dire was the situation in which Herod found himself that he dispatched emissaries to the Nabataeans to sue for peace. But with Cleopatra's reinforcements at their side, they had become confident of victory and killed the envoys. Disaster loomed for Herod, as Cleopatra had planned.

But with his troops very much at the mercy of the Nabataeans, she abruptly transformed the situation. She withdrew the reinforcement units that had stepped in to lead the Nabataean army to battlefield success. They were needed elsewhere because the war Herod had been instructed to launch, over missed Nabataean lease payments, had been a very minor sideshow to the main event, the showdown between Antony and Octavian.

Antony had command of the Roman legions garrisoned in the east and of Cleopatra's Egyptian forces, as well as those of Rome's eastern client kings (other than Herod's) called upon to lend assistance. He and Octavian both deployed large armies on the west coast of Greece for their struggle for supremacy. The opposing land forces at Octavian's and Antony's disposals were evenly balanced in strength.

However, Octavian's commanding general, Marcus Vipsanius Agrippa, his friend and adviser, was a shrewd military strategist and tactician on both land and sea. He blockaded Antony's troops with his fleet, cutting their supply lines, and while methodically avoiding a major confrontation with them, he subjected them to a series of punishing raids.

The result was a stalemate lasting months during which disease ravaging Antony's bivouac areas, and shortages of supplies triggered a hemorrhage of defections from his ranks, sometimes involving whole units. On top of that, Cleopatra's presence as joint, though inexperienced, overall commander of operations with Antony exasperated his senior officers.

Having missed the chance to launch the land assault that would have been his best chance of victory, Antony sent his battle fleet and Cleopatra's warships into battle with Octavian's off Actium in southern Greece. That did not work out well for them either. Though their warships were more powerful than those under Marcus Agrippa's command, they were also heavier. Agrippa's smaller ships were faster and more maneuverable, and there were more of them. While inflicting damage on the larger vessels and their less experienced crews, they easily avoided being rammed and disabled by them. Nor was Antony's hopes boosted when part of his fleet switched allegiance to Octavian.

Cleopatra did not bear up well under the strain of what was happening. As it became clear that she and Antony were being trounced by Octavian and that her precious fleet could be totally obliterated, she briskly pulled her ships out of the line of battle and made off with them back toward Alexandria. Her vision of a reestablished Egyptian empire was dashed for the moment, but she hoped to retain at least her mastery of Egypt while waiting for better opportunities, whatever the outcome at Actium.

Sharing her despair on how the battle was going, Antony also withdrew some of his ships and followed hers with them. He joined her on board her command vessel for the gloomy journey back to Alexandria. Ashore, the men of his legions watched dejectedly as their vessels scuttled off to safety. Instead of withdrawing to regroup to fight Octavian another day, as planned if defeat or stalemate loomed, their commanders negotiated surrender terms, and Agrippa crushed what was left of Antony's battle fleet.

Cleopatra returned to Alexandria to seek a way to salvage what she could. She planned to have her remaining fleet carried overland to the Red Sea to establish a new base of operations for survival against Octavian. But the scheme was abandoned when the first of her ships were set ablaze by the Nabataeans, angry at how they had been used by her in their war with Judaea. In the meantime, Antony went on to Cyrenaica in Libya to rally the five legions he had left garrisoned there and continue his struggle with Octavian. But legion commanders realized he was already the loser in that struggle and refused to obey his orders. He returned to Alexandria to await whatever fate was in store for him.

Octavian did not rush on to Alexandria by sea to put the finishing touches to Antony's destruction, the way Julius Caesar had pursued Pompey fifteen years earlier. He had other problems to sort out. There was unrest in Rome because of the heavy taxes he had extracted to pay for the war, and many of his legionnaires, weary of prolonged duty, wanted their promised land grants and bonuses. It was a month before he embarked in strength on a yearlong tour of some of the eastern territories to familiarize them with the changed circumstances in which they found themselves now that their former overlord Antony had been humbled.

When Octavian finally arrived in Egypt, Antony watched hopelessly on land as the sailors of his last remaining warships, which he dispatched to grapple with his rival's vessels, cheered those they were meant to drive off and defected to the enemy. He then appealed to Octavian to be permitted to live a quiet life in Alexandria or Greece. Receiving no reply, and told that Cleopatra had committed suicide, he took his own life too.

But Cleopatra had not killed herself. She still hoped to salvage something, perhaps permission for her children to succeed her as rulers of Egypt under Roman jurisdiction. When Octavian arrived in Alexandria and went to her palace, she appeared before him. But deploying none of her wiles and dressed in a simple tunic, she made no attempt to seduce him as she had Julius Caesar and Antony. She pleaded that she and her children be left unharmed and claimed that Antony had made her go to war against him.

Octavian rejected her explanation, leaving the question of her fate unanswered. But led to believe she would be made to trudge as a trophy of war in his forthcoming triumphal display in Rome, she committed suicide. The tale that she did so by having a poisonous snake bite her is probably a romantic fiction. It is more likely she took a simpler way out. It was said that when she had returned to Alexandria from Actium, she had "busied in making a collection of all varieties of poisonous drugs and, in order to see which of them were the least painful, . . . she had them tried upon prisoners condemned to die."

The three children she had by Antony were made to walk in Octavian's triumphal procession in Rome but otherwise were considered too young to be punished. Caesareon, the son she'd had with Julius Caesar, was caught fleeing up the Nile and executed. He would have been unlikely to survive even if Antony had not infuriated Octavian by proclaiming him to be Caesar's true heir. He was doomed by the probability that some might say he really was. Octavian was certain to have believed that two Caesars were one too many.

Like the death of Antony, Octavian's consequent absorption of Egypt into the Roman Empire was more than just a triumph for him. It ended a century of civil wars that had cost the people of Rome, Italy, and much of the rest of the empire countless lives, enormous expense, and demoralizing uncertainty.

Octavian now made gestures toward empowering the Senate again and reestablishing the republic. But his objective was to restore stability and order across the vast realm of which he had, in fact, become unchallenged ruler with the consent of the Senate. The stage was set for his transformation into the first Roman emperor within three years of the showdown at Actium. He was already being commonly referred to as Caesar rather than Octavian.

\* \* \*

While locked in the separate conflict with the Nabataeans into which Cleopatra had maneuvered him, Herod had anxiously awaited news of how the Roman civil war was turning out. He knew that if Octavian emerged the winner, his own future would be put in jeopardy. The sudden withdrawal of the troops Cleopatra had sent to reinforce the floundering Nabataeans and defeat his own army had been a clear indication that things were not shaping up well for Antony.

Herod seized on the departure of those Egyptian units to launch an offensive against the Nabataeans. Their ranks depleted, they sustained devastating losses, abandoned plans to invade Judaea, and offered to

surrender. But they had killed the emissaries he had earlier sent to negotiate peace, and Herod refused to accept their submission, forcing them to
continue fighting. An even greater slaughter of their forces ensued until
their inability to mount any further resistance brought the war to a halt.
Herod's triumph was total.

He returned to Jerusalem a military hero. Under his leadership and
personal command, his army had been tested in battle, and neither he nor
it had been found wanting, though it only partially and temporarily over-
rode the continuing antipathy of his subjects.

At that point, the struggle between Octavian and Antony had not yet
reached its climax. Though Antony realized his defeat at Actium was a
devastating setback, he was desperately trying to rally his remaining
forces to fight on. It was not yet thought impossible for him to salvage
something from this conflict. Nevertheless, much had changed since Herod had mobilized his army to fight alongside him and been sent instead
to tangle with his Nabataean neighbors. Antony's final collapse seemed
foretold by the defection of contingents that had originally rallied to his
side. As word of those desertions reached Herod, he realized he also had
to abandon his patron or go down with him. He hurried to join those
joining the side likely to win, sending "some legions and cohorts" to join
Octavian's forces.

There was, however, no guarantee he would be forgiven for having
been Antony's protégé. Siding with the losing side during the succession
of internecine Roman wars had often meant trouble or worse, even for
those who had not been militarily drawn in, as some who had been
among Antony's vassal's now were discovering. Herod's fate was to be
decided at the island of Rhodes where Octavian had paused on his journey through Rome's eastern territories while en route to Egypt to finish
Antony off. He was summoned to an audience with him there.

* * *

Wariness and distrust had become etched into Herod's mindset ever
since the Roman Senate had chosen him to be king of Judaea. Seizing and
securing the crown had been and still was a protracted, wearying experience. The Roman legions had been slow to come to his assistance for the
conquest of Jerusalem, then Cleopatra had blunted Antony's support for

him, and now conflict over leadership of the Roman world seemed to leave his fate in doubt.

In each stage of his rise to power, he had been able to focus on an accessible adversary—the "bandits" in Galilee, the Sanhedrin trying him for exceeding his authority, the Hasmonean loyalists, Antigonus, the Parthians, Cleopatra. But it was difficult for him to attach a palpable identity to the animosity of his subjects, one that he could satisfactorily pinpoint and confront. From the moment he had established himself as king in Jerusalem, he had never been free of the belief that conspiracies were being schemed against him or would be if given a chance. To keep from living in a state of permanent anxiety, he had devised draconian procedures for emasculating potential threats. But they failed to provide the assurances he needed. For much of the rest of his life, he lived in a state of foreboding or actual paranoia.

Preparing to set off for Rhodes for his meeting with Octavian, he was fearful of what might come of it. Octavian might decide to get rid of him because Antony had been his patron. It was true that, like Antony, the new overlord of the Roman Empire would probably wish to maintain order in Judaea under a reliable, subservient king. But for the sake of orderly continuity, Octavian might revert to the established Roman way of choosing a popular local personage with appropriate credentials to be his new surrogate ruler in Jerusalem. Having disposed of Antigonus and young High Priest Aristobulus, Herod could imagine only one figure other than himself who might serve that purpose. The sole remaining senior male Hasmonean dignitary was old Hyrcanus who had settled back in Jerusalem after returning from his Babylonian exile at Herod's invitation.

Hyrcanus was still considered by the Jews more worthy than Herod to wear their crown, but he had shown no indication of wanting to stir trouble. However, his daughter Alexandra, Herod's bitterly disgruntled mother-in-law, was less faint-hearted. She hoped Octavian would ditch Herod because of his earlier attachment to Antony and, if that happened, that her father would be chosen to rule Judaea in his place.

But she feared that, having renewed his residence in Jerusalem, Hyrcanus was in peril because of Herod's relentless suspicions and sporadic rages. She urged him to appeal to King Malchus of Nabataea for refuge in his kingdom. Having been humiliated by Herod in a war not long before, he might prove receptive to such a request. Reluctant as always to take action, Hyrcanus declined to get involved in his daughter's plan. But she pressed him to at least make contact with Malchus.

A trusted intermediary was to carry his message of friendship to the Nabataean king, but he took it to Herod instead. He instructed the messenger to proceed with his instructions, deliver Hyrcanus's message to Malchus. He brought back an offer of Nabataean sanctuary for Hyrcanus. Having the evidence to counter popular outrage, Herod then had Hyrcanus tried for conspiracy by the Sanhedrin, whose current members he had handpicked. Hyrcanus was found guilty of plotting and executed. Thus was the last of the male Hasmoneans of royal rank eliminated. As has been pointedly observed, he had provoked Herod into disposing of him not by making any claim to be the rightful monarch but by being innocently considered by the Jews to be "fitter [than Herod] to be their king."

Having eliminated the threat he believed Hyrcanus might have posed, Herod turned to another problem he believed had to be dealt with before he went off to Rhodes to face Octavian and the consequences of having been linked to Antony. He feared that the ever-troublesome Alexandra, her father having been executed, might try to organize a revolt against him while he was away.

Before setting off to report to Octavian, he installed Pheroras, his last surviving brother, as temporary regent in his place and moved his mother, sister, wives, and children to Masada for safety. Alexandra, Miriamne, and other relatives by marriage were sent to his fortress Alexandreion under supervision of trusted stewards who were to keep a close eye on them. Separating them was acknowledgment that his blood relatives and those he had acquired through marriage disliked each other so intensely that they could not live congenially together and had to be kept apart in his absence. As he had done earlier when he had left Judaea on a risky mission, he gave orders that Miriamne was to be killed if anything happened to him while he was away.

Having taken those precautions, Herod went off to Rhodes and whatever awaited him there. Appearing before Octavian, he was careful not to appear undignified or less than of regal stature. But not wanting to give the impression that he was presupposing Octavian's decision on what to do with him, he carried rather than wore his crown.

Appearing before him, he made no apologies or excuses for his previous allegiance to Antony, though he did say he had advised him to have

Cleopatra killed as an evil influence. His main tactic in Rhodes was to make his loyalty to Antony seem to have been a virtue. Unbidden, he volunteered that he had offered to join the civil war on Antony's side and had been deterred from fighting against Octavian only by being ordered to fight the Nabataeans instead. "I was made king of the Jews by Antony," he said, and confessed that he had "used my royal authority . . . entirely for his advantage." But he urged Octavian to "consider how faithful a friend, and not whose friend, I have been." He would, he swore, be as loyal to Octavian as he had been to Antony.

Impressed by the boldness of his argument, impressed also by Herod's victory over the Nabataeans and recognizing in him the sort of regional factotum Rome should value, Octavian accepted his promise of fidelity. He said he wished Herod to be as much of a friend to him as he had been to Antony. Confirming him as king of Judaea, he reset the crown on his head and assured him that the throne in Jerusalem was now even more securely his than it had been before.

Octavian thus joined the roll call of Romans who had recognized Herod's talents and expected much from him—Sextus Caesar, Cassius, and Antony. He had adapted to the needs of each of them and moved on when it seemed advisable. But his new role as king of Judaea under Octavian would be different in that he would fill it for the rest of his life.

Herod emerged from this watershed moment in his life with his royal status not only intact but enhanced. Before the dust settled on the new order of things, Octavian further confirmed his acceptance of Herod as an esteemed underling by restoring to him Gaza, additional Mediterranean coastal areas, and other territories that Cleopatra had been permitted by Antony to expropriate from him. He also awarded him rule over Samaria and some of the Hellenized, largely pagan cities across the Jordan previously under the jurisdiction of the Roman governor of Syria. There would soon be further additions to his domain, including the territory of Trachonitis in Transjordan, which would later cause him much trouble.

When Octavian subsequently proceeded from Rhodes en route to Alexandria to finish Antony off, Herod received him with lavish hospitality at Ptolemais and escorted him across Judaea to Egypt, bombarding him with extravagant gifts and supplying his accompanying troops with provisions for their journey. Octavian warmly received his attentions. Herod's additional reward from him would be a corps of four hundred

Galatian fighting men who had been Cleopatra's bodyguard and who became among the most elite of Herod's soldiers.

The outcome for Herod was nothing like the ruin Cleopatra had planned for him when she had persuaded Antony to order him to go to war with Nabataea. It might have been different if she had not interceded and he had been permitted, as he had expected, to join Antony militarily in the Roman civil war. He would then have ended up an active foe of the winning side, as did some of the others who had been obliged to lend assistance to Antony in that conflict.

Herod's survival from this brush with disaster dashed the hopes of the many in Judaea who longed for his downfall. Indeed, he had become a more commanding figure than he had been before. The kingdom he ruled was enlarged to become as big as it had been at any time during the Hasmonean dynasty he had consigned to history. He enjoyed the trust, favor, and even the friendship of the new, unchallengeable master of all of the Roman Empire. His audience with Octavian was to prove the turning point in his reign and in his life.

# FOUR

## A New Start

Seven years had passed since Roman legions had helped Herod seize Jerusalem and mount the throne of the Jews. During those years, he had been habitually racked by suspicion and foreboding, sensing challenges even when the defenses he erected efficiently neutered them. But having won Octavian's favor and friendship at Rhodes, where things might easily have turned out otherwise, he returned to Judaea in an exhilarated mood and with a feeling that the period of troubling uncertainty and lurking peril was past.

However, when he reached Jerusalem, his relief and elation quickly turned into fury and frustration. During his absence, Miriamne had discovered he had again given instructions that she should not be permitted to live on if he did not survive his perilous journey. Instead of receiving him with warmth and admiration for the favorable outcome he had achieved at Rhodes, she was cold and censorious. She behaved as if she regretted rather than rejoiced at his survival and success. She berated him for planning her murder and for arranging the death of her grandfather Hyrcanus and brother Aristobulus, and she denied him conjugal contact.

Hers was not the only irritant jabbing at him in his discordant family. His mother, Cyprus, and sister, Salome, bitter at Miriamne's disdain for them because of their less exalted origins, renewed their verbal sniping at her. Salome told her brother that his adored wife was trying to poison him.

His underlying paranoia in abeyance for the moment, he was reluctant to believe it. He loved Miriamne too deeply. But her continuing estrangement and Salome's relentless gibes overcame his disbelief and stoked his outrage. He summoned a council composed of reliable members of his court and had her tried for adultery. Stunned by the intensity of his stoked-up wrath and terrified that her own life was at stake, Miriamne's mother, Alexandra, testified against her, accusing her daughter of being a disloyal, insolent, and unappreciative spouse to her loving and generous husband.

After Miriamne was convicted and sentenced to death, the thought of losing her forever calmed Herod down somewhat. Instead of immediately having her done away with, he contemplated incarcerating her for the time being in one of his palaces. But Salome noted that in addition to being his wife, she was a Hasmonean princess. Confined, she would be even more of a focus of the public's persisting veneration for the Hasmoneans he loathed. Miriamne's survival in prison could well provoke popular unrest. Still reeling from being humiliated by her frostiness, Herod succumbed, and she was executed.

From the heights of exultation over his rapport with Octavian, he fell into an abyss of despair and grief. He loudly lamented Miriamne's death. According to legend, he had her body embalmed in honey to retain her physical presence. But he had feasts and other events arranged to distract him from thoughts of her. They failed to do so.

The poet Lord George Byron tried to capture Herod's sorrow in verse:

> She's gone, who shared my diadem;
> She sunk, with her my joys entombing;
> I swept that flow from Judah's stem
> Whose leaves for me alone were blooming,
> And mine's the guilt, and mine the hell,
> This bosom's desolation dooming;
> And I have earn'd those tortures well,
> Which unconsumed are still consuming!

Herod fled his palace and repaired to the Judaean desert to mourn in private. He turned to hunting to shift his mind from thoughts of his lost love. It didn't help, and he soon moved on. Staying clear of Jerusalem, the place of his deep sorrow, he went on to Samaria where he and Miriamne had been married. There he succumbed to even deeper depression. He also felt physically sick and was subjected to stabbing headaches for which his doctors could do nothing.

Told that he had lost control of his senses and was also deathly ill, Miriamne's mother, Alexandra, saw it as an opportunity to act against him. She sought to assume command of two fortified places in Jerusalem, control of which could be turned into a basis for control of the kingdom. She told those Herod had left in charge of them in his absence that there was no telling who might seize them if the ailing king died. She said it would be best if they were put under the control of herself and her grandsons Alexander and Aristobulus, Herod's next oldest sons, the ones he'd had with Miriamne. (No mention was made yet of Herod's oldest offspring, the banished Antipater II, named after his father. He had been born to Doris before Herod had married Miriamne and was still completely out of the picture.) Alexandra assured those who might be suspicious of her intentions that the fortified locations would be restored to Herod's command if and when he recovered from his ailments and returned to Jerusalem.

Word of Alexandra's request was forwarded to Herod. Smacking of a plot against his rule, it shook him from the depth of his grief and recharged his obsessive vindictiveness, which had been dormant during his breakdown. He hurried back to Jerusalem and ordered that Alexandra be disposed of. But having her dispatched failed to quench his aroused paranoia, and he went on to settle another old score, also partly a family matter.

Costobarus was an Idumaean like himself, a member of a prominent Idumaean priestly clan, possibly having been of more elevated standing than Herod's. Salome had married him after her husband Joseph had been executed by Herod for alleged disloyalty. Herod had appointed Costobarus governor of Idumaea. But though thus favored by the king, he had resented being subservient to him. He also wished to reestablish worship in Idumaea of the pagan god Koze, of whom his forebears had been priests. Years before, he had entered into a conspiracy with Cleopatra to detach Idumaea from Judaea and establish it as a semi-independent Egyptian protectorate, if Antony, still living then, allowed it.

Antony had withheld his approval. But through his spies, Herod learned of the plot at the time and would have had Costobarus killed if his sister and mother had not pleaded for him to be spared. However, Salome had since tired of her second husband and now leveled a new charge against him related to an earlier transgression.

When Herod had captured Jerusalem with the help of Roman legions, he had given Costobarus the task of guarding the city gates. Now Salome told her brother that, back then, he had secretly permitted members of a prominent Hasmonean family, who'd had close ties to Herod's adversary Antigonus, to slip out of Jerusalem and escape the new king's executioners.

His spirits now revived, his health restored, and his vindictiveness in full stride, Herod had Costobarus done away with. He also ordered the execution of some who had managed to survive his earlier purge of Hasmonean-linked figures who might provide the leadership of an organized opposition movement. Never again in Herod's tightly policed Judaea would such a movement be even conceivable.

He married again and would finally have had ten wives. But thoughts of the first Miriamne never ceased to haunt him. They especially tormented him when the sight of Alexander and Aristobulus, the sons they'd had together, sparked memories of her. It was less of a problem for him when he sent them, his likely heirs, off to be educated in Rome when they were aged thirteen and twelve.

The Miriamne and Alexandra episodes dashed all possibility that Herod's paranoia, and his police-state oppression of his subjects, would be tempered by the reassuring warm relationship he had established with Octavian. Indeed, they fueled his suspicions that disloyalty and conspiracies against him were being plotted within his palace as well as elsewhere in the land. Retaining absolute, unqualified control across his kingdom became crucial for his shaky emotional composure.

He had the activities of his subjects kept under the closest possible surveillance, depriving potential subversives of opportunities to organize dissent. People were forbidden to hold meetings, except those officially sanctioned. Spies were planted in the cities and the countryside to monitor their movements and conduct, and they were required to take oaths of loyalty to him. Harsh punishments were meted out to suspected dissidents. Herod was said to change his royal robes for ordinary dress and mingle occasionally with people in the streets of Jerusalem at night to "mix among the multitude in the night-time and make trial of what opinion they had of his government." The merest hint of disapproval could lead to arrests, torture, and execution.

Even criminal activity posing no threat to Herod's rule was punished with extreme severity in his determination to maintain absolute control of the land and its people and preserve order. Thieves were required to pay fines amounting to four times the value of what they had stolen. Those who could not were sold into slavery, even to other lands, though that was against Jewish law. Brigandage, previously widespread, was largely eliminated.

At least one case is recorded in which ten men from Jerusalem planned to assassinate Herod with daggers concealed under their cloaks when he attended a theatrical performance. But one of the king's spies learned of the plot. Brought before him, the conspirators confessed proudly before being tortured to death. The identity of the spy who had foiled their plot was discovered by associates of the plotters and was killed by them. Informed of his spy's fate, Herod had suspects tortured until they revealed these latest perpetrators, who were also tortured to death. Their families were also killed. There is no record of such assassination attempts recurring, though some may have been thwarted before they took credible shape.

It wasn't just the odd miscreant or small groups of malcontents who were to be kept in check. Herod prepared for greater challenges than they could possibly pose. He modernized the network of strategically positioned fortresses and other fortified positions he had inherited from the Hasmoneans, and he built new ones. He had guards posted across Jerusalem to keep an eye on comings and goings and planted military garrisons across the land.

Herod enjoyed a close, direct relationship with his army, having personally led his troops into battle in the war with Nabataea and proved himself an accomplished field commander. He has been described as "not only competent in campaign strategy and in logistics, but also had the ability to communicate with his soldiers and arouse their military prowess." His army consisted mostly of Jewish soldiers, but much of it, and particularly his officer corps, was composed of foreigners free of potentially troubling shared identity with his subjects. They included Greeks from the Hellenized cities within or bordering Judaea, Gauls, Thracians, and Germans. Romans and other Italians held senior officer commands. His elite personal bodyguard unit was entirely composed of foreigners.

Herod established semi-military colonies in which men effectively constituted military reserve units. Their inhabitants were awarded land to cultivate, with the understanding that they were on call for armed service on his behalf. He built the first Judaean navy, and he is known to have at least twice lent military assistance (as expected when required) to Roman operations—into Egypt and as far away as the Black Sea.

His administrative bureaucracy, its structure largely a holdover from the Hasmoneans, contributed significantly to the efficient workings of the police state into which Judaea was transformed. Officials of the major divisions of the land, as well of their subdivisions, held their positions through loyalty to the crown.

That became true also for Trachonitis, Batanaea, and Auranitis, territories all now in Syria and northern Jordan. Lawlessness had been rife in places there, and Octavian had awarded them to Herod to relieve the Roman authorities of the unrewarding chore of policing them. Also awarded to him was Gaulanitis, including what is now called the Golan Heights, parts of which were seized by modern Israel from Syria in a war in 1967. He installed a colony of his fellow Idumaeans to be his reservists in unruly Trachonitis and a colony of loyal Babylonian Jews in Batanaea.

The large, two-dimensional royal court he established in Jerusalem bolstered his image as a commanding figure. His inner court was composed of his senior officials and advisers, his closest relatives and friends, his personal bodyguard, and his personal domestic servants. His outer royal court consisted of hundreds—lesser officials, lesser relatives, and a small army of servants and slaves. Underscoring his uncontestable authority in the land was the absence of the high priest from the court's inner circles. That exalted figure had a court of his own, but it was without the secular significance his predecessors had generally enjoyed.

\* \* \*

Despite the thoroughness and harshness of his security measures, and despite his bouts of murderous fury, Herod was not malevolent by nature. His brutality was guided by his paranoia. It was directed only against those whom his highly charged imagination, spies, and security services led him to believe were or could be plotting against him or might be tempted to. He was highly focused in that regard, displaying much love and warm friendship for those closest to him. The intensity of his feelings sparked his ferocious vindictiveness when he suspected they were betraying him.

He showed great regard for the well-being of his subjects, showing compassion for them and generosity when they were under pressure from such punishing natural events as droughts and an earthquake. He promoted extensive measures designed for the public good. Attempting to establish a bond with his people, he was addicted to calling public gatherings to recount the beneficial results of his policies and programs and to announce, with some measure of accuracy, that he had brought Judaea greater economic security than it had ever before known. That he was unable to gain wide public affection because of it wounded him.

Extreme control was meant to overcome the forebodings that made his peace of mind chronically elusive. It was to provide for his personal safety and continue to secure his position as king. But he had much wider aspirations than mere survival and mental equanimity, and he acted decisively to promote those objectives after he finally recovered from his emotional turmoil over his execution of Miriamne.

The possible threat from Rome to his tenure on the throne having been overcome by Octavian's approval at Rhodes, he embarked on a campaign that would prove him to be a visionary, a masterly administrator, and one of the most accomplished rulers the ancient Jews ever had.

Judaea might easily have remained just another of Rome's assortment of little remembered client states, like Pontus, Commagene, Nabataea, and Thrace. But under Herod, it was transformed into a nation of international repute. He turned it into a secure, comparatively prosperous, bureaucratically efficient land. He changed the face of it, rebuilt and beautified war-ravaged Jerusalem, constructed new cities, and launched state-of-the-art urban renewal projects across his kingdom.

He improved and expanded existing irrigation systems in often-parched regions and introduced new ones in previously neglected areas, notably in the lower Jordan valley. He recruited new farmers and farm laborers from among the landless and settled them in previously uncultivated areas in which he had the soil reclaimed into working farms. Some of the landless were settled in existing agricultural estates appropriated from wealthy Judaeans whom he considered possible opponents.

His reign was marked by a considerable expansion of commercial enterprises and trade. He greatly increased the export of his kingdom's agricultural and other products, including asphalt excavated from the Dead Sea. He promoted the cultivation of lucrative cash crops, including balsam and other medicinal plants and spices, dates, olives, wheat, barley, and grapes. Among the new crops introduced during his reign were rice and cotton. The cultivation of citrus fruit was expanded. In addition to the rewards of broadened agricultural activity, town and village economies were enlivened by greater local market vitality and increased calls on the services of carpenters, blacksmiths, goldsmiths, potters, and other craftsmen.

As a result of Herod's various initiatives, Judaea's overall economy, previously blighted by limited purposeful direction and recurring violent conflict, was rejuvenated. The effect of his measures, and the elaborate building projects he undertook, created great numbers of jobs. Urban renewal was further stimulated as a result, and new centers of urban life were established.

Taxes were high. As well as his own levies, the Romans imposed their steep monetary demands on Herod rather than directly on the people, leaving it to him to collect what they required for forwarding to Rome. The privileged classes appear to have been worst hit by his impositions, but they were not alone in having reasons to complain. However, in years of drought, when crops failed and famine stalked the land, he reduced the taxes on his subjects. To make good his financial shortfall at those times, he sold off precious art works housed in his palaces, "both of silver and gold. . . . He did not spare the finest vessels he had, or that were made with the most elaborate skill of the artificer," and he called on his other personal and official resources.

In hard times, he exploited his contacts in the region to extract priority preference for Judaea in buying corn from Egypt, the major producer, despite the competing heavy demands of the international market. Some of the Egyptian corn Herod was able to acquire was distributed according to need among his most hard-pressed subjects. He had special attention paid to the feeding of the elderly and otherwise vulnerable. The slaughter of sheep for food had caused a shortage of wool for affordable clothing, so he also tried to provide warm clothes for them in winter.

Herod seemed to have developed a planned approach to underlying difficulties. In addition to trying to deal with problems in Judaea, he contributed some of the grain he received from Egypt to neighboring Roman Syria. Much larger than his kingdom, Syria as a whole was generally more fertile but was sometimes equally stricken. In better times, he sent thousands of agricultural laborers, whose feeding and maintenance he funded, to help with the harvests there, from which Judaea also bene-fited.

In his writings, Josephus, who was by no means an unquestioning admirer of Herod and who recounted the worst of his tyrannical conduct, gushes, "There were neither any people, nor any cities, nor any private men who . . . were in want of support, and had recourse to him, but received what they stood in need of."

The Pharisees, the religious sect most respected by his subjects, re-mained unwilling to honor a monarch who was not a descendant of King David. But, his having disposed of or otherwise displaced their Sadducee rivals from positions of authority and prerogative in the land, they had come to treat his rule with forbearance. Indeed, under Herod, schools of Pharisee scholarship flourished in Jerusalem, notably that of Babylonian-born sage Hillel, though one of Hillel's most memorable comments on the law was hardly something the king took to heart—"That which is hateful to you, do not do to your fellow. That is the whole Torah. The rest is commentary."

To Judaea's advantage, Herod's relations with Rome and Octavian turned out to be as agreeable as the latter had said it would be, though their interactions were almost always at long distance, and Herod was always careful to be obsequiously reverential to him. That was especially evident after the Senate, burying the Roman Republic for good, awarded Octavian the name Augustus (the Exalted), and he effectively made him-self the first Roman emperor. Through the warmth of Herod's dealings with Augustus Caesar, he was able to sustain uninterrupted self-rule for Judaea throughout his reign.

That he made a particularly close friend of Augustus's right-hand-man Marcus Agrippa also enhanced his and his kingdom's special status in Rome and throughout the empire. It is questionable whether, as was claimed, he was second only to Agrippa in Caesar's affections and "was beloved . . . by Agrippa next after Caesar." But he was genuinely ad-mired, valued, and even liked by both. Agrippa and other figures at the imperial court in Rome kept him abreast of developments there. He also maintained congenial contact with the successive Roman governors of neighboring Syria and other Roman luminaries posted to the region.

\* \* \*

There was nothing in Herod's background to foretell the development of the most extraordinary aspect of his interests and achievements. He was a rough-and-ready fighting man who, as a boy, had enjoyed, at best, a limited classical education, and he had shown little previous indication of a public service orientation. The opposite was true.

Nevertheless, in addition to efficiently, if despotically, administering his kingdom and the other territories Augustus awarded him, he was a prolific and wide-ranging master builder, one of the most accomplished and aspirational among the rulers of ancient times.

His building projects included new cities as well as state-of-the-art urban renewal for existing ones. He built aqueducts, reservoirs, markets, boulevards, palaces, temples, stadiums, and theaters for them. In Jerusalem, he built a theater, a hippodrome, an amphitheater, improved aqueduct and sewage systems, and an enhanced network of streets. He founded the cities of Antipatris, Cypros, and Phaesalis in Judaea in memory of his father, mother, and older brother.

His extensive municipal projects revived the ancient centers of Jericho, Hebron, Ascalon, and Sepphoris. He rebuilt Anthedon, a Mediterranean shore town ravaged by war, and renamed it Agrippeum in honor of his friend Marcus Agrippa. In honor of himself, he built the fortress of Herodium. It was adorned with a palace within, as well as a theater and other facilities, for an agreeable break away from the palace he erected for himself in Jerusalem less than ten miles distant. Herodium was also designed to be his final resting place.

He transformed the neglected remains of the ancient city of Samaria, which had been the capital of the breakaway northern kingdom of Israel before the Assyrians captured and razed it seven centuries earlier. He turned it into a showplace for his architectural and urban renewal skills and renamed it Sebaste, Augustus in Greek, in honor of the emperor and erected a stately temple there dedicated to Augustus's imperial cult. (The Augustus cult took root and spread throughout the empire as a unifying element during his imperium. In many places, Augustus was absorbed into the pantheon of pagan gods.) Herod awarded patches of land in remade Sebaste to army veterans and fortified it with strong walls. The city became a proud feature of the kingdom Herod had rejuvenated and was transforming.

It was no simple task or process. Many of his building and rebuilding projects, such as those for the Masada, Machaerus, and Alexandrium fortresses, were erected in areas far from ready access to building materials. Carting stones, building blocks often weighing many tons, over large distances was a major challenge in his construction programs.

Herod sought to convince his subjects that his buildings, his upgrading of fortified structures, and his other architectural projects were for their wellbeing rather than for his own safety and glory. He declared, "I have advanced the nation of the Jews to a degree of happiness which they never had before." His most monumental undertaking, the one that most gratified his subjects, was rebuilding the temple in Jerusalem. Just as the Torah was the spiritual heart of the Jewish faith, the temple, dedicated to Yahweh, the one God of the Jews, was its sacred palpable heart and the heart of Jerusalem.

Herod's temple was the third to have been erected on Jerusalem's Temple Mount. Solomon had built the first around the year 950 BCE as a home for the Ark of the Covenant containing the tablets of the law handed down to Moses in the Sinai Desert. The detailed description of Solomon's temple in the Bible made it appear to have been a huge, glorious structure. It lasted almost four centuries until destroyed by invading Babylonians in 586 BCE. The Ark of the Covenant went lost then, never to be seen again.

A second temple rose in Jerusalem after Cyrus, king of Persia, permitted Jews to return to their ancestral homeland from Babylonia to which they had been exiled. Its construction, on the spot where the first temple had stood, was probably completed early in the fifth century BCE. Like its predecessor, it became the central focus of Jewish worship. It also lasted centuries before being desecrated by the Seleucid Syrians in the attempt of their King Antiochus Epiphanes to Hellenize the Jews and obliterate the Jewish faith in 168 BCE. The Maccabees reconsecrated it after the success of their national liberation uprising against the Syrians.

That second Jerusalem temple was far less monumental than King Solomon's. Its grandeur and dimensions fell well short of the earlier structure. Because of the people's lack of sufficient resources and skills at the time, it had enjoyed little in the way of major upkeep. Herod vowed "to correct that imperfection, which has arisen from the necessity of our affairs and the slavery we have been under formerly, and to make a thankful return after the most pious manner to God for what blessings I have received from Him . . . by rendering his temple as complete as I am able."

Herod's announcement that he intended to undertake the project was received with apprehension by his subjects. He gave assurances that essential temple rituals would be observed as usual during the construction, but they did not trust him. They feared he would demolish the existing temple as he said he would, but then fail to build a new one in its place. The structure Herod declared he envisaged would require enormous funding. They doubted he would be willing to provide it. However, his extensive and costly preparations demonstrated his determination to proceed with the project and carry his plan to fruition.

Thousands of laborers were recruited for the work. One thousand priests were also assigned to the project. Some were taught to be masons and others to be carpenters because the law held that only priests could be permitted in certain parts of the temple. A thousand wagons were acquired for the project. They were to bring in the materials for the rebuilt structure after carting away discarded remains of the replaced one as the work proceeded. This would, in effect, be a new temple rather than a rebuilt one, though it would still come to be known as the "second temple" of the Jews.

Herod insisted on a tight schedule for the project and monitored the work as it was being done. Within two years, the walls and the central structure of the temple—much of it built with huge white stones—was completed and consecrated as a cherished place of sacrifice, worship, pilgrimage, and assemblage.

For the new structure Herod planned, he had first to alter the dimensions and shape of the Temple Mount, the high, flat expanse atop Jerusalem's Mount Moriah on which the earlier temples had stood. To accommodate the massive size he planned for the new one, he had the low ground of the existing Temple Mount filled and the higher ground around it leveled. This plateau was turned into a flat, irregular quadrangle of some 1,500 square feet, wider on its west than its east, all of it embraced by huge walls.

Most of the stones used in their construction ranged in weight from two to a staggering fifty tons each; some were even heavier. Broad roads, newly paved, ran along the streets beneath the outside of the western and southern walls. Small shops selling foodstuffs and other staples lined the far side of those streets. The remains of the west wall at the foot of the Temple Mount, a major tourist attraction to this day, is the primary extant Jewish religious site. (The area atop what is left of the wall has been the third holiest Islamic site since the Muslim conquest of Jerusalem in 637 CE. It was from there that the Prophet Mohammad is said to have ascended to heaven.)

The largest part of Herod's temple complex was a large outer court-yard known as the Court of Gentiles. It was the only part of the temple grounds to which non-Jews were permitted access. That it was open to both Gentiles and Jews was an unprecedented experience for both. It permitted rare informal proximity between them and gave Gentiles an acceptance and recognition within a Jewish framework that had never before existed in Jerusalem. According to one historian, "It changed the way Romans thought about Jews and the way Jews thought about Romans." That is probably an exaggeration but not without a germ of truth.

Paved with marble and open to the skies, the Court of Gentiles became a place of assembly where Herod sometimes addressed his subjects on his achievements. But commercial activity also regularly took place there. It was where worshippers could buy animals that would be sacrificed in the temple sanctuary and where visitors from foreign parts could change money to pay for that sort of devotional activity. That accounted for the presence there of the "money changers" Jesus was said to have driven from the temple.

Elegant porches lined long stretches of the temple walls enclosing the Court of Gentiles. Colonnades of tall marble Corinthian pillars supported the flat porch roofs. The porches became popular meeting places, presumably monitored by Herod's spies. Most magnificent among the porches was the Royal Portico running along almost the entire southern wall. Its roof was supported by rows of 162 columns, each 50 feet high. Some of those columns were so wide around that it required three men with their arms extended and hands joined to completely encircle them. An archeologist has suggested this portico was built "to enable Herod to receive, in full majesty," many of the guests and pilgrims who thronged into Jerusalem and up to the Temple Mount for religious festivals. Though the authority of the Sanhedrin was virtually emasculated by Herod, it held sessions in the Royal Portico. Later, Jews who believed Jesus was the Messiah would gather daily at the temple, meeting "together in Solomon's Porch," a smaller portico along the eastern side of the outer court.

Leading from the Court of Gentiles was the temple proper, surrounded by a breast-high marble balustrade through which only Jews were authorized to pass. In 1871, the French archeologist Charles Cler-mont-Ganneau discovered one of the fallen temple pillars bearing the inscription, "No man of another nation may enter within the balustrade around the sanctuary and the enclosure. . . . Whoever is caught on him-self shall be put the blame for his death which will ensue."

The first of the three inner courts of the temple was the Court of Women. It was open to Jewish women who were ritually clean and to Jewish men. But women were not permitted to pass beyond it further into the temple. A rounded stairway from the Court of Women led up to a huge gate of richly ornamented polished brass so heavy that it was said to take twenty men to open and close it each morning and night. Beyond this gate was the Sanctuary, open only to Jewish men and entered through the Court of Men, from which male worshippers could also ob-serve ritual animal sacrifices to God in the Court of Priests rising beyond it. The Court of Priests marked the beginning of the central part of the temple, including the Holy of Holies, the sacred chamber into which only the high priest was permitted to enter.

Herod's temple was "a work of the greatest piety and excellence." According to the Talmud, "He who has not seen the temple of Herod has never seen a beautiful building." On visiting the temple, a disciple ex-claimed to Jesus, "What wonderful stones and what wonderful build-ings!" Even from a great distance, the magnificence of the edifice was apparent.

> The outward face of the temple in its front wanted nothing that was likely to surprise either men's minds or their eyes; for it was covered all over with plates of gold of great weight and, at the first rising of the sun, reflected back a very fiery splendor and made those who forced themselves to look upon it to turn their eyes away, just as they would have done at the sun's own rays. But this temple appeared to strangers when they were coming to it at a distance like a mountain covered with snow; for as to those parts of it that were not gilt, they were exceeding white.

The rebuilt temple would alter the character of Jerusalem. In the follow-ing decades, Jews would be drawn by its monumentality from every-where in the Diaspora. They would come to the city as pilgrims, many to remain as residents. The New Testament says they came from "Parthia, Media, and Elam; from Mesopotamia, Judaea and Cappadocia; from Pon-tus and Asia, from Phrygia and Pamphylia, from Egypt and the regions of Libya near Cyrene" and from Rome, Crete, and Arabia, "both Jews and Gentiles converted to Judaism."

Jerusalem became one of the most awesome cities in the Roman Empire. Visitors marveled at its grandeur. The Roman historian Pliny the Elder calls it "by far the most famous city, not of Judaea only, but of the East." It also would become one of the most cosmopolitan cities of the Empire, a wide assortment of languages sounding out in its streets, markets, and various neighborhoods.

The temple was meant by Herod to be an enduring tribute to his architectural vision, his good works, and his Jewish identity. Among his other major projects in Jerusalem was his spectacularly towered royal palace. Built to substitute for the more modest one in which the Hasmonean kings had lived, the palace was surrounded by forty-five-foot-high walls and capable of accommodating one hundred guests in great luxury with its banqueting halls, courtyards, and cloisters. Towers and cloisters also graced the Antonia fortress adjoining the temple.

The temple and Herod's other projects required the efforts of skilled architects, engineers, sculptors, mosaicists, and other craftsmen. Their presence contributed to an atmosphere of intellectual, artistic, and cultural activity in Jerusalem, promoted also by the presence of ceremonial musicians, scribes, and scholars. Herod imported playwrights and professional orators to provide entertainment within his palaces and theaters. He brought in artists to decorate their walls, though not with forbidden images of humans or other living creatures, except in largely non-Jewish territories in his domain.

Greek intellectuals were respected figures at his royal court. They included the scholars Andromachus and Gemellus, the orator Irenaeus and, most notably, Nicolaus of Damascus, a man of great learning whom Antony and Cleopatra had employed as tutor to their children. Nicolaus became Herod's trusted adviser, taking up residence in his court. He also became Herod's instructor in philosophy and rhetoric. Historian Josephus probably drew on Nicolaus's writings, only fragments of which have survived, for his own accounts of Herod's life and works.

Under Nicolaus's influence, Herod developed a fondness for history meant to help him examine and learn from the deeds of former kings. On a voyage Herod made to Rome, he had Nicolaus accompany him to continue his tutorials aboard ship.

\* \* \*

Notwithstanding the grandeur of the rebuilt Jerusalem temple, none of Herod's building projects displayed as much of the depth and breadth of his visionary imagination, and of his determination to generate enduring esteem for his life and works, as did the city of Caesarea. A state-of-the-art urban creation, it was built on the Mediterranean coast between what are today Tel Aviv and Haifa. It became the largest city in Judaea and one of the largest cities in the Roman Empire. It was second only to Jerusalem in magnificence in the region.

Constructed over a period of twelve years, Caesarea was erected on the site of the ancient Phoenician trading town of Straton's Tower. Herod adorned it with a hippodrome, a royal palace, a spectacular seaside amphitheater, a sewer system, and an aqueduct to bring it fresh water from Mount Carmel some nine miles away.

Caesarea would later become the Roman administrative capital for Judaea. But the city's greatest pride and most remarkable feature was the port Herod built there, the world's first fully artificial seacoast harbor. It was carved out of land where no suitable topography, no bay or natural land protrusion, existed to facilitate construction of a major port. That presented enormous difficulties for Herod and his engineers, "yet did he so fully struggle with that difficulty," Josephus states, that the firmness of the completed structure "could not easily be conquered by the sea; and the beauty and ornament of the works were such, as though he had not had any difficulty in the operation."

He commissioned Italian maritime engineers to create this wonder of the ancient world. Caesarea's large, deep-sea harbor was based on two long breakwaters. The southern breakwater, 200 feet wide, poked about 1,800 feet into the sea, curving north along its extent, angling toward the northern breakwater, which was 150 feet wide and 900 feet long. A sixty-foot-wide gap between their outermost tips served as the entrance into the harbor where vessels were able to shelter comfortably from the strong, wind-driven Mediterranean tides. Those tides swept a continuous flow of silt into the harbor. But an intricate system of sluices kept it washed clean of large deposits.

As was the case with the temple, this unprecedented project of maritime engineering required extensive preparations. Because no small, close coastal islands existed to provide any natural support for constructing the breakwaters, wooden frames had to be lowered into place in the sea into which was poured newly invented hydraulic concrete capable of hardening under water. This provided the essential sturdy breakwater underpinning. The stones of which the breakwaters themselves were constructed were fifty feet by eighteen feet by nine feet, topped with a mixture of limestone and volcanic ash imported from Italy. Six huge statues, visible from well out to sea, were planted at the harbor's entrance. Overlooking the harbor's head was an imposing imperial cult temple.

Named in honor of Augustus, as was the city itself, the harbor at Caesarea gave Judaea direct access to seaborne trade, greatly enhancing its commerce and wealth creation. It came to rival the great seaport of Alexandria.

\* \* \*

The great variety, number, and imaginative quality of Herod's projects were especially remarkable for being the product of a single individual, the subservient ruler of a Roman client state occupying a tiny patch of the sprawling Roman Empire. Ehud Netzer, an archeologist and architect who closely studied Herod's architectural achievements, was much impressed by them.

> Herod's grasp of the realm of construction seems to . . . be beyond the times in which he lived. The combination of a vibrant ruler, having an analytic mind and . . . a pragmatic approach, together with a far reaching imagination, led him to initiate building projects that reflect a line of thought similar to that of an architect acting in the twentieth or twenty-first century CE. . . . [His] building enterprise was impressive not only in its broad scope but also in its diversity . . . above all in its original approach. . . . We are dealing with an architecture that combined an aesthetic appearance, a practical approach and a vivid imagination.

Herod's projects were of many types, functions, and dimensions, and his building frenzy was not confined to his kingdom. In an assortment of locations across the eastern Mediterranean, he built theaters, temples, aqueducts, gymnasiums, market places, parks, cloisters, colonnades, public baths, fountains, roads, and woods.

He graced Damascus with a theater and gymnasium. Berytus (Beirut) received market places, baths, and an amphitheater. Antioch was awarded a boulevard more than two miles long, paved with polished marble along its entire length. Athens received unspecified "offerings" for which Athenians are recorded as having expressed their gratitude "for [Herod's] beneficence and goodwill." The styles of his projects ranged from the utilitarian to the ornamental, from the traditional to the innovative, and from the spectacular to the mainstream.

As to whether Herod's architectural achievements should really be attributed to the architects he employed, Netzer believes the "originality of ideas" that his buildings displayed were "most probably the fruits of a single creative analytical mind—Herod's."

In addition to being a master builder with projects across the region, Herod was an international philanthropist. He became, as one historian put it, "as famous abroad as he was notorious at home." The shipping industry in Rhodes, for example, received financial stimulus from him, as did an assortment of other places in need of project funding. Learning that the ancient Olympic Games were in dire straits because of lack of resources, he rescued them from the terminal collapse that resulted from the repeated disruptions the Roman civil wars had caused. In gratitude, he was proclaimed president of the ancient Olympics for life. It was a particular honor for a man who had been a skilled archer and javelin thrower when younger.

Herod did not stint in pursuing his lavish building programs or on his distribution of lavish gifts to Augustus and others. It required the expenditure of great sums. He must have been extremely wealthy and have had ready access to his financial resources. He is likely to have inherited extensive wealth-producing agricultural land from his father, who had himself been heir to great estates in Idumaea and who also had probably acquired considerable assets in Judaea after Julius Caesar had appointed him its Roman-appointed procurator. It was usual for Roman appointees to accumulate wealth through the power officially vested in them (and still is in countless other cultures).

Herod may also have inherited substantial assets from his mother, who had been from a prominent Nabataean family. The wealth of his Hasmonean princess wife Miriamne had probably become his too upon their marriage and certainly upon her demise. When hard times struck, Herod's act in reducing taxes his subjects had to pay indicated they were otherwise heavily taxed. Those levies also contributed to his considerable income. In addition, he received substantial returns from his investments in Judaea's lucrative trade in balsam and date palm products and revenue from the territories Augustus awarded him. That Augustus presented him with control of copper mines in Cyprus, and a hefty portion of their proceeds, suggests that he was considered an experienced business manager.

Herod's achievements and his display of international generosity won admiration and acclaim across the eastern Mediterranean. Augustus was said to believe "the dominions of Herod were too little for the greatness of his soul" and that he deserved to be king of Syria and Egypt as well. His reputation and his position as king of the Jews enhanced the image of Jewish communities dotted across the empire, bolstering their esteem for him, in contrast to the persistent discontent and disgruntlement of the people of Judaea.

The sums he expended on lavish projects in the predominantly Greek cities and areas he administered for Augustus, and on his international philanthropy, were so great that his subjects felt deprived in comparison. They believed that his funding should have been more extensively directed toward works within his kingdom.

He responded that he was acting on instructions from Augustus. At the same time, he informed the emperor that he undertook his various projects to honor him and established quinquennial games in Caesarea as a tribute to him, making Judaea a center for international athletics and sports. Chariot drivers, wrestlers, discus throwers, and other athletes came from lands all over the Mediterranean region to compete for the lavish prizes he provided and for the international fame victory conferred on them.

That was unwelcome to many of Herod's traditionalist subjects. They abominated many of those athletic contests as incompatible with their Jewish heritage, contrary to acceptable public display, and a spectacular form of the creeping Hellenization they considered cultural imperialism.

# FIVE

## Cultural Divide

Antigonus had been mistaken when he described Herod as a "half-Jew" when defending his position as king of Judaea against him and his Roman allies, and the Jews of the land had been wrong to question whether their king fully shared their religion. Herod had as much claim to a full Jewish identity as they did. His family had been Jewish for three generations: his grandfather had been converted to Judaism; his father, Antipater, had been a practicing Jew; and Herod himself had been raised as a Jew in the Hellenized environment of the Hasmonean aristocracy to which his father had been attached.

Whether Herod's mother, Cyprus, of pagan Arab descent, retained the faith of her forebears is not known. But ancient Judaea was a paternalistic society, and religious affiliation was handed down through the paternal line. The rule that having a Jewish mother determined whether a person was a Jew had not yet been formulated. It was not in the Torah's code of laws. It was not considered the rule until some three hundred years later, possibly introduced then to discourage men from marrying out of the faith. If it had been applicable in earlier times, the children of many iconic Jewish figures, including founders of the twelve original tribes from which the Jewish nation grew, may not have been Jews because no evidence shows that their mothers had been.

Herod personally adhered meticulously to Jewish religious rituals and laws. He refused to allow his sister, Salome, to marry a Nabataean dignitary, giving as the reason the man's refusal to be circumcised as required by Torah law. Even Augustus knew that he obeyed the biblically prescribed dietary restrictions of the Jews. When Herod had two of his sons executed for alleged disloyalty, the emperor mused, "It is better to be Herod's pig than his son," a reference to the dietary restrictions prohibiting Jews from eating pork.

As a symbol of his faith, Herod exquisitely and expensively rebuilt the Jerusalem temple, the heart of his Jewish faith and that of his subjects. Instead of seeking out the best available craftsmen for many of the required construction tasks, he dutifully went through the more complicated process of having priests extensively trained to do the craftwork for parts of the structure where only priests would be permitted access by religious law. He made certain that prescribed religious rules involved in the construction were observed while the work was going on and that basic observances within it were not disturbed during the construction.

Guardians of the faith may have looked askance when he chose and discharged high priests at will, even having one of them—his young brother-in-law—murdered. But though he made certain never to be upstaged by any of them as leader of the people in the minds of his subjects, he did not assume for himself that esteemed priestly role, as previous kings of Judaea had done. Nor did he presume to take on any of their exalted religious functions.

In contrast to the ways of non-Jewish monarchs in those days, Herod did not require an image of himself to be displayed on the coins of his kingdom, nor did he have statues of himself built in areas of his kingdom where Jews predominated in the population. Jewish law forbade such depictions of human form, though he did permit statues of himself to be erected in non-Jewish parts of his domain. In an incident in a corridor of his theater in Jerusalem, when a statue in battle dress representing an opponent he had defeated in battle dismayed people, he calmed their consternation by stripping down the forbidden human likeness to reveal just an innocent wooden frame supporting the armor. His sacrifice to the Roman god Jupiter after being proclaimed king by the Romans could be considered to have been a matter of courtesy, or a sense of obligation under the circumstances, rather than an act of sacrilege against his faith.

It is, of course, possible his commitment to Judaism and its ways was not deeply implanted. His religious observances may have been disingenuous. He may have flaunted his Jewish observances in order to justify being king of the Jews despite having been crowned by the Romans in the hope of moderating the antagonism of his subjects.

Furthermore, Herod was perceived as being "more friendly to the Greeks than the Jews." In two of Judaea's largest cities—Caesarea, which he created largely from scratch, and Sebaste (Samaria), which he magnificently rebuilt—he promoted the growth of Hellenic, rather than Jewish, culture. He also cultivated the Hellenizing process at his royal court in Jerusalem, which he adorned with Hellenic scholars and where Greek was the language spoken. He appointed non-Jews to important positions in his government and to senior command in his army.

Aspects of his character and conduct were those of an Oriental monarch rather than of a traditional Jewish king. He is thought to have been bisexual. He kept eunuchs as personal servants. He made regular concessions to foreign influences, having Greek plays performed in the theaters he built and hosting music recitals by performing artists from other lands. He had inscriptions honoring Augustus affixed to the walls of his theaters, though it was not in the Jewish tradition to immortalize their foreign rulers in such a way.

The amphitheaters and hippodromes he built in Jerusalem, Jericho, and other Jewish cities did not conform to the traditions of the Jews, nor was the use to which they were put easily reconcilable with Jewish sensitivities. He promoted Greek-style athletics, wrestling matches, and chariot races. He gathered a menagerie of fierce animals and put them on show with condemned men who, in Roman fashion, were made to fight them, or for the animals to fight each other. He sponsored gladiatorial spectacles, which Jewish traditionalists considered unseemly at best.

In the manner of a gushing eastern sub-ruler, Herod went to obsequious lengths, contrary to Jewish religious sensitivities, to guarantee that Augustus's patronage, esteem, and trust would never falter. He erected statues of him and temples to his pagan religious cult in Caesarea and Sebaste and in the Greek cities the emperor had put under his jurisdiction. He sent his most loved sons Alexander and Aristobulus to be educated by tutors in Rome rather than by Pharisees in Jerusalem.

His Hellenizing proclivities helped fuel the antipathy that kept his subjects focused dejectedly on the Roman source of his authority and the tyrannical nature of his rule. It undermined the esteem in which they might have held him for the benefits he bestowed on the land.

\* \* \*

Alexander the Great had introduced Hellenic culture to the Middle East in the fourth century BCE. It had deep-reaching impact with comparative rapidity after his conquest of the region. Within a few generations, Greek cultural influences became predominant in many of its areas. The pagan inhabitants of cities on the fringes of Judaea—Ptolemais on the Mediterranean coast, Philoteria on the Sea of Galilee, and the Decapolis of ten cities on the east bank of the Jordan River and in Syria—were readily Hellenized. Many Jews interacted with them, learning their language and their ways.

In Judaea's countryside and small towns, traditional Jewish culture continued to resist the tide of change. But in Jerusalem and other urban centers, Hellenism made deep inroads among the social, intellectual, and commercial elite—senior priests, officials, merchants, landowners, and scribes. While remaining observant Jews, they sought to marry Greek ways to Jewish life.

Many spoke Greek, the lingua franca of the wider region, as their language of choice rather than the Aramaic of the ordinary folk or the Hebrew of their scriptures. Many knew the Bible only, or mainly, through its Greek translation. They called their children by their Greek rather than Hebrew names—Jason or Jesus rather than Yehoshua, John rather than Yohanan, Onias rather than Honiyya, Salome rather than Shlomit. The young people of Judaea were drawn to Greek fashions in clothes and comportment. Greek athletic contests, including nude wrestling, which offended the sensibilities of traditionalists, became popular.

In 175 BCE, well before Herod's time, a gymnasium was built in Jerusalem under the auspices of the Hellenized Jewish High Priest Jason, who had been appointed to his office by the Syrian ruler of Judaea at the time. It became a center for athletic and cultural activities foreign to traditional Jewish practices. According to the Book of Maccabees, "The craze for Hellenism and foreign customs reached such a pitch . . . that the priests . . . disdaining the temple and neglecting the sacrifices, hastened . . . to take part in the unlawful exercises on the athletic field . . . and despised what their ancestors regarded as honors."

Nevertheless, most Jews resisted Hellenic influences at the time and continued to live largely according to their ancestral ways. The popular rising led by Judah Maccabee and his brothers against Syrian king Antiochus Epiphanes when he attempted to Hellenize Judaea and obliterate Jewish religious observances was motivated by cultural as well as religious and nationalist sentiment. Striving to purge the Hellenic influences from traditional Jewish culture, the Maccabees "pursued the wicked, hunting them out." They overthrew Syrian rule and demonized Hellenization. But it soon regained respectability among those who believed such ways did not defile or degrade their Jewish faith.

During the tenure of warrior–high priest John Hyrcanus I, the son of the last of the Maccabee brothers who had led the Jews, Hellenization among their elite classes increased markedly. Though Hyrcanus remained a Jew in belief and practice, his court came to be largely Hellenized in character. He also recruited large numbers of non-Jewish mercenaries for his army.

The guardians of the traditional ways, notably the ultra-pious Hasidim, who were the forerunners of the Pharisees, sought to discourage and repel Hellenizing incursions. But what they dismissed as alien intrusions became attractive to increasing numbers of urban Jews. A split deepened in Judaean society between those who considered Hellenization a welcome, invigorating modernization of Judaism and traditionalists, who saw it as destructive of Jewish identity. It was a division roughly comparable to the rift between Reform and Orthodox Jews in modern times.

By the time Herod became king, Hellenization had long been a matter of contention and discord in Judaea, a class as well as cultural issue. But during his reign, the controversy over its inroads in the land of the Jews was brought into sharper focus. Herod's aim was to transform his kingdom into a glittering modern state in which he would glow in its reflected glory. He accepted without question that the leaders of the Roman Empire, to whom he kowtowed and whose ways he admired, were the masters of the world in which he lived and functioned, and Rome was strongly influenced by Hellenism in the Middle East. Its culture influences there were overwhelmingly Greco-Roman, rather than purely Roman.

Most of Herod's subjects, ill-disposed to him from the start, never came to terms with what was to them his eccentric and often alien interests and enthusiasms. Adapting to his vision and cultural ecumenism would have eroded their biblically established conviction that they were God's people and their assumption that any king of theirs should conduct himself accordingly rather than succumb to foreign ways. They held that Herod's compliant approach to Hellenization undermined the established character of their ancestral homeland. They bridled at his unwillingness as king to commit fully to the traditional cultural patterns of their land. His failure to do so contributed to his inability to win esteem and affection as their ruler.

The situation was different among Jews elsewhere in the Roman Empire where Herod's Jewish identity was not subjected to questioning. Their original Diaspora had been established in Babylonia five centuries earlier. Jewish communities had subsequently developed in other places and, by Herod's time, were long established in many parts of the empire. Though widely open to Hellenic influences through lengthy interaction with their "Greek" neighbors, their inhabitants were emotionally attached to Judaea and to the Jerusalem temple in particular, contributing regularly to its upkeep. They were proud of Herod's positive international standing and of the high regard in which Judaea was held in the region during his reign. It reflected well on them, and they were appreciative of the benefits that came their way throughout the empire as a result of his lobbying on their behalf with his Roman connections. Herod's actions in that respect have had enduring significance over the centuries, cementing to this day the sense of togetherness between the peoples of Jewish Diaspora communities and the Land of Israel.

# SIX

## Palace Intrigue

For Herod to have permitted an assortment of his family members to impinge upon his public as well as his private life was remarkable. He was otherwise a highly focused, authoritarian monarch. But in this, as in other things, the Herod story is special. Both his blood relatives and several he acquired through marriage had a traumatic impact on his life and image. Ultimately, they contributed to deranging the balance of his mind.

In addition to Miriamne and her mother, Alexandra, both of them executed early in his reign, those primarily involved to greater or lesser degree were Herod's sister, Salome, and brother Pheroras; Alexander and Aristobulus, the two sons he'd had with his beloved Miriamne; his first-born son, Antipater, from whom he had earlier been estranged; Glaphyra, wife of Herod's son Alexander and daughter of King Archelaus of Cappadocia; and Herod's niece Berenice, wife of his son Aristobulus.

Unlike Miriamne, most of Herod's other nine wives appear to have had little impact on his thoughts, state of mind, or well-being. But Doris, his first wife whom he married when he was a young man, was an exception. She bore him Antipater, but he divorced her and banished them both before he married Miriamne, permitting them to return to Jerusalem only for religious holiday celebrations. He remarried Doris late in life when Antipater was brought back into Herod's affections and rose in royal favor at the expense of his half brothers, Alexander and Aristobulus. She soon involved herself in palace conspiracies.

Herod's third and fourth wives were a niece of his and a cousin, whose names have been lost. His fifth wife, Miriamne II, was the beautiful daughter of a low-ranking priest whom he had made high priest in order to provide her with the appropriate social credentials for someone who was to be one of his wives. Then came Malthace, a Samaritan woman whose sons Archelaus and Antipas were unexpectedly to become Herod's principal heirs. His seventh wife, Cleopatra, was a Jerusalem woman whose son Philip became the third of Herod's primary heirs. Pallas, Phedra and Elpis, of whom little is known other than their names, were his last wives.

As previously noted, Herod had been badly shaken, became ill, and was reduced to incapacitating grief after having Miriamne killed. But he had recovered from that loss and had proceeded to transform himself into an accomplished national leader. However, family matters began spinning out of control for him again after he returned from a visit to Rome in 17 BCE when he was fifty-six years old and had already reigned for twenty years. He had gone there to collect Alexander and Aristobulus, the offspring of whom he was fondest, just as Miriamne, their mother, had been the only one of his ten wives whom he loved passionately enough for their relationship to have been deeply charged emotionally.

When the two had still been boys, they had been sent off to Rome to be educated. As the sons of an esteemed friend of Roman luminaries, and being royals themselves, they were treated with honor and respect in the capital of the empire. They stayed with a friend of Herod who was close to members of Augustus Caesar's family. Caesar himself took an interest in their education and may have put them up in his palace for a time.

When they completed their studies and Herod went to fetch them back from Rome, Augustus entertained him warmly and personally handed his sons over to him for the return to Jerusalem. Alexander was nineteen years old then, Aristobulus eighteen.

Their celebrity status went back with them to Judaea, as did the aristocratic mannerisms and attitudes they had acquired. As sons of a Hasmonean mother, they were spared the suspicion and antipathy their father inspired among Herod's subjects and were received with admiration wherever they went. Alexander, the more commanding of the two, was particularly popular with the army and was seen as the probable successor to his father on the throne. If he were to inherit the crown, it could lead to a Hasmonean revival.

The presence of the two princes in Jerusalem, and the popular acclaim they aroused, infuriated Salome and Pheroras. Aside from their abiding contempt for the deceased Miriamne and their bitterness about how Hasmoneans scorned their less exalted origins, Herod's siblings were concerned about their own future. They feared that if something happened to their brother, and either of those two princes ascended the throne in his place, he would avenge the way they and others on the Idumaean branch of the royal family had conspired against their mother.

To deal with their disquiet about what might happen to their privileged status if the situation was allowed to run its course undirected, Salome and Pheroras launched a campaign to demonize their young nephews. They, and their partisans at the royal court—including Herod's wives who were held in open disdain by Miriamne's sons—had it bruited about that the young princes hated their father for having had their mother put to death. It was rumored that they considered it immoral for them to have anything to do with Herod other than what was absolutely required.

Salome, who had been instrumental in inflaming his ultimately murderous suspicions about Miriamne, was particularly determined that the late queen's sons be equally disgraced in her brother's eyes. Her malign rumor spreading was skillfully undertaken. The refusal of her proud nephews to stoop to refuting the pernicious tales told about them compounded the effect those aspersions had. Before long, reports filtered through to Herod that his favorite sons were said to hold him in contempt and longed for vengeance for the tragic fate of their mother.

Still afflicted by vestiges of regret over her death and greatly fond of the princes, Herod did not credit such stories when they first reached him and had both sons married off well. He arranged for Alexander to marry Princess Glaphyra of Cappadocia. To Salome's disgust, it put Alexander in line to one day becoming king of that land as well as Judaea.

Herod gave Alexander's brother Aristobulus in marriage to Salome's daughter Berenice. It was an attempt by the king to tighten links between the Hasmonean and Idumaean branches of his family whose continuing mutual antipathy pained him despite his earlier rancor about inherited Hasmonean privilege. Though Salome detested her new son-in-law, she was in no position to challenge her royal brother's matchmaking. However, Aristobulus made no effort to conceal how little affection or regard he had for the commoner, Idumaean cousin his father had chosen to be his wife.

Salome continued to disseminate defamatory rumors about both brothers, as did their uncle Pheroras. His dislike for his uppity half-Hasmonean nephews was magnified by the fact that they outranked him at court and were self-assured, while he, alone among Herod's blood relatives, was not. While he and Salome did their scheming behind-the-scenes so as not to rile their brother, the targets of their backbiting continued to display no such cunning restraint. Alexander and Aristobulus did not condescend to take notice of the damaging rumors circulated about them. But with the arrogance, rashness, and aplomb that came with their noble rank, youthfulness, and advantaged upbringing, they made no effort to disguise what little regard they had for their father's lowborn siblings. Indeed, they were goaded on by "their [seeming] friends" to openly express their scornful feelings about them. Salome's allies and agents at court seized upon their lack of guile and made certain their unconcealed distaste for the king's sister and brother would appear to be directed against the king as well.

The candor and hauteur of the brothers served Salome's purposes. Though they displayed no open disrespect for their father, it was implied in, and could readily be inferred from, their open distress over their mother's execution though it had taken place long before. Soon, the workings of the Jerusalem gossip mills spread the stories beyond the confines of the royal court of Alexander and Aristobulus's anguish over Miriamne's fate. Discord in the royal family became common knowledge across the city. It was particularly pumped up at court while Herod was away from Judaea, traveling with Marcus Agrippa through some of Rome's eastern territories of which Augustus had named Agrippa governor.

Agrippa found Herod to be an agreeable and generous travel companion. Wherever they went, Herod bestowed gifts on the local folk and did whatever else he could to gain their admiration as well as that of his distinguished friend. Agrippa was much impressed with his diplomatic skills. In Ilium (Troy), for example, to the satisfaction of both parties, he reconciled Agrippa with the people who had risked angering him with their complaints.

The tour had the effect of cementing the friendship between the two men. Herod took advantage of it when they reached Ionia on the coast of

Anatolia. Upon their arrival, they were met by a delegation of Ionian Jews who claimed to be mistreated by the majority Greek population. They complained they were being denied rights Rome had conferred on them. They said they were being prevented from being true to their religious obligations, kept from properly celebrating their holy days, and blocked from sending funds for the upkeep of the temple in Jerusalem.

Agrippa was persuaded by Herod to hear their complaint and then announced he was responding sympathetically to it because of his traveling companion's good will and friendship. He decreed that the privileges the complainants had earlier enjoyed under Roman decrees were to be restored.

Throughout the tour, Herod left mementoes of his visit at almost all places they stopped. They included cash gifts and the funding of roads, cloisters, and other projects. He also extracted from Agrippa Roman favors for their stopover localities. He was acclaimed wherever they went, especially in Jewish Diaspora settlements through which word of his achievement in Ionia had quickly circulated. It was a reaction markedly different from the sullen forbearance he experienced from his subjects in Judaea. Agrippa was greatly impressed by Herod's conduct on their journey.

Herod was understandably in good spirits when he returned from his travels. But not for long. Salome and Pheroras had worried that their brother was exposed to danger during his foreign excursion and that if something happened to him, young Prince Alexander would immediately take up his fallen crown, exposing them to troubling consequences. When Herod was back in Jerusalem, they stepped up their efforts to turn him against their nephews.

Abandoning their previous reliance on behind-the-scenes provocation, they directly intimated to Herod that his favorite sons were a threat to him. They led him to believe that during his absence, they had begun openly expressing their conviction that their father had criminally murdered their mother and that her death had to be avenged. Accounts brought to Herod from other sources seemed to confirm that allegation. It included a report that they were thinking of enlisting the support of Alexander's newly acquired father-in-law, King Archelaus of Cappadocia, to take their accusation to Augustus in Rome and ask him for justice.

Herod was outraged that such a move could be even contemplated. If anyone were to presume to inform Augustus of his family matters, it would be himself. Besides, Archelaus was his friend. That he might be drawn into this unseemly squabble was intolerable.

Ironically, despite the murderous fury with which Herod had dealt with relatives he had thought disloyal or a threat (Miriamne; her teenage high priest brother; her grandfather Hyrcanus; Salome's second husband, Joseph; and her third husband, Costobarus), he was very much a caring family man. His strong feelings about the family bond were perhaps a residue of his tribal origins. It had twice been demonstrated earlier when he had taken pains to have his close relatives escorted to safe refuge away from Jerusalem when he thought his own survival and his ability to protect them might be at risk as a result of conflict between Roman luminaries.

He was especially devoted to his blood relatives. But now, because of the sniping of Salome and Pheroras, the tittle-tattle they had inspired, and the indiscretion of the sons of whom he was most fond, the two princes were in jeopardy. He had brought them lovingly back from Rome where they had been educated and had expected Alexander to eventually succeed him on the throne. What should have been a time of fulfillment and contentment for him after his gratifying travels with Agrippa was instead turning staggeringly sour, just as it had with Miriamne after his felicitous meeting with Octavian in Rhodes.

In search of relief from the distress his sons' alleged betrayal was causing him, he turned with a display of affection to Antipater, his firstborn son. Named after Herod's father, Antipater had been born thirty-one years earlier. His mother, Herod's first wife, Doris, had been a commoner like him. They had married when he was a young man just embarking on his rise to power. He had divorced her just before marrying Miriamne and gaining a family foothold in the Hasmonean aristocracy.

Having been banished from Jerusalem with his mother, Antipater had lived his early years and young manhood in obscurity and probably in poverty, in sharp contrast to the privileged upbringing of his half brothers Alexander and Aristobulus. After Miriamne's execution, Antipater and his mother had been permitted to return to Jerusalem, though not to the royal court or high favor.

Salome encouraged Herod to send for Antipater when she believed, gratifyingly, that his suspicions about his two other oldest sons were being stirred. She saw Herod's firstborn as someone who could displace Alexander and Aristobulus in her brother's affections and thus preempt a possible Hasmonean revival at her expense. But Herod's love for the young princes had been shaken, not destroyed. He still preferred them to Antipater, but he made a display of bestowing his good will upon their older half brother with whom he had previously had virtually no contact. He allowed the impression to circulate that Antipater had now graduated to the position of preferred heir to the throne. He hoped the threat of disinheritance would stun the other two, bring them to their senses, and draw their disrespectful shenanigans to an end.

But Herod's ploy failed to produce the intended result. Alexander, now twenty-two years old, and Aristobulus, twenty-one, thought it beneath their dignity to put on an act and respond the way he wished. They had always been lauded and catered to. Their father's gambit presented them with a totally new and unsettling experience. Herod assumed it would make them recognize they had been behaving improperly. Instead, they made no effort to conceal their sense of having been insulted by Antipater's upgrading at court to their disadvantage.

For Antipater, the situation was also new and different. He had long wallowed in resentment at being denied what he considered his birthright as Herod's firstborn. Now emboldened by his enhanced status, he hastened to seize upon the circumstances in which he suddenly had his father's ear, attention, and apparent favor.

Pretending to be above the fray, he sought to deepen Herod's disillusion with his half brothers. He was careful not to appear to be gloating at their increasingly battered standing, acting instead through accomplices at court the way Salome and Pheroras had done. It was easy enough for him to find surrogates in an environment so deeply etched with intrigue. Courtiers prepared to serve him made certain the king was kept regularly informed of the relentless bitterness of the two princes over their father's shameful execution of their mother.

Some at court were willing to serve Antipater's purpose because they had become convinced he, rather than Alexander, would be the next king and hoped for personal advancement through their support for the newly risen star in the Jerusalem firmament; others because they were offended by Alexander's and Aristobulus's ingrained patrician manner.

As Antipater's main rival for the throne, Alexander was the primary target of his vilification. When the tales circulated suggesting he was plotting against their father, Antipater would pretend to be "a kind brother . . . [and] contradict what was said," as if coming to Alexander's defense, before subtly intimating that those stories might actually not be fanciful fabrications. While seeming to be defending Alexander against malicious gossip, he thus, in effect, confirmed that he believed his half brother was conspiring against their father.

His furtive campaign gradually proved effective. Rebounding from what had been his affection for Alexander and Aristobulus, Herod drew Antipater ever closer. At his urging, Herod remarried Antipater's mother, Doris, his once-banished first wife, adding her to the wives he already had, and permitted her a position at court where she helped conspire on her son's behalf.

Herod wrote to Augustus, telling him how much he admired his previously neglected oldest son. He arranged for him to be taken to Rome to meet the emperor, escorted there by no less than Augustus's most trusted aide Marcus Agrippa. Herod also wrote to other distinguished figures in Rome lauding his new favorite offspring, assuring him a friendly welcome and even greater celebrity than Alexander and Aristobulus had enjoyed there as youths.

But Antipater was keenly aware of Herod's mercurial temperament. While relishing the high regard in which he was now held by his father, he knew he could be brought back down as quickly as he had been raised up, while his now floundering half brothers might find themselves on a reverse path. He wrote to Herod from Rome to cover his back, saying he was worried about his father's personal safety. He claimed to have heard rumors in Rome alleging that Alexander and Aristobulus were plotting against him.

Herod's easily aroused paranoia was once more triggered into active play. With such accounts of treason reportedly being heard in Rome as well as in Jerusalem, he began to accept as factual the stories reaching him that the two princes had a scheme actually in the works to bring him down. He was tempted to act as mercilessly against them as he normally did when disloyalty and sedition were suspected.

But Herod recognized that Alexander and Aristobulus were known, even by Augustus, to have been his favorites, just as their mother had been. Augustus had known them as agreeable young princelings when they had been growing up in Rome. It would seem strange—*Herod* might seem strange—if he dealt harshly with them. Instead, he left Judaea and hurried to Rome to properly sort this matter out and then on to Augustus at the seaside town of Aquileia in northeast Italy where he was vacationing. He hauled along his allegedly conspiring sons to explain themselves to the emperor. Bringing them before the startled Augustus, he asked him to offer his judgment in this affair.

Though Augustus could not have been pleased to be thrust into a messy family quarrel, he agreed to hear the details. In a scene very much like a trial, he listened as Herod charged his and Miriamne's two sons with being villains and traitors, seeking to destroy him. He said they had behaved despicably despite his having been their loving father and despite the luxuries he had lavished on them, including the illustrious marriages he had arranged for them.

He said he had long known of their wicked intentions and could have used his own authority to deal with their treachery (as he had with their disloyal mother was the unfortunate if unintentional allusion). He said he had restrained from doing so but could no longer endure the pain of it. It was for that reason he had brought them before Augustus, "their common benefactor," for their foul transgressions to be judged.

The alleged culprits seemed at first shocked into silence by their father's accusation and were reduced to tears by the vehemence of his presentation. But their emotional reaction—distraught and unspoken—evoked sympathy from Augustus and reminded him of the fondness he'd had for them when he knew them as boys. Their verbal restraint and tearfulness even drew pity from their accusing father, leeching the anger from his face.

Alexander finally broke the silence that followed his father's tirade. He said he was grateful to Herod for not having executed him and his brother when he could easily have done so. He denied there was any truth to the accusations that they had prepared poison to kill him or had bribed one of Herod's servants to assist in their plotting or that they had acted against him in other ways. He said the charge that he wanted to kill his father in order to seize the throne for himself made no sense because he and his brother loved their father so deeply that they could not go on living if they believed they had truly wronged him.

He confessed they still openly grieved over the fate of their mother. But he said it was because they sought to defend her reputation. He said that though long dead, she was still being maligned by wicked slander, just as they themselves were being anonymously maligned.

The brothers could not have hoped for a more favorable reaction to Alexander's words. Augustus was openly moved. He had previously doubted the extent of the brothers' misconduct and thought Herod had, in any case, made too much of this matter. He now declared himself convinced of their innocence, though he said the brothers might have avoided being put in such a difficult position if they had taken greater effort to be seen to be acting more properly toward their father. He urged Herod and his sons to apologize to each other and restore their loving relationship.

Responding to a gesture from Caesar, Alexander and Aristobulus began to kneel before their father as a display of their submission, respect, and love. But Herod stopped them. He now accepted his differences with his sons had been blown out of proportion. Raising them up, he embraced each to the gratification of all in attendance, including, it seemed, Antipater. He had been brought along for the proceedings and was silently seething with disappointment at how things were turning out.

Augustus invited Herod to stay on a little while in Italy afterward, signifying his continuing trust in him. Herod did so, and to compensate for having troubled Augustus with a family fuss, he presented him with a sizable gift of money to fund poor relief in Rome and crowd-pleasing public spectacles for the people of the city.

As a sign of the emperor's continuing esteem and confidence in Herod's executive abilities, he awarded him control of lucrative copper mines in Cyprus and a hefty share of their proceeds. Augustus also granted him the right to decide which one of his sons would be his heir or whether he would distribute rule of the different parts of his kingdom among them. Caught up in the spirit of the moment, Herod said he would immediately signify how such a parceling out would be made. But Augustus had no wish to risk prematurely undermining the rule of so efficient an administrator for Rome's Judaea. He ruled out even the suggestion of any division of Herod's kingdom while the king was still alive.

Upon his return to Jerusalem, Herod publicly listed his three oldest sons in order of precedence as his heirs—first Antipater, then Alexander, then Aristobulus. But he made certain his courtiers, senior officials, and senior military commanders understood that they continued to owe allegiance only to him. There was still a kingdom to run and its various difficulties to resolve.

The usually restive people of Trachonitis to the east had revolted during his absence. Though his military commanders had restored order, there was a follow-up to be seen to. Also, the building of the city of

Caesarea was completed about then, and he had to tend to the previously arranged celebrations. The high points were athletic games involving hand-to-hand combat by gladiators, combat with wild animals, horse races, and other contests to which celebrities and officials from around the region had been invited. It was a spectacular extravaganza. Herod was very proud of it and the admiration it elicited. To his relief, the family problems that had caused him so much anguish had been resolved.

Except they had not. Rivalry, mutual dislike, and jockeying for advantage were so deeply ingrained among Herod's closest kin that discord and bad blood continued to fester behind the scenes. The atmosphere at court was soon as poisonous as it had earlier been.

Though relieved to have been spared punishment when brought before Augustus, Alexander and Aristobulus remained resentful at being made inferior to Antipater in the line of succession to the throne. At the same time, Antipater considered his preeminent position most exposed to threat. Though confirmed as Herod's primary heir and though his mother, Doris, newly remarried to Herod, was permitted to rise to a position of respect at court, he feared his impulsive father might find some reason to resume his earlier preference for his downgraded half brothers. He believed it prudent to resort to preemptive defensive tactics and resumed his covert scandal mongering about them.

The wives of Herod's newly reprieved sons also contributed to reviving familial disharmony. Alexander's wife Glaphyra, as spouse of a half-Hasmonean prince and a member of the royal family of Cappadocia, openly poured scorn on Herod's lowborn Idumaean relatives and his assortment of commoner wives. Her sister-in-law, young Aristobulus's wife Berenice, Salome's daughter, was included in the targets of her disdain.

Salome, also one of Glaphyra's pet hates, was similarly incapable of passing up the opportunity to inflame family antagonisms. She poisoned Berenice's mind against her newly acquired son-in-law, easy enough to do in view of Aristobulus's abiding resentment at having been made to wed her. Salome gleaned from her daughter that Aristobulus's bitterness against his father over his mother's fate remained unquenched despite the recent reconciliation in Augustus's presence. Herod was duly informed.

Pheroras, the other royal sibling, also did his bit to keep the cauldron of family discord stirred. Herod was furious when his brother rejected his permission for him to marry one of his daughters. Pheroras had fallen in love with a palace maidservant and wished to marry her instead of his niece. He subsequently also turned down the proffered privilege of marriage to another of Herod's daughters. Risking his brother's disfavor, he wed the maid instead.

To make matters worse, at Salome's coaxing, Pheroras informed Alexander that Herod lasciviously desired Glaphyra. That his father could entertain such squalid lust for his wife enraged the prince. It outraged Herod too when he was apprised of this scandalous rumor about himself. He sharply berated his brother and grew angrier still when Pheroras said their sister, Salome, not only was the source of the allegation but also had persuaded him to pass it on.

Confronted by Herod with the charge that she was trying to cause a new breach between him and his sons, Salome strenuously denied it. She protested that she herself was the target of a plot meant to damage her in her brother's eyes. There was truth to that because Herod's wives complained about her to the king because of the insensitive capriciousness with which she treated then, sometimes treating them as friends, sometimes as foes, often as nonentities. But Salome insisted that she cared for the king's safety more than anyone else, a revelation the ever-suspicious king might not have been completely pleased to hear. He found meeting with his brother and sister ever more distressing and finally ordered them both out of his sight.

By now, every principal member of Herod's family was caught up in intra-family resentments and maneuverings. Their conduct once again had a deeply disconcerting effect on Herod's spirit and psyche. His strong sense of family made it even more unsettling. It subjected him once again to the harrowing mental stress that would plague him till the last day of his life, driving him finally to the brink of insanity.

As always, he was punishingly eager to be informed of all reports and rumors bearing on his personal safety. There were more than enough, and his feverish misgivings brought some who had greatest access to him under his suspicion. They included three long-trusted eunuch servants. Two of them saw to his meals; the third was authorized to deal with various important administrative matters as well as the king's personal care, including arranging for him at bedtime.

Herod was told that Alexander had given money to those eunuchs for undisclosed services. They were said to be attractive in appearance. Questioned, they confessed they had engaged in sex with the prince. Nothing was suspicious about that; Herod is believed also to have been bisexual. But they denied they had been involved in plotting against the king. When tortured, they said more: that Alexander's hatred for Herod was deeply implanted and that he believed the king had lived long enough. The prince had allegedly mentioned to them personal matters about Herod, including that he dyed his hair to conceal his advanced age; he was then sixty-three years old. Alexander was also said to have told them that distinguished foreign figures supported his own claim to the throne and that preparations were in play involving friends "ready both to do and to suffer whatsoever" to gain him the crown from Herod without further delay.

Not only did the torture-driven disclosures put Alexander in jeopardy once more, but Herod was tormented by thoughts of who else at his court might be plotting against him. Only a select few of even the king's most favored officials, advisers, and friends remained above suspicion. Herod's palace spies were instructed to monitor the actions and movements especially of courtiers whose rank, duties, influence, and intimacy put them in a position to harm the king. The royal palace became a place of dread and foreboding. Fewer individuals were now permitted an audience with the king or to be in his presence. Those barred included formerly trusted advisers and previously close friends, sometimes only because they were known to be friends with Alexander, though such a relationship between a courtier and a prince of the royal blood was natural and usual.

Fearful of what anyone might be saying about them in that climate of intrigue, some at court sought to secure immunity to charges of disloyalty to the king by slandering others. Others seized the opportunity to put long-standing rivals in peril by insinuating they were guilty of secret transgressions. Some who had been close friends "were become wild beasts to one another, as if a certain madness had fallen upon them." Some whom Herod previously had no reason to distrust were executed because of what was said about them. In some cases, he subsequently felt guilty for having succumbed to malicious tale bearing and had the tale-bearers put to death as well.

Antipater was one of the few Herod believed he could count on. He had come to consider his firstborn his anchor of fidelity now that it was difficult for him to tell whom else to trust. Unceasingly wary of his father's changeable moods, Antipater sought to cement his acquired privileged standing by encouraging Herod to widen his net of mistrust to include anyone he considered a possible threat to his own improved standing. But he continued to consider Alexander his particular nemesis.

The prince was also the target of those who hoped to deflect suspicion from themselves. He was certainly likely to have thought it unforgivable that his father had killed his mother and may well have detested him because of it. He is sure to have wished Herod would relinquish the throne to him before much longer. But it is doubtful that he engaged in plotting after having already so narrowly escaped execution.

Nevertheless, the tales of Alexander's alleged treachery rattled Herod's mental balance. At times, he imagined his son to be standing behind him with a drawn sword. Finally, exhausted by such unnerving thoughts and by the rumors and reports, he had his once-most-loved son imprisoned pending further action against him.

Bitter, frightened, the balance of his own mind under stress, Alexander composed a long confession of guilt in confinement and claimed that the plot to destroy Herod was widespread. He said many of the king's closest friends and officials were among the conspirators. They were said even to include his uncle, royal brother Pheroras. He also claimed his aunt Salome had come to his chambers and forced him to lay with her.

It may have been that Alexander was hoping the implausibility of these disclosures would finally awaken his father to the realization of how remote from the truth were the accusations of conspiracy and betrayal to which he had been subjected. If that really was Alexander's intention, it failed. A suspected conspirator had said under torture that Alexander had asked friends in Rome to persuade Augustus to summon him into his presence so that he could reveal that Herod had made secret approaches to the Parthian enemies of the Romans. It would be a disaster for his father if such a lie were believed.

In Cappadocia, King Archelaus, informed of the developments in Jerusalem by his daughter Glaphyra, feared for the life of his imprisoned son-in-law. He hurried to Judaea to use his friendship with Herod to try to calm the situation. Archelaus knew Herod well enough to believe that trying to convince him no plot existed would only lead him to conclude that he was in on it. Fixing on a different approach, he denounced Alexander as an ingrate and a traitor. He intimated he would force Glaphyra to divorce this wretched figure and would be taking her home to Cappadocia. What was more, he would punish her severely if he discovered she had known of Alexander's plot against his father and had not exposed it.

Archelaus told Herod Alexander's villainous conduct had put him beyond the call of mercy. He asked to be permitted into his presence in his confinement so that he might kill him for his treachery. He said Herod's restraint in not yet having disposed of his ungrateful and perfidious son was admirable but excessive, unwarranted, and astonishing.

The tactic worked. Even before Archelaus had finished with his litany of condemnation, Herod began defending his disgraced offspring and suggesting he probably wasn't really as bad as he had been made out to be. He urged his friend not to be so hard on Alexander and to leave his son's marriage to Glaphyra intact.

Having achieved his immediate purpose, Archelaus turned his attention to Herod's brother Pheroras who was already out of favor with the king. He approached him and accused him of having tried to damage the Herod-Alexander, father-son relationship. Taking Archelaus's advice now that Herod was in a forgiving mood, Pheroras went to his brother, declared himself responsible for some of the unfortunate developments, and begged forgiveness.

Herod was pleased to give it and also to free Alexander from confinement. He felt relieved that things were out in the open and that he had been able to act the wronged but merciful father and brother, in command of a complex situation. This display of compassion after so much tension at court was much welcomed there. Examining what was transpiring, Antipater was prudent enough to back quietly out of the situation for the moment. The edge taken off family turmoil, Herod was able to concentrate once more on affairs of state.

# SEVEN

## Crisis

Herod's relations with Judaea's Nabataean neighbors should not have been as fraught as they turned out to be or to have caused him as much bother as they did. His mother was from a high-ranking Nabataean family. His father had enjoyed mutually agreeable relations with the Nabataeans, once negotiating a tricky dispute between them and the Romans. He had even spent some of his childhood years in the Nabataean capital of Petra. He and his siblings were left in the care of the king of Nabataea while their father was tied up trying to resolve (to his own advantage) the dispute about which of Queen Salome Alexandra's sons would succeed her on the throne of Judaea.

Though a Jew rather than a pagan like the Nabataean Arabs, Herod was of Idumaean Arab descent, making him ethnically related to them. But there was friction between them from the moment of their first important contact during the early days of his rise to power. They had refused him sanctuary when, as Roman-appointed tetrarch of Judaea, he had been forced to flee Jerusalem by royal claimant Antigonus, his Parthian-backed Hasmonean adversary.

That Nabataean rebuff ultimately worked out well for Herod, prodding him to journey on to Egypt and then to Rome, where the Senate, seeking a compliant alternative to Antigonus as king of Judaea, chose Herod and supplied him with the necessary military muscle to make it happen. But the Nabataean brush-off had occurred at a stressful moment for him and had, for a time, put his advancement, and even his life, at risk. It was not easy to forgive.

As related earlier, when Herod ruled Judaea, Cleopatra arranged through Mark Antony for Herod to be responsible for the collection of debts the Nabataeans owed her. She subsequently forced him, again through Antony, to go to war with them to extract the withheld payments. Herod trounced his Arab neighbors in battle and earned their abiding hatred. Their disgrace was compounded when Augustus later awarded him Transjordanian territories that the Nabataeans believed should have been theirs.

As harmony finally returned to the dysfunctional royal family in Jerusalem, or at least the illusion of it, a personal rebuff to a Nabataean luminary provided them with still another reason to want to avenge their humiliation. Syllaeus, chief minister of Nabataean king Obadas, had earlier visited Jerusalem to negotiate a large loan. While there, he established an intimate relationship with thrice-widowed Salome. But Herod told him it would be impossible for him to marry the sister of the king of the Jews unless he was circumcised. Syllaeus declined, saying such an act, effectively declaring himself a Jew, would not be acceptable to his fellow Nabataeans. Although ostensibly acting for religious reasons, Herod may have insisted because he believed his would-be brother-in-law wanted entry into the royal family to further his own dynastic ambitions.

Whatever the reason, it was not the last Herod heard of Syllaeus. Nor was it the first. Years earlier, the Nabataean had played a shady role in a Roman military expedition into Arabia by way of Egypt in which Judaean troops had participated.

Egypt, with its great wealth and huge expanse, had fallen to Augustus as one of the prizes in his victory over Mark Antony in the last Roman civil war. Seizing control of that ancient kingdom broadened the emperor's territorial horizons still further, and he dispatched a military expedition to explore regions south along Egypt's east coast. Aside from wanting to make new conquests and/or alliances, he was hoping to discover a land route to southern Arabia.

Separated from southern Egypt by the narrow Red Sea, Arabia and particularly Arabia Felix further south (Yemen) were known to be the source of the spices and perfumes used in great quantities by the Romans in their temples and to disguise disagreeable odors in their homes and meeting places. They had long acquired them at great cost from Nabataean middlemen. Southern Arabia was also believed to be a source of precious gems, which, in fact, were imported by Arabian merchants from India.

According to the Roman geographer and historian Strabo, "It was [Augustus's] intention either to conciliate or subdue the Arabians. . . . He was . . . influenced by the report . . . that this people were very wealthy. . . . He hoped to either acquire opulent friends or overcome opulent enemies."

On the basis of the inconclusive report he received from the expedition, Augustus dispatched a larger force into the region. Consisting of ten thousand men, it was meant to initiate the process of bringing the Arabian Peninsula into the Roman orbit. Rome's proconsul of Egypt, Aelius Gallus, led the operation. Augustus advised him to employ Nabataeans as his guides because they would know the territory well.

Syllaeus, already chief minister at the Nabataean court at the time, offered himself for that role and promised full cooperation. His actual purpose was to prevent the Roman expedition from succeeding. If it were to go well, the Romans might proceed to seize control of Nabataea's lucrative spice trade and perhaps of Nabataea itself.

Syllaeus advised Gallus to launch his expedition by sailing down the Red Sea with his men to avoid a more difficult and dangerous land route at the start. But the route he charted for their large vessels, to a port city far down on the Nabataean coast, was through shallow waters spiked with coral reefs. The Romans might have marched there overland far more easily.

According to Strabo, "[Syllaeus] neither guided [Gallus] by a safe course by sea along the coast, nor by a safe road for the army as he promised, but exposed both fleet and the army to danger by directing them where there was no road, or the road was impracticable, where they were obliged to make long circuits, or to pass through tracts of country destitute of everything; he led the fleet along a rocky coast without harbors, or to places abounding with rocks concealed under water, or with shallows. In places of this description particularly, the flowing and ebbing of the tide did them the most harm."

Directed along a tortuous route after landing, much of it through Arabian desert wasteland, Gallus lost a great number of his men because of contaminated drinking water and the inedible plants they found to eat to supplement their meager rations. They were forced to make camp for an extended period to assist the recovery of those who were also stricken but had survived.

His supplies running out, Gallus finally felt obliged to turn back. Now properly guided, the return journey was completed in a fraction of the time the arduous outward expedition had consumed. The only resistance Gallus met was from bands of warriors wielding primitive weapons. His men easily scattered them.

Strabo believed Gallus probably would have successfully completed the operation with which Augustus had entrusted him if he had received the same guidance from Syllaeus at the beginning of his operation as he received at the end and had not felt it necessary to cut it short. Strabo thought all of Arabia would have become part of the Roman Empire. That he was a personal friend of Gallus may have colored his judgment. But if he had been right about that, the subsequent history of Arabia might have taken a markedly different course. Roman colonization, administration, city building, and architecture would have made it a different place.

Herod had contributed a unit of five hundred Judaean troops to the Gallus adventure. But he knew nothing of Syllaeus's earlier duplicity when, after being denied the right to marry his sister, the Nabataean again came to his attention, featuring in a dispute between Judaea and the Nabataeans over Trachonitis.

That craggy patch of territory in Transjordan was a hotbed of unruliness. Over Nabataean objections, Augustus may have awarded it to Herod because he considered him capable of taming its troublesome nomadic inhabitants. Settling down, growing crops, and paying taxes were foreign to their culture. Herod performed his assigned task in Trachonitis with his customary harsh methods and settled three thousand Idumaeans in the territory in an effort to change the character of its population.

But a rumor that he had died triggered an upsurge of unrest among the Trachonites. In an effort to reclaim the area for Nabataea, and possibly also out of enduring bitterness at Herod's refusal to let him marry his sister, Syllaeus helped promote the disturbances. Herod's commanders on the spot quickly crushed the outbreak. But some of its leaders fled across the border into Nabataea where Syllaeus, acting in the name of King Obadas, provided them with a sanctuary from which they mounted raids back into Trachonitis.

Aware of Syllaeus's involvement, Herod demanded that he deny the raiders refuge in Nabataea. He also called for repayment of the substantial loan he had made to Nabataea's king. He was supposed to have received it back by then. Careful not to offend Augustus, he informed Saturninus, the Roman governor of Syria, responsible for the maintenance of *pax romana* in the region, of his intention to mount a cross-border raid to wipe out the marauder base and collect the money owed him. But a pledge by Syllaeus to repay the debt at a fixed date, and his denial that the Trachonite marauders had been given sanctuary, persuaded Saturninus to forbid Herod to send a task force into Nabataea to achieve his objectives.

However, the date for the promised repayment passed with no further word from Syllaeus, and the marauders not only continued their activities in Trachonitis but also extended their raids into Galilee and Syria. Herod appealed to Saturninus again. This time he was given permission to take armed action against the marauders, and he dispatched a contingent of troops into Nabataea to wipe out their base of operations.

Syllaeus, who had already gone to Rome to protest Herod's threats, complained to Augustus about the cross-border raid, greatly exaggerating its results. He said the Judaean strike force had devastated Nabataea. Instead of the 25 Nabataeans who had been killed in the attack, he claimed the figure was 2,500 and said they included many of Nabataea's most prominent figures. He claimed, furthermore, that its treasures had been pillaged. He protested to Augustus that only the assurance that Rome would prevent such things from happening had kept him from remaining in Nabataea to personally prevent Herod's rampage from succeeding.

On Augustus's immediate agenda at the time was an elaborate celebration of how he had established peace and order across the empire. Having long relied on Herod to impose and sustain calm in the patch of the Roman realm that he administered, Caesar was angered by what Syllaeus had tearfully alleged was the destruction that had been inflicted on his land. Refusing to hear any explanations, he wanted an answer to only one question: had the Judaean army crossed into Nabataea? It could not be denied that it had.

Augustus was incensed. He had Herod informed that from then on he was to be treated as a subject rather than a friend. It was a punishing downgrade and a warning that worse might be in store, possibly involving increased tax demands and the extent to which Judaea would be permitted continued self-rule. Herod sent emissaries to Rome to challenge Syllaeus's account of the Trachonitis affair, but Augustus refused to see them. After basking so long in Caesar's favor, he was being abruptly thrust out into the cold, confronting him with his greatest challenge since securing the throne in Jerusalem almost three decades earlier.

Syllaeus wasn't finished with his mischief making. Having achieved his objective in Rome, he sent a message back to Nabataea that Herod had lost the emperor's patronage; the Nabataeans should feel free to take advantage of the changed situation as best they could. The Trachonite marauders regrouped in their Nabataean sanctuary and resumed their cross-border marauding. At the same time, the people of Trachonitis took heart from Herod's fall from Roman favor to rebel against his rule.

Being subjected to Augustus's wrath cast a shadow over the relief Herod had felt when harmony in his family appeared to have been restored. What little remaining satisfaction he could manage to draw from that was soon also denied him as unsettling familial matters again forced themselves on his attention. The catalyst for this renewed vexatious distraction was Gaius Julius Eurycles, one of an assortment of well-connected adventurers who wandered the Roman Empire at the time in search of greater contacts and riches than they already enjoyed.

Eurycles was the son of a Spartan of distinguished rank who was accused of piracy and executed by Mark Antony. He first came to wide notice when, perhaps to avenge his father's execution, he gathered and commanded warships to fight on Augustus's side during his victorious clash with Antony at Actium. It earned him Augustus's gratitude, Roman citizenship, and the title of ruler of Sparta. But he had greater aspirations.

He showed up in Jerusalem when Herod was reeling from Augustus's rebuff in the affair of the Trachonitis marauders. Eurycles gave the impression he was on intimate terms with the emperor. Feeling perilously estranged from Augustus, Herod received him warmly. Besides, Judaea had enjoyed friendly, if thin, diplomatic relations with Sparta since the days of the Maccabees. The effusive praise Eurycles heaped on Herod and the rich gifts he delivered earned him the king's good will as well as presents from him even more extravagant than those he had brought.

Having thus established his credentials in Jerusalem, Eurycles quickly sought out Antipater, whom everyone knew had become heir to Herod's throne. He ingratiated himself with him and was offered accommodation in his palace quarters. Then, having quickly apprised himself of the recently patched-up relationship between Herod and his son Alexander, he proceeded to wreck it.

Claiming to be a friend of Cappadocia's King Archelaus, Eurycles struck up a friendship Alexander, Archelaus's son-in-law, and soon presumed to scold the prince. He told him it was inexcusable for him to permit a mere commoner like his father to wear the crown of the Jews when both his mother, Miriamne, and his wife, Glaphyra, were of royal blood, as he himself was. Wounded by the rebuke and deluded by Eurycles's flattery and his expressions of sympathy, Alexander unburdened himself of his catalog of complaints about Herod.

His new friend listened supportively. Using similar tactics with Alexander's brother Aristobulus, he extracted similar grievances about Herod from him. He then went off to delight Antipater with what he had learned from his disgruntled half brothers. He added that they were also deeply bitter about how he had replaced them in line for the throne and were planning his elimination.

Eurycles's next audience was with Herod again. This time, he said that, to repay the kindnesses the king had heaped on him, he had come to save his life. He said Alexander intended to assassinate him and would have already tried to do so if he, Eurycles, had not delayed him by pretending to be his collaborator in the plot.

He claimed Alexander had complained that his father was not merely content to sit on a throne that did not rightfully belong to him but that he had named a bastard son of his as his successor. Alexander was also said to have told him Augustus permitted Herod to remain king of Judaea only because he was not yet aware of his true character or of the "gross wickedness that was in the kingdom" during his reign. He claimed that after Herod died, Alexander intended to publicly reveal the disaster Herod had been for his subjects, how they had been taxed to death, how Herod had stolen the great wealth he had accumulated and the crimes he had committed in having murdered Miriamne and her grandfather Hyrcanus.

Herod's rage rose in stages as these alleged transgressions and shortcomings of his were recounted. Eurycles followed his provocative recital by changing pace and offering extravagant praise for Antipater, who, he said, had nothing but affection for his father. Having stirred the pot of discord in Jerusalem, he moved on. Before leaving, he received a handsome reward from Herod for exposing the supposed disloyalty of his two targeted sons and for testifying to Antipater's supposedly wholesome character. He then went on to Cappadocia where he offered King Archelaus a fabricated account of what he had accomplished in Jerusalem. He claimed to have restored peace and love between Herod and Alexander. He earned a handsome reward for that too before shifting on to cities in Greece, where he sought to use his wiles to accumulate further riches. Complaints about him from those he deceived would finally reach Augustus who had him banished.

But the damage he had done in Judaea was beyond repair. It had become open season again for plotting against Alexander and Aristobulus. The distress Herod felt over having fallen from Augustus's good graces was exacerbated by the heartache he suffered over his revived belief that he was being betrayed by sons he had loved, for which further alleged evidence was provided.

Antipater seized the moment to step in and press the case against his half brothers while still not exposing himself as their accuser. He had confederates at court confirm all that Eurycles had said against them. An intercepted letter supposedly revealing a new scheme by them to kill their father was brought to Herod's attention. Antipater arranged for two men, said in the letter to be central to the plot, to be eliminated before they could deny the missive was genuine. But others alleged to be involved were taken into custody and questioned. What they said under torture reinforced Herod's certainty that Alexander and Aristobulus were bent on destroying him and that they had plans in the works to do so. Alexander was supposed to have arranged for his father to be killed while out hunting. He was to appear to have been run through by his own spear while falling from his horse. It would seem credible because he had once actually come close to suffering such a fate.

Herod was now unwilling to listen to anyone who might have come to the defense of Alexander and Aristobulus. He had them confined while he pondered how to punish them. Many at court had long known and liked them but were disinclined to expose themselves to Herod's wrath by speaking in their defense when he was unshakably convinced of their duplicity.

All the while, he had been anxious about the possible consequences of having fallen from Augustus's favor over the Syllaeus-Trachonitis affair. Caesar still sternly refused to hear any argument defending the action he had taken in the matter. In desperation, Herod dispatched his tutor and adviser Nicolaus of Damascus to Rome to try to do something about that.

Augustus knew and respected Nicolaus and permitted him into his presence. Knowing the emperor would forbid any direct attempt to justify Herod's invasion of Nabataea, he instead concentrated on undermining Syllaeus's credibility. He forced the Nabataean to admit he had magnified the extent of the damage done to Nabataea in the affair. Follow-up questions by Augustus forced Syllaeus to concede he had exaggerated substantially, claiming it was because he had been misinformed. It was enough to awaken the emperor's interest in the details of the incident, permitting Nicolaus to proceed to his main purpose, defending Herod's actions in the Trachonitis issue.

He explained that Syllaeus had promised, in the presence of unimpeachable witnesses, that he would repay the debt owed Herod and would close down the base in Nabataea of the Trachonite marauders. But he had done neither. Nicolaus recounted how Syria's governor Saturninus, acting on behalf of Rome, had then reversed his earlier refusal and had permitted Herod to take action against Nabataea. Only then had he dispatched his task force to wipe out the marauder base and claim the overdue debt repayment.

Syllaeus's position was further undermined by rows within his own delegation, members of which had concluded that his duplicity had become insupportable. At the same time, Aretas, who had just been crowned new king of Nabataea, accused him of having poisoned his predecessor Obadas in an effort to claim the crown for himself.

Augustus realized he had been tricked by the power-hungry Nabataean and accepted that Herod had been justified in acting the way he had in the affair. He expressed regret for having treated him unfairly and restored his status as a friend of Rome. Unlike most Roman luminaries, he was capable of admitting mistakes and forgiving suspected offenders. The biographer Suetonius observes that Augustus "did not readily make friends, but he clung to them with the utmost constancy, not only suitably rewarding their virtues and deserts but even condoning their faults, providing they were not too great."

Syllaeus was ordered to return to Nabataea to arrange for the repayment of the debt owed to rehabilitated Herod. He was then to return to Rome to face punishment. But he failed to make the required financial amends. What was more, the insidious way he had sabotaged Gallus's expedition into Arabia years before came to light again. He was seized and executed.

As for Nabataea, Augustus considered awarding the land to Herod for having treated him unjustly. He could be trusted to bring order to its troubled state of affairs. But news reached the emperor from Jerusalem that the agony Herod had gone through with his once-favorite sons had been revived, and he held back. It was not a time for him to be given additional responsibilities.

# EIGHT

## The End Looms

Herod was delighted to have regained Augustus's high regard and for the fuss over Nabataea to have been sorted out. But it did nothing to relieve him of indecision over what to do with his imprisoned sons. Having earlier drawn Caesar into passing judgment on their purported disloyalty to their father, he felt it would be improper not to consult Caesar again about how to deal with what he once more believed was their treachery. Though still shaken by the memory of having been denied the emperor's approbation over the Syllaeus situation, however briefly, he had the details of the incarcerated princes' new alleged transgressions forwarded to Rome.

Augustus had been pleased to be reconciled with Herod. He still highly valued his administrative skills and trustworthiness. But he must have been dismayed at being dragged once more into his personal affairs. He had known the accused princes since they were boys and was still fond of them. He sent word to Jerusalem that he was saddened to hear of the latest charges made against Alexander and Aristobulus. However, he was reluctant to undermine Herod's authority over his family. If his sons were guilty of disloyalty or sedition, they deserved extreme punishment. But they should be permitted a hearing rather than being summarily executed.

He advised Herod to call together an assortment of respected personages of the region. Those invited were to be informed of the details of the troubling situation and asked to offer their views for Herod's consideration on how it should be resolved. He did not want to get personally involved again but believed it would be wrong for the father of the accused to be the judge in this matter without first hearing the thoughts of other respected figures.

Accordingly, a group of dignitaries of various levels were called together by Herod to examine the situation. They gathered near Berytus, as suggested by Augustus, rather than in Jerusalem. Among them were Saturninus, the governor of Syria, and Volumnius, its military commander, but also lesser officials from the cities of the region. Herod's advisers were there too, as were Salome and Pheroras. Despite Augustus's suggestion, Herod chose not to invite Alexander's father-in-law, King Archelaus of Cappadocia, who might prove biased in his daughter's husband's favor.

The accused were brought from Jerusalem and held in confinement not far away from the hearing but ultimately were not permitted to appear before the assemblage to refute the charges against them. Five years before, Alexander, then also facing accusations of disloyalty, had tamed Herod's fury while tearfully defending himself before Augustus. Herod had no wish to offer the opportunity for the accused to escape justice that way again. Nor was anyone else on hand to plead their innocence.

As a consequence, the main feature of the hearing was an impassioned speech from Herod in which he made clear his conviction that he had been criminally betrayed by his sons and conveyed his intention to have them pay the extreme penalty for it. He presented no specific evidence of their alleged crimes. Instead, his presentation implied that the hearsay of others concerning their perfidy sufficed to prove their guilt. He noted that Augustus agreed he had the right to act with the utmost rigor against his wayward offspring and also that the laws of the Jews would justify such action. Indeed, he said it would be wrong for him not to act sternly against the criminality of his sons.

None of those Herod had invited to offer an opinion questioned their guilt, but not all were of one mind on whether they should be executed. Saturninus said the conduct of the accused, as described by Herod, could not be overlooked or forgiven but that their young lives should not be terminated. He said he had three sons of his own and believed that to kill any one of them would be the greatest tragedy he could imagine for himself. His sons, also in attendance, felt the same way. The implication was that confinement or banishment would be punishment enough for the brothers. However, the soldierly Volumnius, a friend of Herod, spoke up to say execution was the only proper conclusion to this matter. That was the view of most of the assembled.

The verdict aroused much grief and disquiet in Judaea. It caused particular distress in the army where the brothers were popular. The view in Rome, reported to Herod by a trusted adviser, was that imprisonment of his sons or their banishment was a better course of action for him to take if he could not tolerate the thought of forgiving them but that it was his right to deal with the accused as he chose. He returned to Judaea undecided but believing he enjoyed enough support for Augustus to believe that whatever course he took would be appropriate.

Once he was home again, as were Alexander and Aristobulus, waiting for their fate to be determined, he was fed further reports of their plotting against him. Torture was once more applied to suspected witnesses. Among those subjected to it was a plain-speaking old army friend of Herod's whose crime was to dare to tell the king in strong terms that he was being manipulated by malicious family plotters and that his sons had been wrongly accused and prosecuted. The torture drew the required confession from him about conspiracies.

Herod's vindictiveness was once more inflamed. He dismissed thoughts of leniency and ordered that Alexander and Aristobulus be killed, as well as the soldier friend who had admonished him and three hundred soldiers who were also accused of disloyalty for speaking out in defense of the brothers. His sons were taken to Sebaste where, when it had still been called Samaria, Herod had married their late mother and where public outrage was likely to be more subdued than it would be in Jerusalem. There they were strangled, a form of execution not uncommon for condemned dignitaries. Thus ended the last possibility of a Hasmonean revival, though Herod permitted them to be buried alongside their Hasmonean forebears.

Their execution provided Herod with no mental relief. It soon began haunting him almost as much as did the killing of Miriamne so long before. It compounded the physical pain and discomfort to which he was being increasingly subjected. He was now sixty-six years old, and age was taking its toll. His health had been seriously deteriorating, and he was increasingly subjected to physical frailty, stomach pain, and itching across his once robust body.

Herod's last years—three in all—after the execution of Alexander and Aristobulus were a forlorn and wretched period for him. Final fringe work continued on the temple he had rebuilt, but he had little interest anymore in architectural projects or administrative innovation.

Antipater, the key figure instrumental in forging the terminal fate of his half brothers, was the chief beneficiary of their demise as well as of his father's bodily decline and mental anguish. Herod wrote a new will confirming him as his primary heir and permitted him to exercise much of the authority over the administration of the land and its resources.

The king's manipulative firstborn was now recognized as empowered to act on his father's behalf in matters of state though he had to tolerate being held in as little public esteem as Herod. Even in death, Alexander and Aristobulus retained the affection of the people, and it was commonly understood that Antipater had played no small part in their downfall and termination. As heir apparent, he was able to exercise authority over senior figures at court, but his efforts to gain their affection through the distribution of lavish gifts was not overly successful.

He had other concerns too. Two of his young half brothers, Herod's sons Philip and Archelaus, had been sent off to Rome to be educated, a sign of the king's particular affection. Antipater feared either of them could become a candidate to replace him as primary heir to the throne if Herod lived on much longer. Also, the children of the executed Alexander and Aristobulus, who included five boys, were growing up. Herod's fondness for them was openly displayed, as was his bouts of remorse at having had their fathers killed. In an effort to make amends, he declared his intention to be a "better grandfather" to their offspring than he had been a father to their fathers and arranged suitably advantageous betrothals for them, children though they were.

The fear that he still might not inherit the crown goaded Antipater to action to secure his position as king-in-waiting. He cultivated a close relationship with Pheroras, whom he thought might help him firm up his position as Herod's favorite. Unlike his royal brother, Pheroras had long shown himself to be a weak, malleable character. He was widely known to be submissive to the domineering former maidservant he had taken as his wife over Herod's objections. He was also under the thumbs of his wife's sister and mother.

Antipater sought to work through their influence to guarantee Pheroras's support in his campaign to keep his path to the throne unobstructed. He also had the assistance of his mother, Herod's once-banished first wife, Doris, who had become a figure to be reckoned with at court.

The newly developed close relationship between Antipater and Pheroras was kept secret for fear of arousing Herod's readiness to suspect conspiracies. But Salome learned of their covert alliance from her spies at court and concluded that it was directed at Herod's overthrow. She had always been intensely protective of her older brother, aside from which, if anything happened to him, her own privileged status might be put in jeopardy. She told Herod that their younger brother and his oldest son were joined in plotting against him at secret meetings and at drinking parties.

Despite her affection for him and his for her, Herod had long known of Salome's habitual malicious rumor mongering. But in this case, he had already known that Pheroras, whom he loved despite his conspiratorial shenanigans, and Antipater had become suspiciously close while making a public display of disliking each other. He had cautioned them to distance themselves from each other, but they continued surreptitiously to maintain close conspiratorial ties.

The atmosphere at court had again grown venomous, and Herod was once more drawn in, despite the authority he had conferred on Antipater to relieve himself of the burdens it entailed. An open conflict arose when the Pharisees, the popular, tradition-bound religious sect, offended by Herod's Hellenizing, refused to swear the oath of loyalty both to him and to Augustus required of all people of the land. Reluctant to treat the Pharisees more harshly, Herod limited himself to imposing a fine on them and was outraged when the woman Pheroras had married against his wishes paid it on their behalf. He was even more livid when, as Salome informed him, the Pharisees, in gratitude to their fine-paying benefactress, publicly predicted that Herod's reign would end imminently and that Pheroras and she would next ascend the throne of Judaea.

No longer concerned about offending the religious sect, Herod executed those among them accused of making the offending prediction, as well as those at court suspected of being pleased by it. He summoned Pheroras and told him to get rid of his wife if he wished to continue to be his beloved brother. Pheroras refused, saying he would rather die but did not want to forfeit his brother's love either. For the moment, Herod confined himself to formally prohibiting his defiant brother from further contact with his oldest son and heir whom he still deemed trustworthy.

Nevertheless, Antipater was worried that the situation had developed the potential for chipping away at his favored position at Herod's court.

Fearing he was beginning to walk a fine line in his relations with his father, he wrote to well-connected friends in Rome, urging them to suggest to Herod that he send him there. Once he was in Augustus's presence, the emperor might be encouraged to confirm his status as heir to the throne of Judaea. His safety would be secured and his future elevation guaranteed before the situation for him in Jerusalem could slip out of control.

His ploy succeeded. Herod was persuaded to send him off to Rome together with sumptuous gifts for Augustus and the draft of a new will, again naming Antipater his primary beneficiary.

But Herod remained upset by Pheroras's refusal to obey him. Exasperated by his brother's marital arrangement, he ordered him to remove himself from Jerusalem and take up residence across the Jordan River in Peraea, of which Augustus, persuaded by Herod, had earlier made him tetrarch. Furious at such a dismissal, Pheroras swore not to return until Herod died. But he himself fell ill and died first. Herod, who had gone to Peraea to see that Pheroras was properly cared for when he was ailing, had his body brought back to Judaea to be buried with honor.

While he was still grieving over the death of the last of his brothers, Herod received reports that rather than illness, poison disguised as a love potion from Arabia may have killed him. Resorting to torture of the people who might have been involved, Herod was stunned by the extent of the intimacy that had developed between Pheroras and Antipater and how he had figured in that relationship. He was told that while professing great love and honor for his father, Antipater had confided to Pheroras that he hated him. He was said to have complained that Herod was living too long, keeping him from the throne while grooming his other sons as candidates to inherit the crown rather than himself.

Once more, Herod was shaken by evidence that a favored offspring neither returned his affection nor refrained from plotting against him. Torture extracted the testimony that Antipater had arranged for Pheroras to be supplied with a drug to poison Herod but that he had been so touched by his brother's concern for him, despite their estrangement, when he had fallen ill in Peraea, that he'd had the poison destroyed.

Further torture of suspects left Herod in no doubt that Antipater was continuing to conspire against him and was attempting to involve others at court in his plotting. Salome, who had formerly favored Antipater, added her warnings to her brother about what his heir was up to. Despite having worked so assiduously to achieve preference, Antipater fell irredeemably under a cloud in Jerusalem. He was no longer able to enlist even his most meticulously cultivated friends there to be caught up in his schemes and risk Herod's murderous fury.

Enjoying life as an honored guest in Rome, Antipater was oblivious of the sharp reversal of his fortune at home. But he remained apprehensive of his father's suspicious and impulsive nature and worried that one or another of his half brothers, cozying up to Herod in Jerusalem, might snatch from him the prize of being his father's successor. He urged friends in Rome to write to Herod, accusing the most likely ones of plotting against the king.

But the situation had developed beyond his ability to influence it. Without letting on that he had turned against Antipater, Herod instructed him to return from Rome, advising him to hurry in case anything suddenly happened to him, leaving the throne vacant. Unaware of how deeply he had come under suspicion, he headed home. Word reached him at a stop en route that his mother was suspected of having been involved in some way in a poison plot against Herod. She had been banished from the royal court again, and her possessions had been confiscated. It should have made him understand how seriously he himself had fallen into jeopardy.

Some in his entourage advised him not to proceed to Judaea but to await news of further developments. Others told him he had to continue with his return journey in order explain away any of Herod's suspicions about him that might have been aroused. Fearing that his chance of eventually succeeding to the throne might otherwise slip away from him, he chose the latter course.

When he arrived by sea at Caesarea en route to Jerusalem, Antipater finally realized that he was in trouble. Instead of being ceremonially greeted as the presumptive next king of Judaea might expect to be, his reception was low-keyed, even hostile. Herod had also journeyed to Caesarea to receive Quintilius Varus, the visiting new Roman governor of Syria. His son's realization that things had turned against him was confirmed when, though he was permitted into his father's presence, his entourage was pointedly kept out. When he tried to embrace him, he was pushed away and told that Herod knew of his plot to have him killed. Varus would be informed and asked to pass judgment on him at a hearing.

Witnesses aplenty were summoned to attend. Promised immunity for what they were obliged to disclose, many revealed in detail what they knew about Antipater's machinations to secure his position as his father's favorite, including his participation in the events that led to the execution of Alexander and Aristobulus.

Though Herod had previously been informed of what their testimony was likely to contain, he was so overcome by how unscrupulous Antipater had been in planning his destruction, and the destruction of the sons he'd had executed, that he broke down in tears. His friend and adviser Nicolaus of Damascus took over from him in the role of chief accuser, charging Antipater with planning "such a sort of uncommon parricide as the world never yet saw."

For Varus, sitting in judgment, the conclusive evidence, when the hearing seemed to have bogged down in repetitive detail, was a confiscated dose of poison Antipater was said to have supplied to kill Herod. A prisoner condemned to death was brought in, made to drink it, and immediately expired. Antipater's guilt could no longer be denied.

Herod had him chained and imprisoned. He thought of sending him back to Rome, together with all the evidence against him, for Augustus to decide on whatever punishment he thought warranted. But he was persuaded that the connections Antipater had made there might intercede in his favor. He kept him imprisoned and sent word of the proceedings to Augustus, intending to await his response before acting further.

The Antipater episode deepened Herod's despair over his growing physical incapacity. It affected his thoughts and reactions after he returned to Jerusalem and was informed of what he deemed an outrageous deed. He'd had a golden eagle placed on the temple's main gate in honor of Augustus, despite the Torah's injunction against images of any living creature. It was widely seen by the Jews as a desecration of their holiest site. Particularly incensed were two highly regarded religious scholars and teachers who spoke to their students of their disgust. They said that tearing the eagle down would be a worthy and memorable act, even if execution by Herod would be the consequence. Prompted also by a rumor that the sickly king had suddenly died, a group of their students converged on the temple gate, climbed up, pulled the offending image down, and hacked it to pieces.

Guards rushed to the scene, seized the young men and brought them before Herod, who was lying on a couch in pain from his illnesses. Enraged by their claim that they had acted for the greater glory of God in destroying the eagle, whose installation at the temple he had approved, he hoarsely recounted the benefits he had bestowed on his people, in particular rebuilding the temple, whereas his Hasmonean predecessors had achieved nothing comparable. He ordered that the perpetrators be brought before magistrates who, too terrified to decide otherwise, ruled that they deserved extreme punishment. Herod had them executed, along with those who had encouraged them. Some were burnt alive. Though he was never squeamish about such matters, the particular savagery of that punishment may have been influenced by the physical agony he was enduring and his realization that his own life was drawing to an excruciatingly painful end.

# NINE
## Closure

Historians and medical scientists have long sought to identify the medical conditions that tormented Herod during his terminal decline. The earliest diagnosis, written not long after he died, was that his bowels were ulcerated and that the "chief violence of his pain lay on his colon; an aqueous and transparent liquor also had settled itself about his feet, and a like matter afflicted him at the bottom of his belly. . . . His privy-member was putrefied, and produced worms; and when he sat upright, he had a difficulty of breathing, which was very loathsome on account of the stench of his breath. . . . He had also convulsions in all parts of his body."

In recent times, medical scientists have suggested he might have suffered from any of an assortment of identifiable maladies, including various types of cancers, cardiovascular disease, advanced renal failure, syphilis, chronic amoebic dysentery, type 2 diabetes mellitus, and extreme asthma.

According to A. T. Sandison, who has studied the pathology of diseases of antiquity, "Herod was very probably a hypertensive who in the last decade of his life had suffered from progressive cerebral arteriosclerosis. His death may have been due to a combination of congestive cardiac failure and terminal uraemia with traumatic myiasis of the genitalia. Alternative diagnoses which merit consideration are hepatic cirrhosis and amoebic dysentery."

Jan Hirschmann, professor of medicine at the University of Washington, wrote that Herod was probably afflicted by chronic kidney disease complicated by Fournier's gangrene, an infection afflicting male genitalia. The early mention of "worms" in his genitals may have been a description of larvae of flies infecting his private parts.

In addition to the various natural shocks to which flesh is heir when a person reaches an advanced age, the possibility also exists that Herod suffered from the consequences of having been poisoned.

He submitted to all medication and therapy prescribed by his doctors. He moved from Jerusalem to the winter palace he had built at Jericho, just fifteen miles away but, at 1,300 feet below sea level, had a markedly warmer climate. It did nothing to relieve the intensity of his pain or his extreme discomfort. At his doctors' advice, he went to Callirhoe on the northern tip of the Dead Sea for hot baths and treatment with warmed oil. No relief for him there either. At one point, he fainted during treatment. Those attending him believed he had died. Their shouts of alarm wakened him.

Herod's mental shakiness may well have had psychosomatic consequences contributing to his physical decline. A recent study analyzing the likely emotional impulses that drove his actions and attitudes concludes that paranoia had been a dominant aspect of his personality, that from childhood he suffered "from a profound sense of inferiority which turned into an obsessive complex that never left him."

Realization that his death was imminent drew conflicting reactions from him, murderous vindictiveness, generosity, and agonizing soul searching. He gave instructions that large gifts of money should be distributed to the officers and soldiers who had served him faithfully and to friends whose loyalty he had not doubted. But his sense of impending doom did not temper his fury over real or imagined conspiracies against him or diminish his determination to crush all suspected disloyalty. His physical decline appeared to accelerate his mood changes and intensify his bitterness and paranoia, leaving him teetering on the brink of insanity.

During what he knew were his last days, the long-exasperating recognition that he had never been popular with his subjects particularly enraged him. Expecting them to shed few tears when he died, he resolved to keep them from celebrating the occasion. He issued orders for the army to round up revered figures from around Judaea and corral them in the hippodrome he'd had built at Jericho. He then instructed Salome and her third husband Alexas, a loyal friend of his, that when death finally claimed him they were to immediately pass on his command for his soldiers to massacre them all.

Suspecting the possibility of betrayal to the last, he told them the soldiers were not to be informed that he had died before they had followed their orders. They might disobey and refuse to go through with the mass execution of the respected eminences if they knew he was gone. Kept in the dark for the moment, they would do as commanded. Word of the slaughter would spread through the land before popular elation at Herod's passing could be generated. Rather than jubilation over his death, the people would be stricken with grief. They would wail rather than cheer.

Guilt as well as vindictiveness troubled his thoughts as the end neared. He brooded ever more over thoughts that he'd had Alexander and Aristobulus executed for no good reason while permitting the treacherous Antipater, still imprisoned in a chamber of the royal palace in Jericho, to survive. He had already drawn up a will to replace the one in which he had declared Antipater his primary heir. His teenage son Antipas, who does not appear to have featured much in the king's life, had been elevated to that position.

Word finally reached him from Rome that Augustus had given permission for him to determine Antipater's fate—either to have him executed or driven into exile. Antipater forced the pace of Herod's decision before he could choose the course to follow.

As Herod was about to peel an apple, he suffered a sudden pain so agonizing that it drove him to try to stab himself with the fruit knife he had been handed by his cousin and carer, Achiab, commander of the royal guard. Shouting in alarm, Achiab grabbed his hand before he could do himself much harm.

His shout reverberated through the castle where it led retainers nearby to believe Herod's expected demise had finally occurred. Their loud cries of grief and Achiab's cry of alarm led Antipater, in his palace confinement, to believe Herod had at last died and that, despite all that had happened, he was about to be catapulted into place as king of Judaea. He summoned his jailer and offered him a rich reward to free him at once so that he might take immediate charge of the situation.

But the jailer was not as willing to leap to conclusions. He rushed off to learn what, in fact, the noise was about. Seeing Herod still alive, he told him of Antipater's evident satisfaction over what he thought had occurred and of the bribe he had been offered to set him free. In a rage aggravated by his physical agony, Herod ordered members of his body-guard to dash off at once and rid him for good of his firstborn son.

His pain, convulsions, and breathing problems grew worse and came to dominate his thoughts as his end neared. Five days after he'd had Antipater killed, death finally relieved him of his physical and mental torment. It was the year 4 BCE. He had lived sixty-nine years.

Thus ended the story of the tyrant, visionary, statesman, and master builder who had reigned for more than three mostly eventful decades. If Herod had been a man of lesser abilities and more modest aspirations, he might have ended just a historical footnote, perhaps more remembered than so many of the now-forgotten titular heads of imperial Rome's client states but only because of his ruthless cruelty, though such behavior by rulers at the time was not uncommon.

Despite his tyrannical conduct, emotional instability, and dismal final years on the throne, he had translated his subservience to the Romans, whose military-based supremacy could not have been successfully chal-lenged, into a mutually advantageous relationship. He skillfully rode the shifting waves of Roman politics to the benefit of his kingdom and him-self, using the resulting security of his position to bring his creative and constructive aspirations to fruition. His death marked a watershed in the history of Judaea and the Jews.

# TEN

## Herod: The Image

That Herod the Great was a wicked ruler has been conventional wisdom since ancient times. *The Assumption of Moses*, believed written not long after his death, refers to "an insolent king," who was "bold and shameless" and who killed "the chief men" of the Jews, slew "old and young," and brought fear to the land. Another early account depicts him as behaving with "great barbarity towards all men equally."

But though Herod's positive achievements as a national ruler were also chronicled by Josephus, as were other less repugnant aspects of his character, over the centuries, those redemptive features were consistently eclipsed by the portrayal of him as a malevolent figure and nothing more.

Virtually all people for whom the name Herod had, or has, any resonance have known him exclusively for his having committed one almost unimaginable atrocity. He is said to have ordered the slaughter of all boys under the age of two in the city of Bethlehem, considered the birthplace of Jesus Christ, when informed that a new king of the Jews had recently been born there.

Herod lived in a violent age. He lived in a Roman world where "brutality was not only normal but a necessary part of the system." Nevertheless, the Massacre of the Innocents was seen as bearing witness to the great depth of Herod's extraordinary personal iniquity and culpability. The third-century Christian historian Eusebius attributes the agonizing pain he suffered from illness during his last days as "just punishment for his slaughter of the children of Bethlehem."

That abominable act was repeatedly depicted and resurrected in works of literature and art, perpetuating the image of Herod as heartless and depraved. It featured in paintings by such master artists as Giotto, Cranach, and Breughel, in the works of less celebrated painters, and in countless church murals. Actors representing the villainous Herod in all his maliciousness were central characters in popular religious "mystery plays" of medieval Europe. Berlioz recounted his child-killing inhumanity in his opera *The Childhood of Christ*. When Shakespeare's Hamlet advises touring actors not to "out-Herod Herod" in reciting their lines, he is referring to a figure given to indulging in feverish, emotional ranting.

Herod can justifiably be charged with numerous appalling acts, but it is ironic that the bloodbath of children in Bethlehem, the evil deed for which he is most notorious, is unlikely ever to have happened. A mention of it in the Gospel of Matthew is the only indication that the massacre might actually have occurred. There is no other word of it in any of the other gospels or elsewhere in the New Testament, though, if it had taken place, such an attempt to destroy Jesus when he was a child would certainly have been thought worthy of more than a single passage of a few lines.

Josephus, whose writings are the main source of information about Herod and who was not loath to record examples of his brutality, makes no reference to the supposed Bethlehem slaughter. Augustus Caesar made a cutting remark regarding Herod's execution of his own sons, but there is nothing in accounts of Augustus's well-chronicled life that refers to the Bethlehem episode, though such a barbaric act would surely have been brought to his attention. Nevertheless, because of the one mention of that supposed atrocious deed, Herod has been judged over the centuries as utterly evil and vicious, bordering on the diabolical, by most people for whom his name has any meaning.

Not until almost two thousand years after his death did reappraisals of him begin to appear. In the nineteenth century, writers and scholars, while recognizing Herod was a cruel tyrant, gradually began looking beyond the established public image of him as a villain without redeeming features. In retelling the fate of Miriamne at the hands of her husband, an episode of great dramatic imagery, some began seeing him as a tragic victim of his passions as much as a depraved murderer. Lord Byron portrays the depth of Herod's grieving anguish after he had executed the wife he loved so deeply.

Oh, Mariamne! now for thee
The heart of which thou bled'st is bleeding;
Revenge is lost in agony,
And wild remorse to rage succeeding.

Acknowledgment of Herod's laudable achievements slowly also began to take hold. In 1885, *The History of Herod; Or Another Look at a Man Emerging from Twenty Centuries of Calumny* appeared. Its author, John Vickers, contends, "The preservation of order in the various provinces of Palestine immensely outweighed whatever harm or wrong [Herod] occasionally inflicted in the punishment of individuals who were falsely accused."

Though contrary to prevailing thought at the time, that was hardly a ringing acknowledgment of the breadth of his achievements. But soon, recognition began being paid to a wider range of Herod's accomplishments. In 1890, a study credits Herod with being "animated by a sincere desire to promote the welfare and prosperity of his subjects. . . . Under his rule, Palestine . . . entered upon an era of unwonted affluence. Measures were put in operation to augment the productiveness of the country. Trade was encouraged, new commercial centers were established."

Though still confined to a small group of specialist historians, and though the name Herod still evoked an image of unmitigated wickedness except to very few, the door was slowly opening to a wider reappraisal of the long-reviled figure. A subsequent study of the Herodian dynasty maintained that though considered by his subjects "an alien, a usurper and a creature of the Romans, . . . his aim was at bottom sane and enlightened and if they could have learnt from him, the Jews would have been saved much suffering."

In his epic poem *For the Time Being* (1944), W. H. Auden went further than anyone earlier in absolving the infamous king of his shortcomings by portraying him in poetic imagery as an effective social reformer.

Things are beginning to take shape. It is a long time since anyone stole the park benches or murdered the swans. There are children in this province who have never seen a louse, shopkeepers who have never handled a counterfeit coin, women of forty who have never hidden in a ditch except for fun. Yes, in twenty years I have managed to do a little. . . .

Growing numbers of historians began looking beyond the accounts of Herod's unconscionable deeds to determine what he really did and did not do. Stewart Perowne (1956) admires his "administrative vigor," saying, "His famine relief measures, for instance . . . have never been equaled in the Levant." Maurice Sartre writes, "Despite a tradition that is unanimous in its hostility, Herod appears to have been an effective ruler who took his responsibilities seriously."

Géza Vermes declares, "Thanks to [Herod] Judaea became a richer, more civilized and definitely more beautiful country" and because of his "unquestionable achievements . . . deserves to be known as . . . Herod the Great." Samuel Sandmel states that the unrelievedly disparaging image of Herod is "simply [an extension] of the animosity which the ancients felt for [him] which have prevented modern historians from a balanced appraisal. . . . That Herod was guilty of needless killing is beyond challenge. But . . . these killings were never without some direct relation to events and crises; there is no single incident . . . which would represent mere wanton, unrelated and unmotivated killing."

In *Judaea's Most Able but Most Hated King*, S. G. F. Brandon calls Herod "sagacious and far-sighted" despite his failings. Peter Richardson writes that despite his tyrannical rule, "Herod . . . had the good of his people at heart." Ehud Netzer calls Herod "a practical and thorough man, with a broad world view, outstanding organizational talent and improvisational ability (in the best sense of the term), able to adapt himself to his surroundings and to changing situations—a man who anticipated the future and had his two feet planted firmly on the ground."

Byron McCane dismisses the idea that Herod was a man for whom the description "renowned for his ruthless exercise of power" is adequate.

> More than most in Palestine during the late first century BCE, he correctly understood which way the winds were blowing. Recognizing that old political, religious, and cultural patterns were passing away, and that a new synthesis—a first-century Mediterranean version of globalization—was on the way, Herod saw the Roman Empire coming. So he decided to get out front and help Augustus lead the parade.

None of that is likely to change the impression of Herod held by those who continue to know him only through the one questionable account of the slaughter of the Bethlehem infants. Nevertheless, an understanding of the man and ruler he actually was is finally consigning to fiction the one-dimensional portrayal that has long distorted the image of this complex, driven, dynamic, and largely constructive tyrant, statesman, and visionary.

# ELEVEN

## Herod's Heirs

Despite never having gained the affection of the people of Judaea, Herod had been the architect of the kingdom's long period of stability and security and the anchor at the heart of its administration. His passing inflicted paralysis on the governance of the land he had efficiently, if tyrannically, ruled. It spelled the end of its cohesion. As death had beckoned, he had realized none of his surviving sons would be sufficiently mature, adequately experienced, or of sufficient toughness to govern a territory as large as the extended one with which the Romans had entrusted him. It would have to be split up.

Beset by family traumas over the years, he had written and torn up several successive wills during his reign. In the final one, drawn up after he had ordered his son Antipater put to death, and just before his own quietus, another of his offspring was placed center stage. His oldest surviving son, Archelaus, was revealed as his primary heir. Antipater had previously poisoned Herod's mind against him to block any possible challenge to his own ascendance.

But though Archelaus was only nineteen years old, Herod had chosen him to be king of Judaea. His brother Antipas, who was seventeen, was to rule Samaria, Galilee, and Peraea. Both were the sons of Malthace, Herod's sixth wife. Their half brother Philip, only sixteen, son of Herod's seventh wife, Cleopatra, was to be tetrarch of a patchwork of thinly populated territories north and northeast of the Sea of Galilee.

All of this required Augustus's approval. But some matters required immediate attention, and Salome, Herod's only surviving sibling, took charge as soon as her brother gasped his last breath. As instructed by him, she and her husband Alexas made their way to the hippodrome in Jericho where respected figures from all over the land had been confined to be executed on the day of Herod's demise to sadden his subjects and divert them from celebrating the news that they were rid of him. But instead of having those confined there killed, they had them freed and allowed to go home. Salome announced that Herod had so commanded, which was possible as a last minute spark of the empathy and compassion that had marked his actions from time to time. But it is also possible that she decided herself that the consequences for public order of such a massacre would have been disastrous.

That danger having been averted, she assembled Herod's troops in the city's amphitheater, such as were present in Jericho, and informed them of Herod's passing. She read out a letter to them that Herod had composed thanking them for their loyalty and urging them to be equally loyal to his successor. Then Ptolemy, Herod's chief minister, stepped forward to read out Herod's will, noting that its implementation was subject to Augustus's sanction. When he named Archelaus as Herod's primary heir, the troops responded with loud acclaim. It was a matter of form rather than an indication of his personal popularity among them. But unit-by-unit they swore their allegiance to him.

Herod's funeral was suitably lavish. His body, wrapped in crimson fabric, was carried in procession on a golden bier in which precious stones were embedded. A gold crown was on his head and a scepter was in his hand. His children, his wives, and other relatives escorted the bier. They were followed by his closest aides, then his personal guard followed by his elite corps of Thracian, German, and Galatian bodyguards, then by regular units of the army, all attired as if for combat. Hundreds of Herod's servants brought up the rear. The body was carried in procession to Herodium, the fortress/palace Herod had built to be his sanctuary and ultimately his final resting place. In 2007, after years of digging in the remains of the structure, Israeli archeologist Ehud Netzer uncovered Herod's tomb there.

* * *

Despite his youth, heir apparent Archelaus was at the heart of the events that unfolded in Jerusalem as the focus shifted from Herod's death and burial to the future of Judaea without him. After the religiously pre-scribed seven days of mourning, and after he had provided a feast for the people as was customary on major occasions, the presumptive new king, still awaiting confirmation from Augustus for his elevation to the throne, addressed his prospective subjects from a golden throne set up on an elevated platform at the temple. He promised to be a gentler ruler than his father had been, a declaration that was greeted with cheers. It was also received with requests that he immediately fulfill that promise by releasing men wrongfully imprisoned by Herod and by lowering taxes.

Wanting to shore up public support, already forthcoming because of his lofty pledges, and anxious to hurry off to Rome for Augustus to confirm him as king, Archelaus announced he would grant those re-quests. The effect was not what he expected. The crowd immediately sized him up as weak and malleable. His eagerness to please the people who had been used to a ruler who brooked no such audacity was met with further demands.

Punishment was insisted upon for the officials who, at Herod's in-structions, had tortured and killed the young men who had pulled down the golden eagle installed on the temple gate and had their teachers burned alive. What was more, a call was issued for a new high priest to be appointed to replace the last one Herod had chosen, deemed to have been the late king's meek accomplice in his acts of brutality.

The barrage of demands left Archelaus shaken. The cheers with which he had been initially received were replaced in the streets of Jerusalem with unruly clamor that threatened to turn into violent demonstrations. Fearing that disorder would force him to delay his crucial trip to Rome, he sent the commander of the army he had inherited to calm the leaders of the malcontents. But they would not be placated. His emissary was stoned and forced to flee.

So promising at first, the situation had suddenly become precarious for Archelaus. Passover was imminent and great numbers of people were converging on Jerusalem to celebrate the holiday. The unrest in the city could prove infectious. Mass rioting could result, not something that would commend Archelaus to Augustus at this critical moment. He dis-patched a small unit of troops to single out and arrest leading trouble-makers. Barrages of stones greeted the soldiers, killing several of them.

His relatively low-keyed attempt to deal with the situation having failed, Archelaus saw no alternative to escalating his response. The vision he had of an easy and orderly transition between his father's rule and his own was dissolving. He ordered a much larger army contingent, including mounted troops, to crush the demonstrators. By the time they had done their work, three thousand people had been massacred, and the celebration of Passover at the temple had been effectively cancelled—a very serious matter—despite the huge influx of pilgrims into Jerusalem from all over the land. Archelaus had outraged the people he had expected to make his loving subjects. The hope he'd had of an untroubled ascension to the throne had been lost.

In vigorously suppressing the rioting, he had also exposed himself to another problem. Though Augustus had not yet confirmed him as king, he had acted as if he were already ruler of Judaea. It was something to which the emperor might not take kindly. Further trouble plagued him when, leaving his brother Philip in charge in Jerusalem, he hurried off to cross the Mediterranean to Rome to seek Augustus's blessings despite his unfortunate debut as king-in-waiting. Before he could board his ship at Caesarea, Sabinus, the Roman official who was treasurer for the province of Syria, confronted him with a power grab.

A grasping, greedy figure, Sabinus claimed the right to act on behalf of Augustus's financial interests in Judaea. He said his position authorized him to take charge of Herod's properties and treasures until the emperor sorted the situation out. In fact, he was seizing an opportunity to acquire a fortune for himself. At the same time, his action suggested that Archelaus would not be deemed worthy of being confirmed as Herod's successor and main beneficiary.

What could have become a serious complication for him was averted by the intercession of Sabinus's superior, Varus, the Roman governor of Syria. Varus decreed that everything had to await the emperor's decision about Archelaus and ordered Sabinus to desist. That he did, though only for the moment.

Archelaus, in the meantime, had to contend with still another challenge. Discord was too deeply entrenched in Herod's family to be buried with him. Archelaus's younger brother, seventeen-year-old Antipas, named after Herod's grandfather, was not content with having been nominated in their father's final will to be ruler only of Samaria, Galilee, and Peraea. He also hurried to Rome to claim that he, rather, rather than Archelaus should be king of Judaea.

In Herod's penultimate will, drawn up just after Antipater had been disowned and imprisoned, Antipas had been named primary heir to the throne. But then Herod, in those tormenting last days of his life, realized that Archelaus had not been the disloyal plotter Antipater had made him out to be and, in his final testament, chose him to be his main heir instead of Antipas.

But the latter now insisted that the earlier will, naming him, was Herod's legitimate last will. He maintained that the later one, choosing his older brother Archelaus, was invalid because it was a product of their father's mental decline and confusion.

That wasn't the only challenge for Archelaus as he arrived in Rome. He had brought his mother Malthace along to provide him with maternal support. But Malthace, mother also of Antipas, decided to back her younger son's claim to throne. Herod's chief minister, Ptolemy, and other court officials did so also.

Those who favored the younger claimant may have been influenced by Archelaus's dismal performance in Jerusalem after Herod's burial. But intrigue and power games were so much a part of the environment at Herod's court that personal animus or hope for reward was likely to have been motivation enough for some.

Among those supporting younger Antipas was his aunt Salome, who had joined the others in Rome for reasons of her own. Herod had bestowed several lucrative properties on her in his will, as well as sums of money. Augustus's approval was required. She hoped also to receive additional awards through the influence of Augustus's wife Livia, who was an even closer friend of hers than Cleopatra had been.

The squabbling in the royal family over who would rule Judaea would have enraged Julius Caesar or Mark Antony and possibly would have led them to replace them all. But Augustus retained his characteristic cool-headedness. He was concerned only that strategically positioned Judaea, like all of Rome's other territories in the region, remained properly administered in an orderly fashion and that tax revenues continued to flow uninterruptedly from it.

When the suppliants from Judaea appeared before him for his decision on what the listed beneficiaries of Herod's estate would or would not receive, frontrunner Archelaus immediately came under blistering criticism. Salome's sharp-tongued son Antipater, of whom little is otherwise known, led the attack. (Then as now, imagination in naming chil-

dren seemed to have been in short supply. Antipaters, Ptolemys, Sa-
lomes, Alexanders, and Archelauses proliferated.)

This Antipater charged his cousin with presuming to be king of Judaea without Augustus's assent, sitting on the royal throne, and appoint-
ing new army commanders for Judaea. He charged him with impiety for
the slaughter of the thousands of people killed at his command in and
near the temple on the eve of the Passover holiday, as if they were human
sacrifices. He said Archelaus had celebrated Herod's death with singing
and dancing, "as though an enemy of his were fallen," hardly the proper
behavior of a son in mourning. He echoed the assertion that Herod had
not chosen Archelaus as his heir until illness had disturbed the balance of
his mind.

That barrage of criticism and denunciation rattled Archelaus. But he
was not without defenders, notably Herod's esteemed counselor Nicolaus of Damascus. With regard to the disputed state of Herod's mental
powers when he drew up his final will, could it really be questioned,
Nicolaus asked, when it included the caveat that all of its provisions
would require Augustus's sanction. And was it wrong for Archelaus to
have dealt firmly with the unruly demonstrations in Jerusalem when that
had been necessary to prevent a total breakdown of order?

Nicolaus noted that many who now accused Archelaus of having exceeded his authority, as well as acting brutally, had advised him at the
time to do exactly what he had done to cope with the problems that
confronted him after Herod's death. He accused those now criticizing
Archelaus of siding with would-be disrupters of *pax romana*.

Archelaus and Antipas were not the only ones who had come to Rome
to submit arguments to Caesar about how Judaea should be governed
now that Herod was gone. A group of Pharisees had journeyed there to
try to sway the emperor along different lines and to say things none of
the others would. They said Herod had been the most ruthless oppressor
that had ever lived, that he had tortured and executed great numbers of
his subjects, that he had denied Judaean cities resources they deserved in
order to fund his building projects in other lands, and that he had reduced his people to poverty.

They said Archelaus had already proved he was cut from the same
cloth as his wicked father. They wanted no king for Judaea other than
God. Supported by the large Jewish community in Rome, they pleaded
that the land should be turned into a Jewish province of the Roman

Empire rather than a semi-independent client nation. They pleaded that its high priest and Sanhedrin should guide it, according to the laws of the Torah. But theirs was a lost cause. Augustus needed greater assurance of stability and military reliability in Judaea than religious sages could provide.

Still another petition came from envoys representing the Greek cities of Gaza, Gadara, and Hippus, which Augustus had awarded Herod and in which he had built pagan temples and generally promoted Hellenic culture. They wanted to be free of rule from Jerusalem and to be answerable instead to Rome through the governor of Roman Syria. Augustus saw sense in that proposal, and Nicolaus advised Archelaus not to object to what he knew the emperor would consider a reasonable plea.

Nevertheless, Archelaus sensed that the tide was flowing against him, and he sank to his knees in submission before Augustus. The emperor drew him up and told him that if chosen, he would make a worthy successor to his father. But before he announced his decision, word reached him that rebellious violence had broken out in Jerusalem and across Judaea. It was the most severe challenge the Romans had experienced there since their legions had put Herod on the throne of the Jews.

Responsible for the eruption was Sabinus, the Roman treasury official who had earlier been blocked from seizing deceased Herod's treasures. Governor Varus, who had ordered him to desist at the time, had also garrisoned a legion of troops in Jerusalem to guarantee the maintenance of order. But as soon as Varus had turned his attention elsewhere, Sabinus, in command of those legionnaires, tried to gather in those elusive treasures, and he deployed some of those troops to assure that he would not be thwarted again. In effect, he was trying to introduce direct Roman rule in Jerusalem, in the person of himself, for the first time since the days when Rome had appointed foreign procurators to govern Judaea.

His action coincided with the Shavuot holiday celebrating the anniversary of the day God is said to have given the Jewish people the Torah. It again brought great numbers of worshippers to the holy city. They included large groups from Idumaea and Galilee, which were becoming hot spots of anti-Roman religious ferment, as well as from Jericho and Peraea. It had been a long time since Roman troops had been seen in the streets of Jerusalem. Outrage at their reappearance, and at Sabinus's seizure of the royal palace, sparked a violent crowd reaction. Angry Jews seized control of the temple area, Herod's hippodrome, and other major sites in the capital.

As the unrest spread, civilianized veterans of Judaea's army, their own grievances unanswered, took up arms against the Romans. Across the Jordan in Peraea, Simon, a former slave with royal aspirations, gathered a band of rebellious fighters and marched with them on Judaea where they ransacked and burnt buildings in and near Jericho, including Herod's former royal palace there. He and his followers were not brought to heel until units of the Judaean army joined forces with Roman legionnaires to deal with them.

In various other parts of the land, anti-Roman sentiment and the collapse of Herod's security systems brought forth assertive and charismatic figures who claimed to lead national liberation movements like that led by the apotheosized Maccabees of long before. A towering shepherd named Athronges proclaimed himself king of Judaea and set out to be master of the land with the aid of his four brothers, all also of formidable stature, strength, and legendary fearlessness and each with his own band of fighters. Their resemblance to the Maccabees, who had also been five brothers resisting foreign oppression, drew many recruits with whom they mauled the legionnaires sent to end their rampage.

Varus was apprized of the disastrous turn of events by Sabinus, who locked himself in for safety in a tower Herod had built in Jerusalem. Varus feared for the fate of the legion he had earlier garrisoned in Jerusalem. Bringing two other legions to combat readiness, he led them into Judaea to deal with the crisis. He was joined in the campaign to obliterate rebellion by fighters sent by the king of Nabataea, hungering to avenge the humiliation Herod had inflicted on him years before.

The bolstered forces dealt harshly and quickly with the trouble in Jerusalem. Having restored Roman control there, Varus sent troops out into the countryside to crush the unrest and dispose of its leaders. By the time they had done so, thousands of Jews had been killed, many of them crucified, and others had been sold into slavery.

What later came to be called Varus's War had a bearing on the interrupted proceedings before Augustus in Rome. He was given additional reason to believe extreme measures would continue to be necessary if order was to be maintained in Judaea. Installing an on-the-spot Roman administrator in Jerusalem was made to seem inadvisable by the reaction of the Jews to Sabinus's power grab. Retaining Archelaus seemed a better idea. The disturbances appeared to justify the stern action he had taken against the rioters and protestors after his father's death.

For organizational convenience and continuity, Augustus would have preferred the kingdom to continue to be governed as a single entity but decided it would be more prudent to validate Herod's final will, with modifications. Archelaus would rule Judaea, Samaria, and Idumaea. But he would do so as ethnarch rather than king, to which position he would be raised when he proved himself worthy of the crown. Governing those territories would be enough of a trial for him. He would not administer Galilee and Peraea as well. Those two areas would come under Antipas, who would be awarded the title tetrarch. Archelaus and Antipas would each adopt the patronymic Herod as a prefix to their names.

Young Philip was made tetrarch of sparsely settled Batanaea and Trachonitis, as well as the Golan Heights. Gaza, Gadara, and Hippus, once part of Herod's realm, were to be confirmed as independent cities within the empire.

Salome did well in the settlement. Augustus confirmed her brother's proposed bestowal upon her of the cities of Jamnia (Jabneh), Azotas (Ashdod), and Phaesalis (Fasayil) and the lucrative proceeds therefrom. He also added a royal dwelling for her in the seaside town of Ashkelon, as well as a cash bestowal from the sizable gift of money Herod had bequeathed him. He distributed the rest of that sum among Herod's other beneficiaries, keeping only a few artistic mementos of the late king's reign.

Barely had Augustus's decision been announced when much excitement was caused by the arrival in Rome of a young man who looked very much like Herod's executed son Alexander, whom he claimed to be. He confirmed that he and his brother Aristobulus had been sent to be strangled in Sebaste for disloyalty, as Herod had ordered, but that their executioners had taken pity on them and let them escape. He and his brother had then gone to the islands of Melos and Crete where the Jewish communities had received them ecstatically and lavished gifts of money on them. He said he had left Aristobulus in Crete for fear they might both be lost at sea, bringing an end to the line of their mother Miriamne that their amazing survival was perpetuating.

The Jews of Rome warmly received him and paraded him through the streets of the city when he appeared among them and told his story. Young Alexander had been an admired figure when Herod had sent him to be educated there, and his reported execution had grieved them deeply. The belief that the royal Hasmonean line had miraculously escaped extinction revived questions about who really should rule Judaea now that Herod was dead.

Informed of his story, appearance, and reception, Augustus had this Alexander brought before him and agreed he greatly resembled the young man he had known. But in contrast to the executed prince whom he pretended to be, he was well built and sturdy. His hands were rough, like those of a laborer, not like those of a pampered member of a royal family.

Augustus offered him a deal. If he told him who he really was and who had put him up to this charade, he would spare his life. The imposter complied and was sent off to be a galley slave in Augustus's navy. The man whom he said had devised the plot, someone familiar with the ways of Herod's court, was tracked down and executed.

\* \* \*

Of the three brothers Augustus authorized to rule their father's divided dominions, Philip, the youngest, enjoyed the most untroubled reign. The Babylonian Jews who had been settled in Batanaea by Herod did not share the nationalist cravings of their coreligionists in Judaea and were less bothered by Roman overrule. They caused him little bother. The inhabitants of his Trachonitis territory had moderated their unruly ways since their resistance had been crushed by Herod years before, and peaceful Nomadic pagan Arabs predominated in the rest of Philip's realm. He was a popular figure, admired by his subjects for coming among them to hear their petitions, often out in the open at the side of a road.

Herod Antipas, tetrarch of Galilee and Peraea, is best known for the references to him in the New Testament where he is usually and confusingly called only by the name Herod. He is described as being responsible for the execution of John the Baptist and of being complicit in the crucifixion of Jesus.

Antipas sought to emulate his father's architectural achievements. In addition to the new towns he built, he created the city of Tiberias on the Sea of Galilee to be his capital, named it after Tiberius Caesar, Augustus's successor, and adorned it with a palace, a stadium, and other impressive structures. It was his most enduring achievement. He would end in exile, of which more is said in the following chapter.

Of Herod's three main heirs, Herod Archelaus, the primary one, did worst. He was fated never to recover from his dismal start as his father's successor as ruler of Judaea. Like Herod, he failed to gain the respect or admiration of his subjects. Unlike Herod, he was unable to maintain a police-state structure to crush and stifle disorder or dissent. To repeated outbursts of unrest in his diminished realm, he responded with mass slaughter. According to the New Testament, it was during Archelaus's reign that, because of his brutality, Joseph and Mary traveled to Galilee rather than settle in Judaea with baby Jesus when returning from exile in Egypt.

Ultimately, emissaries of the Jews and Samaritans, in rare agreement, joined in complaining to Augustus about Archelaus's oppression and cruelty. He was summoned to Rome to explain and to hear himself exiled to Gaul, where he lived out his life in obscurity.

After banishing him, Augustus might have adhered to Roman tradition and found another prominent Jewish figure to rule Judaea on his behalf. But facing a rebellion in Dalmatia and unrest in other corners of his empire, he wanted to make certain his control of that strategically important patch of territory would be properly secured.

The first procurator of Judaea, appointed by Julius Caesar fifty years earlier, had been Herod's father, Antipater, grandfather of the disgraced Archelaus. Now a procurator was again appointed to administer Judaea, Roman cavalry officer Coponius, who took up official residence in Caesarea rather than Jerusalem. Coponius was given "supreme power" over Judaea but in times of trouble would be answerable to the Roman governor of Syria. The land of the Jews was, in effect, reduced to the status of a sub-province. Coponius was the first of the Roman procurators who would include the infamous Pontius Pilate and who would govern Judaea for almost four decades before the Jews again had a king of their own—Herod's grandson Herod Agrippa.

# TWELVE
## The Other Herodians

The route Herod Agrippa I took to the throne of Judaea was very different from that taken by his grandfather. Though he revived the Herodian dynasty, by nature and through experience Agrippa was markedly unlike Herod, and the circumstances of his elevation contrasted sharply with those of his infamous forebear.

Marcus Julius Agrippa, born in 10 BCE, was named after Herod's high-ranking Roman friend Marcus Vipsanius Agrippa. When he was three years old, Herod executed his father, Aristobulus, and his uncle Alexander for allegedly plotting against him, having earlier executed their mother, Miriamne, Agrippa's grandmother. She had been descended from Hasmonean monarchs. He was, therefore, descended along both the Herodian and the Hasmonean lines.

While Agrippa was still a boy, his widowed mother, Berenice, daughter of Herod's sister, Salome, took him off by to be educated in Rome. There he enjoyed a highly privileged upbringing in an environment nothing like that of Jerusalem. As he grew up, he was assured a pampered life among the elite of Roman society. His grandmother Salome was a friend of Augustus Caesar's widow Livia. Berenice, equally well connected, was a friend of Antonia who was sister-in-law of Tiberius Caesar, Augustus's successor as emperor. Moving in such exalted circles, young Agrippa established a close friendship with Tiberius's son Drusus and associated with other youthful members of the imperial family, including future emperors Caligula and Claudius.

As Agrippa grew into young manhood, his connections, charm, easy manner, and exotic origins made him a popular figure in Roman high society. While his mother was alive, he lived comfortably, though not lavishly, on the family's considerable means. But when she died, he was drawn into squandering his resources in a way that he believed was required if he was to keep up with the cream of Rome's aristocracy and its hangers-on like himself. He entertained, gambled, drank, and caroused with his upper-crust friends whose means were far greater than his own.

After Augustus died, Agrippa hoped his friend Drusus would arrange for his father, new emperor Tiberius, to award him a lucrative sinecure. As a scion of Herod's royal family, he might have hoped the emperor would name him tetrarch of one of the territories on Judaea's fringes, a money-spinning appointment that would not necessarily require him to leave Rome and forgo its pleasures. But Drusus died and Tiberius was so stricken by his son's death that he refused to have anything to do with anyone who could stir memories of him.

Agrippa's remaining resources were soon exhausted, and he plunged so deeply into debt that he had to flee Rome. With his wife Cyprus, the granddaughter of King Herod's deceased older brother Phaesal, he made for Idumaea, the place of his grandfather's origins. But he had no idea how to recoup his losses there. Despairing of having to live frugally in a place whose features were in sharp contrast to the splendors of Italy, he contemplated suicide.

His wife came to his rescue. Cyprus wrote pleadingly of their plight to Agrippa's sister Herodias. She was the wife of Herod's son Antipas who had been obliged to settle for the position of tetrarch of Galilee and Peraea, rather than ruler of Judaea, when Augustus had doled out Herod's legacy. Though Antipas was Agrippa's uncle as well as his brother-in-law, he was openly contemptuous of his wastrel ways. However, he was persuaded by Herodias to come to her brother's assistance by granting Agrippa a sinecure in Tiberias, the new city he had created on the shore of the Sea of Galilee and named in honor of the emperor.

Though saved from penury, Agrippa still had difficulty reconciling himself to a dreary life in the boondocks. Feeling humiliated by his appointment as mere overseer of Tiberias's markets, he found life there unendurable when Antipas, drunk at a feast, publicly ridiculed him as impoverished and dependent on his handouts, even for the food he ate.

Now almost forty, he sought escape again by calling on the hospitality of Pomponius Flaccus, Roman governor of Syria. Flaccus was a friend from their rollicking Rome days and happily put him up until he learned his guest had accepted a bribe to try to influence him in a local territorial dispute he was attempting to resolve.

Hurriedly on the move again, Agrippa made for Alexandria, where he borrowed a substantial sum from a senior figure in the Jewish community and made his way back to Italy. Once there, in search of the rewards imperial favor might bring him, he managed to persuade Tiberius to grant him an audience at the island of Capri where the aged emperor had begun to reside permanently. But before they could meet, Tiberius learned that he was on the run from outstanding debts and refused to receive him until he paid off what he owed.

Agrippa managed to do so by tapping the resources of his Roman connections. Delightedly back in the swing of things in Rome, he imagined all obstacles to his advancement had been cleared, and they would have been if an eavesdropping chariot driver had not informed Tiberius that Agrippa had uttered a treasonable remark. While drunk in the man's chariot, he had told his old friend Caligula, Tiberius's nephew and heir, that he hoped the emperor would die so Caligula would not be kept waiting to inherit the empire. An outraged Tiberius had Agrippa jailed.

His imprisonment was not overly onerous. His late mother's friend Antonia made certain he was comfortable in his confinement and well-enough fed. Nor did he have to suffer imprisonment very long. Tiberius died a few months later to be duly succeeded by Caligula, who ordered Agrippa's immediate release. The new emperor also replaced the iron chains that had shackled him in prison with a gift to him of a chain of gold.

The path to good fortune had finally reopened for Agrippa. Another of his uncles, Herod's son Philip, tetrarch of Trachonitis and other territories north and east of the Sea of Galilee, had recently died. Caligula now awarded them to Agrippa. But in contrast to Philip, he was spared being lumbered with the comparatively humdrum title of tetrarch of those territories. Instead, the Jews suddenly found themselves with a crowned king again, though not of Judaea, which continued to be administered by Roman procurators.

Arriving in his northeastern "kingdom," Agrippa clamped down hard on brigands and marauders who had begun being active there, emulating the actions of young Herod when he had been given his first official appointment. But in contrast to the hostility his grandfather had generated as governor of Galilee so long before, by restoring order to his remote realm, Agrippa earned the respect of his subjects.

However, his good fortune riled his sister Herodias. She was mortified that her ne'er-do-well brother had been crowned a king while the Romans had awarded her husband, who had rescued Agrippa from poverty and despair a few years earlier, only the more modest honorific of tetrarch. She was especially upset because the realm Caligula had capriciously conferred on Agrippa was a poor excuse for a kingdom compared to the more deserving and more important territories of the tetrarchy of Galilee and Peraea that her husband ruled. What was more, they bordered each other, accentuating the significance of the contrast in their titles. Herodias felt she could not bear living with such an insult.

Antipas had by now been tetrarch for some forty years. Regardless of how more brightly fortune now smiled on Agrippa, he was satisfied with his privileged life in Galilee. Besides, he knew that Caligula's Rome could be a treacherous place for petitioners. But his wife insisted it was only his laziness in not making himself a presence in the capital of the empire that had kept him from higher rank. She persuaded him to go to Rome to seek the kind of recognition her less worthy brother had received and win a royal crown too.

Tipped off about their doings, and recalling how demeaningly Antipas had earlier treated him, Agrippa wrote disparagingly of him to his friend Caligula. He accused his uncle of treason and said he had gathered a suspiciously huge store of arms, was allied to the Parthian enemies of Rome, and had participated in a plot against the deceased Emperor Tiberius.

Questioned, Antipas denied the worst of the charges. He admitted he had gathered a sizable armory but for no particular purpose, certainly not to go to war with Rome. Nevertheless, Caligula banished him and Herodias to Spain. When the emperor was informed that Herodias was Agrippa's sister, he relieved her of the requirement that she join her husband in his banishment. But she proudly rejected Caligula's reprieve for herself, accepted that her demands were responsible for her husband's downfall, and went into exile with him.

Antipas removed, Caligula added his former tetrarchy of Galilee and Peraea to Agrippa's existing kingdom, making it far larger and more substantial. He also awarded him his banished uncle's personal fortune. Now enormously wealthy, he was in no hurry to relocate to his newly acquired hinterland. He preferred life in Rome where his continuing closeness to Caligula, and the friendships he had made while growing up there, made him a figure of considerable influence. However, living in Rome had taken on a dimension of peril for high-profile personages. Caligula had long displayed signs of mental aberration and was now increasingly subject to sudden, violent mood changes and irrational conduct. Passing whims of his could prove lethal, even for his friends. Suetonius observes that they could be rewarded "for their kinship and their faithful services by a bloody death."

Unlike emperors Augustus and Tiberius, who were declared divine and worthy of worship by many in parts of the superstitious east, Caligula began actually believing the adoring declarations made by sycophants both east and west that he was a god. He readily granted requests from those seeking to be in his favor for permission to erect statues of him to be worshipped in pagan temples.

Their devotions had a bearing on the simmering anti-Jewish sentiment that had developed in Greek communities in the Middle East. The Greeks found the monotheism of the Jews among whom they lived strange and abhorrent, so different to their own paganism. They also considered Jewish, biblically prescribed circumcision of boys to be mutilation of the body and their dietary restrictions irrational. They also objected to the legal dispensations Jews had enjoyed in some places under Roman rule since the days of Julius Caesar.

In the largely Jewish city of Jamnia, some Greeks erected an altar for worship of the divine Caligula. When local Jews tore it down, the emperor was furious at this sacrilege perpetrated against his godliness. He angrily ordered that a magnificent statue be made of him and installed in the temple in Jerusalem. Publius Petronius, the governor of Syria, was instructed to organize its carving and erection. He was to deploy two legions to crush any problems that might arise as this task was carried out.

Petronius was aware the Jews would consider placing the statue in their holiest site an intolerable desecration. It could provoke an uprising that, in addition to other consequences, would interrupt the flow of highly valued Judaean grain shipments to Rome and interfere with the collection of taxes. He had no doubt that Caligula would hold him responsible.

He also was sympathetic to the feelings of the Jews. Nevertheless, he could not risk defying the emperor with regard to the statue. He, therefore, followed Caligula's instructions. But he made certain there would be no rush job. The sculptors were told to spare no effort in making certain the statue was an absolutely exquisite, flattering likeness of the divine emperor. It was to be perfect. But artistic masterpieces take time to create, and Petronius hoped the mercurial Caligula might change his mind about the project before the statue could be finished and ready for installation.

Agrippa, in Rome, was aware of what Caligula had demanded and the possible consequences in Judaea. He had been Hellenized by his education and general upbringing, but he had retained his Jewish religious identity as well as his personal bond with Judaea and the heritage of the Jews. He now interceded in the affair, at great personal risk. Caligula's murderous rages over imagined slights had grown terrifyingly frequent. He had been targeting even those closest to him. Nevertheless, Agrippa brought the matter of the statue up at a lavish dinner to which he invited the easily enraged emperor, risking that their long friendship would see him safely through.

At the dinner, at which his imperial guest liberally imbibed fine wines, Caligula expressed his pleasure at how close he and Agrippa were and how much he prized their friendship. He insisted he had not done enough to reward him for it. He now offered to grant him any wish, "to make amends for everything in which I have been formerly deficient."

Knowing better than to press his case too soon, Agrippa replied that Caligula's friendship, and what he had already given him, were beyond the hopes of any man. He said their continuing friendship was enough of a gift. But the emperor kept pressing him to ask for something more, and he finally allowed himself to be persuaded to do so. What he wanted, he said, was something that was not for himself but would glorify the emperor and demonstrate to all that he was a man of great piety and justice. His wish was that Caligula would withdraw the command that the statue of him be erected in the Jerusalem temple.

Caligula was disappointed. He had assumed his friend would ask for something more substantial, perhaps an additional territory to be incorporated into his kingdom. But he had offered Agrippa anything he wanted and, restraining his homicidal impulses, stood by his offer—partially. He sent word to Petronius that if the statue was already in place, it should stand; if it was not, the project was to be scrapped.

However, Petronius had already dared to write to Caligula suggesting that the Jews might go to war against Rome unless the statue project was aborted. There had already been some disorder among them because of it. That report so infuriated the emperor that he wrote back advising Petronius to commit suicide and thus avoid being tortured to death.

Fortunately for him, this latest instruction from Rome reached him in Damascus after he learned that Caligula had been assassinated in a plot organized by officers of Praetorian Guard, members of the Senate, and others. They had grown increasingly concerned about his bizarre and murderous behavior to which none of them had come to feel immune.

Some of the senators involved in the conspiracy, and some who had not been, had pined for the restoration of the pre-Caesarian Roman Republic. They now believed the moment had come for their wish to be fulfilled. But Praetorian Guard commanders, who had been nibbling at the fringes of political involvement, wanted no such revival. Their corps had initially been established to serve as personal bodyguard for Augustus Caesar. A restored republic would rob them of a reason for existing. They argued that the empire was too vast and complex to be run as a republic again. They insisted that a new emperor be chosen to succeed Caligula, and they wanted to be influential in deciding who he would be.

They favored Caligula's uncle Claudius despite his having been a much-derided figure. He seemed likely to be docile and accommodating to them. He limped, suffered a speech impediment, and was something of a family embarrassment despite a scholarly turn of mind. Suetonius states that he had suffered so severely from various medical disorders during his childhood that his mind and his body were dulled and that even when he was an adult, "he was not thought capable of any public or private business." His mother Antonia spoke of him as "a monster of a man, not finished but merely begun by Dame Nature."

Claudius was the brother of the deceased Germanicus, the idolized commander who had led Roman legions in battles with the Germans in forests to the north. But Claudius was not cut from the same cloth. He was nowhere in sight when, in the uproar sparked by Caligula's assassination, he had remarkably emerged as favored by the Praetorians to be next to don the imperial purple. A soldier found him cowering behind a curtain in the palace and hailed this terrified figure as the new emperor.

Claudius considered it a questionable honor. Having never been held in high regard, the idea of becoming the focus of public attention did not appeal to him. His reservations were understandable. Caligula's gruesome fate suggested being emperor was not necessarily a prescription for a long life. He was inclined to make his apologies and slip back into the shadows.

Learning of the latest developments and of Claudius's inclination to play no part in them, Agrippa hurried to the side of his boyhood friend to urge him not to back away from the great distinction and opportunity offered him. His was not completely selfless advice. His friendship with the murdered Caligula had been rewarding. He hoped to do as well if Claudius assumed the imperial throne. Nor was the alternative attractive to him. If the Republic-espousing senators had their way, they were unlikely to have much regard for someone like himself who had been so close to Caligula.

Claudius may have by then already been persuaded that becoming the fourth Roman emperor had much to commend it. He made a gift of a considerable sum of money to the Praetorians, which may have firmed up their positive feelings about him. But doubts about his elevation were still being expressed in the Senate where some continued to believe a revival of the republic would be preferable. Over several days, Agrippa, who still circulated in the most elite Roman circles, helped negotiate differences between the parties, and Claudius was duly confirmed as the new emperor.

One of his early acts was to reward Agrippa. He added Judaea and Samaria to the fringe kingdom Caligula had established for him. It was more than an act of gratitude for the role he had played in the aftermath to Caligula's assassination. He recognized that direct administration of Judaea by Roman governors had not been a success, certainly compared to the conditions that prevailed during Herod's reign when the Jews were permitted self-rule under a king of their own faith. Furthermore, Claudius had no doubt that his friend Agrippa would serve Rome loyally.

Administration of Judaea by procurators was suspended, and Agrippa was entrusted with the authority they had wielded. With the territories Claudius added, his kingdom became as large as the one Herod had ruled. As another gesture of gratitude, Claudius named Agrippa's brother Herod II to be king of the region of Chalcis in southern Lebanon.

The first time Agrippa left Rome, he departed as a destitute scrounger not knowing what fate awaited him and fearing the worst. This time, he left not only as a king but also as one much favored and generously rewarded by the master of the Roman Empire. His arrival in Jerusalem in 41 CE was a joyous event. In contrast to the hostility with which his grandfather had been received by his subjects when the Romans had appointed him their ruler a century earlier, Agrippa's elevation was received with elation throughout Judaea. People were relieved to be rid of their Roman-appointed procurators and to again have a monarch of their own faith, and they were aware he had earlier dissuaded Caligula from desecrating the Jerusalem temple.

Now fifty-one years old, Agrippa was much transformed from the freewheeling, often duplicitous figure he had once been. He was said to have become genuinely pious and respectful of his religious obligations. Upon his arrival in Jerusalem as king, he dutifully offered sacrifices at the temple. As a symbol of his dedication to his faith and to his people, he deposited in the temple treasury the gold chain Caligula had given him when he was released from the Roman prison to which Tiberius had consigned him.

But he was still uncertain of his reception when he first attended a holy day service at the temple. He was seen to be weeping when reciting the Torah passage that admonished Jews, "not to set a stranger over you who is not your brother." But whatever their forebears had thought of his Idumaean grandfather, other worshippers called out to assure Agrippa that they considered him one of their own. From then on, his visits to the temple became celebratory affairs.

Agrippa quickly demonstrated that he was dedicated to the welfare of his subjects. His popularity soared when, in view of the great wealth he was accumulating through the territories that he had been awarded, he reduced taxes. During the first harvest festival of his reign, he was admired for behaving as an ordinary pilgrim at the temple by carrying a basket of fruit on his shoulder to hand to the priests as part of the service.

Though Agrippa played fast-and-loose with the appointment of high priests, he solicited the support of the still-influential Pharisees and received their backing. The Sadducees had earlier been largely reduced to silence by the end of the Hasmonean dynasty with which they had been close and by the anti-Hellenic sentiment that had prevailed in Judaea since Herod's death. Agrippa's building projects, a bid to emulate his grandfather's architectural genius, drew less acclaim because he devoted more of his resources to architectural adornments in Berytus than in Judaea, though that was not a calculated snub.

His personal Roman connections, even greater than those Herod had enjoyed, gave him special recognition among the empire's other client states. That displeased Vibius Marsus, the governor of Syria, who resented Agrippa's ready access to eminences in Rome who were senior to him. When Agrippa organized a conference in Tiberias to be attended by other of Rome's client kings in the region—an indication of his high standing among them—Marsus intervened. He suggested to Rome that it might be intended as a secret prelude to a bid by conference participants to establish separate relations with the Parthians at a time when Parthian friction with the Romans was again escalating.

The proposed conference was a bold gesture by Agrippa. He may have wanted the gathering to formulate a common policy among the client states if a new war affecting them did develop between Rome and Parthia. If that had been Agrippa's intention, it did not succeed. Despite their friendship, Claudius authorized Marsus to cancel the Tiberias meeting. Marsus also blocked Agrippa's request to Rome for permission to strengthen the walls around Jerusalem. He may have suspected Agrippa of trying to make alterations in the relationship between Rome and Judaea, superseding his own role as official intermediary between them.

As king, Agrippa grew increasingly mild mannered and sought to conciliate rather than crush those who were critical of him. They included the Hellenized majorities in the Judaean cities of Caesarea and Sebaste, who might have preferred a Roman procurator for Judaea rather than a Jewish ruler. In addition to being popular with his subjects, Agrippa was held in high regard in the Jewish Diaspora throughout the empire because of how, like his grandfather, he gained special Roman recognition for them.

But Agrippa was distinctly unaccommodating to at least one group among his subjects. By the time he had become king, the disciples of the crucified Jesus, though still comparatively few in number, had become a recognizable presence in Jerusalem. This was before differences among them developed when Paul of Tarsus disputed with Jesus's brother James and the Apostle Peter over whether Gentiles could be accepted as fellow members of the Jesus movement without adhering to Jewish religious observances. Considering these early Christians to be trouble-making instigators of sacrilegious controversy, Agrippa persecuted them. The Apostle James the Greater was executed, and Peter was briefly imprisoned, accounting for the New Testament suggestion that Agrippa's early agonizing death was divine punishment for his wickedness. In 44 CE, a mere three years after he had become king of Judaea, he was stricken with severe abdominal pains while attending the quinquennial athletic games in Caesarea, originally established by Herod in honor of Augustus. He might have been poisoned. Agrippa was carried back to his Caesarea palace where he died five days later.

His passing would prove a disaster for the Jews. Though he had ruled Judaea for only three years, he had achieved the unique feat of being extolled both by his Jewish subjects and Roman luminaries. Given more time, he might have laid the groundwork for long-term peace and economic fortune for his kingdom, as his grandfather had tried to do, but without turning it into a brutal police state. In his "most determined effort . . . to settle the differences between the Roman Empire and Judaism," he might have changed the course of Jewish history, steering it away from the catastrophe that would soon overtake it.

* * *

Agrippa's son, Herod the Great's great-grandson, was also called Marcus Julius Agrippa. He would be the last king of the Herodian dynasty and the last king of the Jews though he never became king of Judaea. Seventeen years old when his father died, Agrippa II was raised and educated in Rome. He was looked on with favor by his father's friend Claudius Caesar and, like his father, grew up associating with the offspring of Rome's upper crust.

Claudius considered letting young Agrippa succeed his father on the throne of Judaea. But advisers persuaded him the boy was neither old nor experienced enough for responsibility in a land that had so recently been subjected to much mayhem and disorder. It was remembered that when Augustus permitted Herod's young son Archelaus to rule Judaea when Herod died, it proved a fiasco. Claudius's advisers may also have felt that, through his imperial connections, Agrippa I had been permitted too much leeway as king of Judaea and that his son might be tempted to try to follow suit.

But Claudius did award Agrippa II a royal crown, though only that of Chalcis when its king, his father's brother Herod II, died. Though denied the crown of Judaea, he also was granted custodianship of the temple in Jerusalem with authority to choose the high priest of the Jews. The Romans did not want to offend them and stir trouble by letting supervision of their temple fall to a procurator who did not share their religion.

Claudius subsequently decided young Agrippa deserved still more. So did Claudius's wife Agrippina, who had appointed herself his sometime patron, and he was awarded a much-expanded royal realm by imperial decree. In place of diminutive Chalcis, he was to be king of large, if sparsely populated, territories north and northeast of Judaea that had earlier been part of his father's domain. Still more was added to his realm, including the city of Tiberias in Galilee and parts of Peraea, after Claudius died and Nero (Agrippina's son) succeeded him on the imperial throne.

But Agrippa still was entrusted with no authority or official position in Judaea other than with regard to the temple. He did, however, establish an official residence in Jerusalem in the old Hasmonean royal palace. His sister Berenice briefly lived there too, sparking tittle-tattle that they were in an incestuous relationship. But he soon took to spending much of his time in Caesarea and in his kingdom in the north rather than in the holy city. Judaea had been reabsorbed into direct Roman jurisdiction, and he had no wish to displease Rome by leading fellow Jews to think of him as a rival focus of governance through his residence among them.

The procurators were now back in command. They came; they went. There were seven Rome-appointed procurators of Judaea from the death of Agrippa I till the start of the war between the Jews and Rome two decades later: Cuspius Fadus, Tiberius Julius Alexander, Ventidius Cumanus, Marcus Antonius Felix, Porcius Festus, Lucceius Albinus, and Gessius Florus. Each served between two and four years before moving on. Some were corrupt or incompetent, but despite the efforts of those of them who had constructive intentions, none contributed meaningfully to the well-being of the people or to the maintenance of peace and order among them. Aside from the wealth some of them accumulated while in Judaea, their experiences in office generally proved almost as unsatisfying to them as it was for the people they governed.

Agrippa tried to promote the interests of the Jews where he believed his influence might be effective. But in contrast to his father, he made no attempt to retrieve from the Romans a measure of self-rule for Judaea, nor did he take any step that might have been deemed contrary to Rome's wishes as his father had in organizing the aborted gathering of regional client kings. He conformed to religious observance that displayed his fellowship with other Jews, but he remained very much a creature of his Roman upbringing and of his fidelity to the imperial family.

\* \* \*

The return of the procurators to Judaea had brought Roman soldiers back to the streets of Jerusalem. Their presence did not sit well with the Jews. Though they considered themselves the people chosen by God, alien pagans were manifestly their masters. It reawakened nationalist sentiments among them. That Agrippa wore a royal crown had little meaning for them.

The Roman soldiers sent in to deal with disturbances or just patrolling their streets were mostly recruited from among the Greeks of Sebaste, Caesarea, and Syria, whose congenital antipathy to the Jews compounded the climate of disquiet. Incidents involving them inflamed the situation—a soldier publicly tearing up a scroll of the Torah, another exposing himself to a group of worshippers near the temple, another desecrating a synagogue. Attempts by the authorities to calm the outrage such acts provoked often only drew angrier responses from the people. These were in turn met with heavy-handed crowd-control measures that worsened the situation still more. Claudius had been alerted to the problem—possibly by Agrippa—and considered replacing those chronically hostile units with unbiased troops from elsewhere in the empire. But he was persuaded the situation was under control.

Famine from failed harvests and increasingly onerous taxation compounded a mood of foreboding in Judaea. The gap between the poor and the rich grew ever wider, exacerbating popular discontent. Completion of work on architectural projects raised unemployment levels. Thousands of men were made jobless when the final touches to the rebuilding of the temple were finally completed. Agrippa tried to alleviate their difficulties by putting them to work repaving the streets of Jerusalem.

Procurator Fadus discovered how demanding his assignment would be when he brought Roman rule back to Judaea upon the death of Agrippa I. He wanted to make the transition of rule to him from that of the late esteemed king as unobjectionable to the people as he could. But he quickly felt obliged to deploy force to crush anti-Roman disorder in parts of the land.

Tiberius Julius Alexander, who succeeded Fadus, was from one of Egypt's leading Jewish families. His uncle was the renowned philosopher Philo of Alexandria, who did much to blend traditional Jewish and Hellenic approaches in philosophical analyses. But Tiberius was an apostate, and the Romans were mistaken if they believed he would be more acceptable to the Jews. Though he respected the people's continuing observance of their traditional ways, the appointment of someone who had abandoned the faith of those he was to govern was not greatly appreciated by them. He further alienated them when he dealt harshly with incipient insurgent movements.

Agrippa, a friend of the new procurator, distanced himself from this difficult situation. However, he did intercede when Tiberius's successor, Ventidius Cumanus, found himself caught up in a violent contretemps between Jews and Samaritans. Their mutual enmity was historically implanted, dating back to the Assyrian conquest of part of the divided kingdom of the Jews eight hundred years before. The latest clash between them erupted when Galilean pilgrims passing through Samaria on their way to the temple in Jerusalem were killed.

Cumanus sided with the Samaritans in the situation. He and prominent Jews critical of his judgment were summoned to Rome for the affair to be sorted out. The procurator had strong support at Claudius's court. But Agrippa, in Rome at the time, spoke up in favor of the Jews, and Claudius found in their favor. He ordered Cumanus removed as procurator, to be succeeded by Antonius Felix.

Although he intervened against Cumanus and sought to further the interests of his fellow Jews, Agrippa generally gave unquestioning support to the procurators in their often-fumbling efforts to govern Judaea. (His sister Drusilla was the wife of Procurator Felix.) At one point, friendly relations between Agrippa and Procurator Festus brought him into passing contact with a seminal figure in the birth of Christianity.

Paul of Tarsus had, by then, devoted much of his adult life to evangelizing for belief in Jesus as the Messiah among Jews and pagans in Greek areas of the Middle East outside Judaea. On his final visit to Jerusalem, Paul went to the temple where his presence offended many of the worshippers who considered him an apostate. He might have been killed in the resulting hubbub if Roman soldiers had not taken him into protective custody. Accused of causing a disturbance and defiling a holy place, he was sent by the Romans to Caesarea where he was imprisoned for two years before being brought to trial.

By then, Felix, who had been procurator when Paul was arrested, had died and the affair was to be judged by his successor, Porcius Festus. Although Festus tried to be an honorable and effective governor, his task was formidable. He inherited a milieu awash with insurrectionists and would-be spiritual leaders. He had already felt obliged to dispatch "both horsemen and footmen to fall upon those that had been seduced by a certain imposter who promised [the Jews] deliverance and freedom from the miseries they were under if they would but follow him."

When Paul was taken from his cell and brought before Festus to be judged, he invoked his right as a Roman citizen to appeal to the emperor against the accusations made against him. Fed up with having to deal with such disruptive figures, Festus was delighted. The case would be removed from his jurisdiction. But he was in some confusion about it. The charges against Paul were so vague that he had no idea how to frame the documents that would have to be passed along to Rome with the prisoner. He brought the matter to the attention of Agrippa, who was in Caesarea at the time for Festus's official inauguration as procurator. He considered him better able to explain the offenses Paul had committed against the Jews in the temple that had led to his arrest.

Agrippa agreed to see what he could do. When interrogated, Paul told him that rather than being a disorderly troublemaker, he had been trying to bring spiritual salvation to the Jews through belief in Jesus. Agrippa was not impressed, but he told Festus the defendant seemed not to have done anything for which he should be either executed or confined to prison. "This man," he said, "might have been released if he had not appealed to the emperor." But he had done so and, therefore, could not be released. He was sent on to Rome to be dealt with there and where it was said he was ultimately martyred.

The small Jesus movement continued to cause something of a stir in Jerusalem after Paul's demise, as was demonstrated when Lucceius Albinus was sent to succeed Festus as procurator. Albinus took up his post in Caesarea at a complicated moment in Rome's dealings with the religious authorities in Jerusalem. High Priest Ananus had chosen the interregnum between the departure of one procurator and the arrival of another to convene a session of the Sanhedrin in Jerusalem. It was a minor act of defiance. Calling such conclaves was supposed to require the approval of the procurator. Officially, Ananus should have waited till Albinus had arrived and given his authorization.

On the high priest's agenda at the Sanhedrin session he unlawfully called was crushing the Jesus movement. Its members had taken to meeting at the temple to the annoyance of the priestly authorities. Though Jesus's disciples in Jerusalem were pious Jews, Ananus, a Sadducee, considered their belief in a Messiah to be sacrilege contributing to public disorder. Biblical prophets had predicted the appearance of a Messiah among the Jews one day, but there was no specific reference to such a figure in the Torah. To deal with what he considered a vile heresy, the high priest had James, the brother of Jesus, arrested. James had become leader of the Jesus movement after the crucifixion. He was tried and condemned to death by stoning, a punishment also meted out to some other members of what later came to be described as the original Jerusalem Church.

Leading Pharisees, rivals of the Sadducees, called the execution of their fellow Jews a travesty of justice, no matter how errant their beliefs seemed to have been. The Pharisees were less inflexible in their attitude toward the peculiarities of pious spiritual movements that had begun springing up among the Jews during the turbulent period of direct Roman rule. They protested to Agrippa, who was also offended, possibly because the convening of the Sanhedrin session without official sanction by the procurator had been in disregard of Roman regulations. Acting on his authority as Roman appointed overseer of the temple, he replaced the presumptuous Ananus with another high priest (who was no more sympathetic to the Jesus movement than his predecessor but who refrained from having its leaders killed).

When Albinus finally arrived to take up his procuratorial office, public unrest, fueled by increasing rancor over the Roman occupation, led him to order a harsh crackdown. Like the similar responses of some of his predecessors, it proved counterproductive. Discord in the religious leadership in Jerusalem diminished what influence it might have had in promoting support among the people for order to be maintained, especially when Gessius Florus arrived to succeed Albinus as procurator. Florus was openly unresponsive to the drift toward crisis in Judaea. Indeed, he deepened the alienation between the Jews and the Roman authorities. Using the powers of his office, he brazenly dipped into the treasury at the temple in search of a personal fortune. His venality triggered public protests. Some youths carried a begging bowl through the streets of Jerusalem, pleading mockingly for contributions for the "destitute" procurator. Enraged, Florus sent troops to rough up his critics. The soldiers saw it as a license to murder and loot.

Florus did not object. He encouraged the anti-Jewish sentiments of the Greek majority in Judaea's administrative capital Caesarea, fueling violent sectarian strife. He made no effort to curb it as it spread to other cities as well. Moderate Jewish leaders sought to channel popular fury at Florus's conduct into appeals to Emperor Nero for him to be recalled or reined in. But Nero was trying to cope with difficulties in Rome and elsewhere in the empire of far greater concern to him than what might be transpiring in Judaea, and their efforts to take the edge off the anger of the people had little effect.

Public order in Judaea continued to unravel. Religiously driven and nationalist movements attracted ever more recruits. Together, they became the driving force promoting armed defiance of Rome. Their followers were increasingly well organized and grew ever bolder, notably in Galilee, Paraea, and Idumaea, where Rome's armed presence was not as palpable as in Jerusalem. The countdown to insurrection had begun, and it was apparent that neither the procurators nor the moderate Jewish leaders had any idea how to defuse the developing tempest. Nor did Agrippa. He was scorned by rebel leaders and continued to be held in little regard by the people of Judaea. Unable to contribute anything toward curbing the escalating tide of the insurgency, he felt obliged to support the Roman authorities in Caesarea in their failing efforts to do so.

But when he came to Jerusalem after a visit to Alexandria, where he had gone to congratulate former procurator Tiberius on his appointment to be Roman governor of Egypt, he recognized how volatile and imminently combustible the atmosphere had become. The Jerusalemites were demanding action against Florus's corruption and malfeasance. They called on Agrippa, whose connections in Rome were well known, for firmer support than he had yet provided. But, though still linked to the imperial family, he had a less close relationship with Nero than he'd had with Claudius. He also realized Nero would be enraged rather than sympathetic if warned that an insurrection could be taking shape in Judaea because the complaints of the Jews were not being addressed.

Agrippa did, however, feel obliged to try to keep the situation from erupting out of control. Though not much given to public speaking, he told a large crowd he had called together at the gymnasium in Jerusalem that he understood and sympathized with their grievances. But he pleaded for recognition of the realities. He told the assembled that an uprising would be a catastrophe for the Jews. He was scathing about those who spoke of making war against Rome, demanding to know what resources they had for such an undertaking.

> What sort of an army do you rely on? What are the arms you depend on? Where is your fleet that may seize upon the Roman seas? Where are those treasures which may be sufficient for your undertakings? Do you suppose . . . that you are to make war with the Egyptians and with the Arabians? Will you not carefully reflect upon the Roman empire . . . [which is] invincible in all parts of the habitable earth?

Agrippa warned the assembled that they were not as rich as the Gauls, or as strong as the Germans, or shrewder than the Greeks, all of whom had been conquered by the Romans, as had even the British who should have been unconquerable on their island.

Agrippa's words had a sobering effect. For the moment, those listening to him realized defiance of Rome's would be unrealistic and could be calamitous. Gestures were made at withdrawing the challenges made to Roman rule. Money was to be raised to make good suspended tax payments. Plans were mentioned for restoring the passage between Jerusalem's Roman-occupied Antonia Fortress and the temple that had been destroyed by mob action.

But the rapport Agrippa had managed to establish with the people of Jerusalem was shattered by what else he had to tell them. He said the appointment of Florus as procurator of Judaea had been an aberration, but his authority should be respected until the Romans sent a suitable replacement. It was not what they wanted to hear, and their mood again turned hostile. It was made clear to Agrippa that his advice was not needed. He was denounced, and stones were thrown at him. Realizing his efforts had failed and that his personal safety was compromised, he quickly fled Jerusalem for his kingdom in the north.

Developments elsewhere in the land made the situation even more explosive than it had become in Jerusalem. Charismatic, articulate figures had emerged to provide dynamic leadership for increasingly assertive rebellious militias that were determined to drive the Romans from Judaea. The first major blow was struck by the Zealot Menahem ben Judas and his band of followers. In 66 CE, they overwhelmed and slaughtered the Roman garrison at the Masada fortress in the south and claimed it as a trophy of war. Though an audacious challenge to Rome's authority, Masada was a remote outpost, easily isolated. The Romans judged the event an intolerable act by a small band of outlaws. They would get around to dealing with them after they attended to more pressing control issues.

What happened soon afterward, the first major act in the war between the Jews and Rome, might seem to have been comparatively innocuous, but the Romans could not have as easily put it aside for score-settling later on. It took place at the temple in Jerusalem where the captain of the temple guard Eleazar ben Ananus (son of the high priest who'd had Jesus's brother James executed) took it upon himself to issue a symbolic but intolerable challenge to Roman rule. Eleazar persuaded like-minded junior temple priests to disregard the objections of their seniors and suspend the regular animal sacrifices made in honor of the Roman emperor. The cancellation amounted to no less than an insult to Nero and a declaration of independence from Rome. A strong response was inevitable, especially after a subsequent public gathering cheered the act and issued a furious condemnation of Procurator Florus.

The high priest, Pharisee leaders, and other leading figures called a public meeting in the outer courtyard of the temple to try to stem the tide of rebellion. But the popular mood of defiance had gathered unstoppable momentum. An outbreak of open rebellion seemed imminent. Messages were dispatched to Florus and to Agrippa, pleading for strong forces to be hurried to Jerusalem to prevent an uprising there.

Florus, in Caesarea, did nothing. He feared his troops might sustain casualties for which he would be held responsible. Besides, his administration of Judaea was already under unsympathetic examination in Rome. He hoped the deteriorating situation would demonstrate that despite the accusations of unwarranted brutality leveled against him, he had been justified in having used harsh methods to maintain order.

However Agrippa responded to the appeal by dispatching two thousand cavalrymen from his northern territories to do what they could to maintain order in Jerusalem. But by then, the uprising had gained large numbers of recruits, and Agrippa's men were substantially outnumbered by insurgent fighters converging on the city from Galilee and elsewhere to seize the temple and its surroundings and make their stronger presence felt. Agrippa's men were forced to take refuge in a palace Herod had fortified long before and then to leave the city under safe conduct. But Roman units that had also taken refuge in the palace were slaughtered as the insurgents who, preparing for a Roman onslaught, substantially increased their numerical strength in the city and firmed up their control of its walls.

It now fell to Cestius Gallus, Roman governor of Syria, to deal with what had become an intolerable situation for him. Rome held him responsible for the maintenance of order in the region. Gathering a force consisting of a legion, parts of others, and units supplied by the heads of other client states in the area, including Agrippa, he marched on Jerusalem to lay siege to the city. Agrippa sent two emissaries up ahead to the insurgents to seek a way that would spare Jerusalem and its people another bloody Roman conquest. But his peace bid was again fruitless. The insurgents gave his envoys no hearing, killed one of them, and wounded the other.

The possibility of negotiations eliminated, Cestius sent his army storming into the city. The outnumbered insurgent fighters were forced back to where they could better stand their ground. That gave Cestius pause. In their new defensive positions, the insurgents would be able to put up formidable, prolonged resistance, and the autumn rain season was beginning. Fighting into the winter was not an attractive prospect. Cestius decided to withdraw his forces, intending to resume the assault later under more favorable conditions.

But his men were not permitted to pull back unchallenged. Insurgent fighters rushed out of Jerusalem to pounce on his withdrawing army. They badly mauled it and humiliatingly captured his legion's treasured standard. The success of that attack had two important consequences. It convinced the insurgents that, having once trounced the Romans, they could keep on doing so. At the same time, it made the Romans even more determined to obliterate the insurgency thoroughly and ruthlessly. Agrippa saw no meaningful role he could any longer play in the situation.

In Rome, Nero was stunned by what was happening in Judaea. He summoned Titus Flavius Vespasian, a distinguished former senator and general, out of retirement and commanded him to crush the rebellion. It took Vespasian several months to leave retirement behind and gather the resources he required to fulfill his assignment. During that time, the insurgent militias consolidated their control of much of Jerusalem. They were strong in resolve though small in number compared to the population of the city. Most Jews shared their wish for independence from Rome, but the prospect of a war to achieve that objective alarmed them. Their history told them of the death and destruction Roman legions on the attack were capable of inflicting. But they were also uneasy about how the rebels had seized control of the temple and other parts of Jerusalem and were attempting to extend their authority to all of it. They were troubled too by the assertive conduct of the insurgents and the feuding for supremacy between insurgent leaders.

Men of senior priestly rank and others in Jerusalem who had a personal stake in the maintenance of peace and order were prominent among those who had little sympathy for the strong-willed insurgents in their midst. They feared defiance of Rome was leading the Jews to disaster. They came to consider that the corrupt and brutal Procurator Florus was less of a threat to the people than the insurgent militias and that he was also less of a threat to what was left of their own privileged status. They believed Rome could eventually recognize the justice of their complaints about procuratorial shortcomings and might also permit them one day to rule Judaea again within the Roman orbit, as Herod and Agrippa I had. As Vespasian prepared for conquest, the lull in the confrontation with the Romans provided them with an opportunity to examine how to counter the insurgent power grab, end the spiral toward all-out war with Rome, and work toward a mutually acceptable solution to the situation.

They did, however, recognize that belief in the objectives of the uprising, if not in its means, was shared by most of the people embittered by heavy Roman taxes and the disrespect of Roman officials. In the heady atmosphere that had developed in Jerusalem, they concluded that the only way to undermine the insurgency was to assume leadership of it. If they could accomplish that, they would provide the Romans with a negotiating partner with whom the conflict might be resolved without much bloodshed.

Calling on their traditional positions of authority among the people and the greater numbers persuaded to follow them, they formed what was, in effect, a provisional government and claimed command of the insurgency from the squabbling insurgents.[1]

The insurgents did not readily surrender control of Jerusalem. But teams of fighters organized by the provisional government successfully drove them back into the temple and confined them there. However, they managed to slip a message out to insurgent leaders in Idumaea claiming that the provisional government, now in charge in Jerusalem, was collaborating with the Romans and intended to surrender the city to them. Believing that to be true, ten thousand Idumaeans marched on Jerusalem to free and reinforce the beleaguered insurgents, who then made short work of the senior figures of the provisional government. Taking control of the entire city, they ended all possibility of negotiating with the Romans and halting the advance toward open war with them.

Having gathered an army of sixty thousand men, Vespasian, his logistics in place, was now on the move. Marching his legions through Syria, he first wiped out stiff resistance in Galilee and then quickly overran most of Judaea. He then took a break to refresh himself and escape the searing heat in the south by spending some time as a guest of Agrippa at Caesarea Philippi, his capital in the hills to the north. Before he could return to his campaign and mount an assault on Jerusalem, a further delay in operations became necessary. Word came that Emperor Nero, whom the Senate had declared a public enemy, had committed suicide.

Offensive military action in Judaea and elsewhere in the empire was suspended while the consequences were sorted out. Vespasian now devoted his full attention to questions related to the imperial succession. He sent his son, Titus, his leading general, back to Rome for the inauguration of a new emperor. As a client king of the Romans and a friend of both Vespasian and Titus, Agrippa went with him. So did his sister Berenice, who had become Titus's mistress.

The contest to succeed Nero as emperor became a tortuous sequence of developments involving shifting allegiances among Roman luminaries

---

1. Young Joseph ben Matityahu, of priestly ancestry and later to be known as the historian Josephus, was appointed commander of official resistance forces in Galilee. He took up his position there and, he said, performed his task well. But he soon concluded resistance was futile and counterproductive and changed sides to become an aide to the Romans.

and military commanders at home and in the field. The year 69 CE became known as the year of the four emperors. Galba, then Otho, and then Vitellius each emerged victorious in succession. But each, in turn, ran into strong opposition from within the army and was deposed before Vespasian himself, having skillfully patched together sufficient military backing, left Judaea for Rome to be acclaimed emperor himself.

Titus, who would succeed him as emperor ten years on, had been in operational command of much of the fighting across Judaea. Back in Judaea from Rome after his father's enthronement, he now took on the task of finally obliterating the heart of the insurrection in Jerusalem. Agrippa also returned to Judaea to see what he might do to resolve the conflict before more blood was spilled. Whatever his anguish about the imminent fate of the people of Jerusalem, he was so fully committed to the Romans that he was unable to play any role whatever when Titus laid siege to the holy city in 70 CE, overran it, and destroyed the temple Agrippa's great-grandfather had magnificently rebuilt. Ironically, he had himself superintended completion of the final touches to Herod's temple project just a few years earlier.

The insurgent leaders were cut down or captured. Great numbers of their followers and others in Jerusalem were killed, and parts of the city were ravaged. The Zealots at Masada held out for another three years before each committed suicide rather than surrender. Only two women and five children survived to tell the story.

Though retaining his northern kingdom, Agrippa, Herod's great-grandson, later settled in Rome where he continued to be a respected, well-connected, if innocuous, figure. Emperor Vespasian added additional territories in Syria to his kingdom. He may have visited them from time to time, but Rome, where he was appointed an honorary magistrate, became his primary home, as it had been when he was growing up. He may have observed Titus's triumphal celebration in Rome in which Jewish prisoners taken at war's end and temple trophies were paraded in procession. He is believed to have died childless in Rome around the year 100 CE, when he would have been seventy-three years old.

There were other "Herodians" during that period, mentioned in passing in the New Testament. They were probably an amorphous group of individuals who favored the perpetuation of the dynasty founded by Herod the Great. But Agrippa II was the last of the Herodian kings to function, however marginally and ineffectively, in the land of the Jews.

# Afterword

## The Dawn of Christianity

The birth of Christianity was the most significant episode of the Herodian period though Herod the Great played no part in its creation, nor had the other Herodians much to do with its founding. Christianity grew from the conviction of a small group of Jews in Galilee that a charismatic, fellow Galilean was the Messiah sent by God to herald the imminent end of time and the establishment of God's kingdom on Earth.

Jesus Christ was born shortly before or shortly after Herod died. He was a child when Herod's inept son Archelaus governed Judaea as its Roman-appointed ethnarch, and he grew up during the time when a succession of Roman-appointed procurators administered the land. Jesus is believed to have been around thirty years old at the high point of his ministry when he and his twelve Apostles journeyed from Galilee to Jerusalem to celebrate the Passover holiday. He was arrested there for blasphemy and judged guilty by the Sanhedrin. He was then handed over to Procurator Pontius Pilate to be dealt with, as required by Roman administrative procedures. That suggests sedition may have been the Roman charge against him or at least one of the charges.

After Jesus's crucifixion, his original Apostles and other early followers continued to preach that he was the Messiah. They were all devout Jews. In his *Christian Beginnings*, Géza Vermes observes that they "thought as Jews, lived as Jews, and shared the aspirations of their fellow Jews." James Dunn, author of *Jesus Remembered: Christianity in the Making*, writes, "Earliest Christianity was not yet seen as something separate and distinct from Judaism. It was a sect, like other sects within first century Judaism." In his *Church History*, Eusebius states that four "popular" sects existed within Judaism at the time, in addition to the better-known Pharisees, Sadducees, and Essenes. Not until later did the Jesus sect begin its transformation into Christianity, a religion distinct from its Jewish origins. How that happened was a subject of controversy then and continues to be a matter of conflicting views today.

* * *

The kingdom of Judaea had been at peace during the reign of Herod the Great for three reasons: (1) Herod's tyrannically efficient ruthlessness made popular unrest, insurrectionary movements, and the conspiracies of individuals unsustainable and futile; (2) relative prosperity promoted by agricultural innovation, expanded commercial activity, and low unemployment levels dampened economically motivated unrest; and (3) Herod's submission to Rome spared Judaea the foreign meddling in its affairs that would have inspired the faith-driven nationalist uprising that direct Roman rule subsequently did.

The succession of procurators appointed by Rome to govern Judaea ultimately proved as incapable as Herod's son Archelaus had been in taming the turbulence that convulsed the land after his father died. Some of them were dedicated civil servants who sought to perform their duties honorably. Others had little concern for the well-being of the people they governed.

Taxes, already considered punitive, increased. Landlords pressed their tenant farmers for greater crop tithes. Joblessness grew as construction projects were completed, cut back, or phased out. Poverty was rampant as the gap between rich and poor grew ever larger. The result was widespread uncertainty and unrest.

Robber bands roamed the land, their leaders sometimes claiming to be king of Judaea. Even main roads were no longer safe for travelers and commerce. Violence stalked the cities. Acts of oppression, incompetence, and the venality by some of the procurators stoked Jewish resentment of Roman rule. The anxiety and agitation of the people were compounded by outcroppings of anti-Jewish actions and feelings among the Greeks of the region and sometimes among the Roman soldiers who patrolled trouble spots.

Judas the Galilean, a firebrand who denounced Roman taxes as little less than slavery, stirred a violent revolt. It gathered some momentum before he was killed and his followers dispersed. Other such rebels similarly appeared and were similarly eliminated. But craving for national liberation spread among the people and could not be easily extinguished. Religious zealotry played a central role in the movement.

Zealotry was an honored tradition in Judaea. The biblical prophet Elijah had been taken up to heavenly reward because of his "burning zeal for the Law." After killing a Syrian officer sent to force him to worship a pagan god, Mattathias, father of the Maccabee brothers and instigator of the Maccabee uprising against Syrian oppression, said, "Let everyone who is zealous for the Law follow after me" into the Judaean hills for armed resistance to foreign rule.

The leaders of the Zealots were among the most assertive of the nationalists in the build-up to the war with Rome. They considered themselves and other Jews answerable only to God and bound to obey only his laws and their decrees. They abominated Roman rule and objected to the incursion of Greek language and Hellenic ways into traditional Jewish society. They would provide the main spark for the war that would result in the destruction of the ancient Jewish nation. Among the Zealots were the Sicarii, assassins who concealed small daggers called *sicas* in the folds of their cloaks. In the streets of Jerusalem, they sought out those they considered collaborators with the Romans and stabbed them to death. They then blended into the clusters of bystanders that gathered around their fallen victims, one of whom was a former high priest, and pretended to share their horror at their bloody deeds.

But the aftermath to Herod's death also had another, very different, dimension. For some Jews, the response to the troubled times did not come in the form of rebellion, nationalist fervor, or despair. Instead, they viewed the disquiet and anxiety gripping the land, troubling as they were, to be hopeful and promising. They saw the convergence of violence, oppression, and social decay as the prelude to the arrival of a Messiah whose appearance would be the prelude to the end of days and the beginning of sublime divine rule on Earth.

There would be "no Satan any more nor any evil destroyer. For all their days shall be days of blessing and healing." "The days will come in which vines shall grow, each having ten thousand shoots, and on each shoot ten thousand branches, and on each branch ten thousand twigs, and on each twig ten thousand clusters, and on each cluster ten thousand grapes, and each grape when pressed shall yield five-and-twenty measures of wine."

The belief that a Messiah would one day bring eternal relief from adversity had long been part of the Jewish mind-set. Biblical prophets had planted a hope that a charismatic spiritual savior would appear in times of supreme distress to herald a new, glorious age and rescue the Jewish people from all that was wrong in the world. The Messiah was not expected to be divine but a direct mortal descendant of the apotheosized King David who had welded the twelve original Jewish tribes into a nation.

The prophet Jeremiah quotes God as saying, "A time is coming when I will raise up a true branch of David's line. He shall reign as king and shall prosper, and he shall do what is just and right in the land. In his days, Judah shall be delivered and Israel shall dwell secure."

According to the prophet Ezekiel, God saw his people as a flock for which the future would be idyllic. "I will appoint a single shepherd over [the Jews]. . . . I the Lord will be their God and my servant David shall be a ruler among them." Through the prophet Malachi, God is said to have promised, " I am sending a messenger to prepare the way before me. "

The Messiah-will-come theme, imbedded in the psyche of the Jews in biblical times, rose to the surface in the troubled post-Herod period. For many, it was a time of spiritual questing, a time of yearning for the promised marvelous figure with powers to bring relief from existential troubles, a time of belief that the long-awaited moment of his messianic appearance had finally come. Such figures were Abba Hilkiah, who was reputed to be able to make rainfall at times of drought, and Hanina ben Dosa, another rainmaker who was also said to be capable of curing people of illness. It was this feverish period that saw the dawn of the Jesus movement from which Christianity would emerge.

The earliest figure in this developing phenomenon was John the Baptist. In the tradition of the prophets of old, John, the son of a local priest, lived ascetically and called on his fellow Jews to obey God's laws and repent their sins. Josephus describes him as "a good man who commanded the Jews to exercise virtue both as to righteousness towards one another and piety towards God."

Some saw John as the Messiah, but he disclaimed any such role. Instead, it was he who first saw Jesus, the son of his mother's cousin Mary, as the one whose arrival at that time of lawlessness and tension would be the prelude to the establishment of God's kingdom on Earth.

John went to an early death. Herod's son Antipas, tetrarch of Galilee and Peraea, had imprisoned him after being accused by him of violating Mosaic Law in marrying the former wife of his still-living brother Philip. According to the New Testament, John was then killed when Salome, the daughter of Antipas's new wife Herodias, was granted her wish for him to be beheaded for his impertinence. However, Antipas may instead have had him executed for fear that his preaching would be seen by his Roman masters as promoting insurrection and would provoke them into taking harsh preemptive measures.

The situation with Jesus was different. He won the devotion of a core of followers, most notably the twelve Galilean Jews who came to be known as his Apostles. What was more, he did not confine his ministry to remote Galilee but spread his message in Jerusalem, the urban center of the Jewish nation and the heart of its religious establishment.

The priestly leadership at the temple and the sages of the Sanhedrin jealously guarded their roles as guardians of the Jewish faith. Jesus's preaching, and the belief of his followers that this eccentric upstart from Galilee was the Messiah, outraged them. Nor would they have taken kindly to the claim that he was a blood descendant of the revered King David and, therefore, spiritually outranked them. Like Antipas in the case of John the Baptist, they may also have been concerned that the ever-watchful Romans would believe he was promoting unrest in Judaea with his declaration that the arrival of God's kingdom on Earth was imminent.

The Sanhedrin condemned Jesus for blasphemy and handed him over to Pontius Pilate for judgment and sentencing. Upon learning that Jesus was a Galilean, Pilate had him delivered to Tetrarch Antipas, who was also visiting Jerusalem from Galilee. But failing to get Jesus to attempt to perform any of the miracles of which it was said he was capable, Antipas declined to free or condemn him and sent him back to Pilate to be dealt with.

Accountable for the maintenance of civil order in Judaea, Pilate could have decided on a sentence for Jesus short of execution. But as a stern governor who would later be summoned back to Rome to be tried for the brutal nature of his administration of Judaea and Samaria, he handed down the death sentence.

More than brutishness may have motivated Pilate in this case. As has been pointed out, "[i]n the existing permanent state of tension, any Roman administrator, taught by the experience of other messianic commotions, must have seen red at the mention of a new movement spreading. . . . The procurator must have considered it a matter of sheer prudence to suppress the agitation before it got out of hand."

After Jesus's crucifixion, the apostles gathered daily "with one mind in the temple," the center of Jewish worship. Jesus's brother James, who had not been one of them but who was also considered a descendant of King David, assumed leadership of the Jesus sect. Together with the Apostles, he established what came to be described as the Jerusalem Church, the cradle from which Christianity would emerge into an organized religion. Its core principles were belief that Jesus was the Messiah and strict observance of Mosaic Law. Whether this church was a fixed venue, perhaps a synagogue, or merely a concept, can only be guessed. Aside from James, the church's preeminent figure was Peter, the apostle with whom, according to the New Testament, Jesus was particularly close.

However, Paul, a Jew from the city of Tarsus in what is now Turkey, challenged the preeminence of James and Peter among the followers of Jesus. Paul was a Roman citizen by birth. Though he had grown up in a Hellenized setting, he had been a deeply pious youth. While still young, he had migrated to Jerusalem where he studied under Gamaliel, a Pharisee scholar and religious luminary.

The son of a Pharisee and a Pharisee himself, Paul later describes himself as having been "extremely zealous for my ancestral traditions." At first, he abominated those who claimed the crucified Jesus was the Messiah and describes how he had persecuted them "beyond measure." Indeed, "entering house after house," he dragged out believers in Jesus and threw them into jail. He watched when Steven, a convert to belief in Jesus, was stoned to death in Jerusalem for blasphemy and believed he deserved the punishment meted out to him.

It is unclear what authority had been conferred on Paul to punish blasphemers. But he was apparently so successful in rooting them out that he was authorized by the high priest and Sanhedrin to journey from Jerusalem to Damascus to arrest and bring to justice devotees of Jesus who might be found among the Jews there.

But Paul's epiphany, the dazzling vision he had of the crucified Jesus calling to him while he was en route to Damascus, affected him so profoundly that he dedicated his life to spreading what he took to be Jesus's message. He began this new mission immediately in Damascus to which he had originally traveled to protect Jews there from blasphemous messianic delusions. But he aroused such fury among them with what they considered his apostasy that he had to flee for his life.

He spent his next years wandering, often alone, in prolonged spiritual cleansing before beginning his ministry among pagan Gentiles. He had come to believe that people should not be excluded from the rewards and comforts offered by belief in Jesus only because they did not abide by the laws governing Jewish religious observance. He declared that a person is not put right with God by doing what the law requires. It would happen only through "faith in Jesus." That assertion thrust the Jesus movement into internal controversy. Although he had never known the living Jesus, Paul claimed equivalent standing with the Apostles, declaring, "By God's power, I was made an apostle to the Gentiles, just as Peter was made an apostle to the Jews."

Paul had earlier met in Jerusalem with James and Peter and established his credentials with them as a fellow Jewish follower of Jesus. When he began seeking converts among Gentiles in Antioch, one of the largest cities of the Roman Empire, he met with censure from Jews there. Among the detractors were those who, though remaining observant Jews, agreed with him that Jesus was the Messiah but who objected to his recruiting Gentiles to the Jesus movement without requiring them to join them in observing Torah Law as they were convinced Jesus had done.

Paul considered his critics in Antioch to be dangerous enemies of the mission with which he believed Jesus had entrusted him. "Pretending to be believers, these men slipped into our group as spies. . . . They wanted to make slaves of us but . . . we did not give in to them."

In an effort to end the friction, Paul journeyed from Antioch to Jerusalem to meet with the leaders of the Jerusalem Church and resolve outstanding doctrinal questions, in particular on whether Gentiles who were converted to belief in Jesus were required to obey Torah commandments. Paul insisted they did not.

The leaders of the Jerusalem Church had largely resisted the cultural inroads of Hellenization, which had become a key cultural aspect of the embryonic, Greek-speaking Christianity for which Paul, equipped with the Hellenized familiarities of his early years, was evangelizing. Having lived all their lives as pious Jews, James and Peter were not easily persuaded to agree that Paul's Gentile converts should be welcome in the Jesus movement if they did not accept Torah Law.

But Paul was a forceful and resolute figure, not readily given to submission. He appears not to have held the leaders of the Jerusalem Church in high regard, saying they—Jesus's brother James and the Apostles Peter and John—only "seemed to be [its] leaders." The New Testament indicates that at that Jerusalem meeting, Paul won his argument that Gentiles who joined the Jesus movement were not obliged to be circumcised or observe most other Mosaic Laws.

Nevertheless, the issue continued to trouble the leaders of the Jerusalem Church. After Paul had returned to Antioch, Peter went to see what was happening there. His reception by Paul and Gentiles he had converted presented no problems at first. They ate agreeably together, which was unusual. Because of their dietary restrictions, Jews rarely practiced table fellowship with non-Jews.

But the situation in Antioch soon highlighted persisting differences between Paul and the Jerusalem Church. When other members of the church, sent by James from Jerusalem, arrived there, Peter immediately distanced himself from Paul's uncircumcised converts. So did other Jews there. Paul reacted to their conduct by leveling scorn at Peter, accusing him of hypocrisy. "I opposed him in public because he was clearly wrong. . . . The other Jewish brothers [in Antioch] also started acting like cowards along with Peter" (Gal 2.11).

The impression left by the New Testament account is that Peter did not challenge that rebuke and that he, like Paul, became a pillar of the new Christian faith, shorn of its original Jewish elements and "transformed [from] the God-centered religion of Jesus into a Christ-centered Christianity." During the following two centuries, the new faith survived persecution, schisms, and bitter internecine theological conflict to establish itself throughout the Roman Empire, subsequently to spread across the world and become in time, in its various denominations, the world's largest religion.

There is no evidence testifying to the ultimate fate of Peter and Paul. According to Christian doctrine, both ended up in Rome where both were martyred, Peter crucified and Paul beheaded. However both remain figures of puzzlement. Ever since the sixteenth-century Protestant Reformation, Paul's contributions to Christian thought have come under critical review, not least by those who have considered him to have been a "corrupter of the doctrines of Jesus." Nevertheless, even biblical scholars who reject such a disparaging and dismissive judgment, and who consider Paul the most influential figure in originally defining fine points of Christian doctrine, have been engaged in recent times in exploring "new perspectives on Paul" to reexamine and reinterpret his original teachings.

Peter is even more of an enigma. It seems strange, as is implied, that he did not challenge Paul's harsh and religiously significant rebuke to him in Antioch, or respond to it in any way. It also seems odd that Paul would have criticized Peter so abrasively in view of the latter's more senior standing within the Jesus movement at the time. Unlike Paul, he had enjoyed a personal relationship with the living Jesus who had chosen him to be the "rock" on which "I will build my church."

After his confrontation with Paul in Antioch, there is little more of Peter in the New Testament. He subsequently "disappears into legend" in which he is said to have later become the bishop of Antioch and then the first Christian bishop of Rome before being martyred there.

* * *

Even before the death of Peter and Paul, it was becoming clear how the Jesus movement was developing. While increasing numbers of Gentiles in Syria and elsewhere in the Middle East were converting to the new Christian faith, the efforts of the remaining leaders and congregants of the original Christian church—the Jewish Christians—to convince significant numbers of other Jews that Jesus was the Messiah was proving unrewarding. Though they continued to adhere to Torah Law, they were ostracized, harassed, and increasingly isolated in Judaea. The priestly authorities in Jerusalem considered them a disruptive, heretical sect. The Apostle James the Greater was executed for blasphemy. Jesus's brother James was subsequently similarly charged with transgressing the law and stoned to death. According to the historian of the church Eusebius, a conclave of senior Jewish Christians then met in Jerusalem and chose Symeon, a cousin of Jesus, to succeed James as leader of the Jerusalem Church.

The Jewish Christians managed to survive as a small, tight-knit community despite the relentless pressures they were under. But as the anti-Roman national liberation movement grew increasingly volatile in Judaea, they were troubled by the rising tension in the land. As the Jews edged toward war with Rome, Symeon is said to have led his Jewish Christian congregants out of jittery Jerusalem to the city of Pella on the far side of the Jordan River.

Symeon remained titular head of the church and may have led his followers back to Judaea after the Romans crushed the Jewish rebellion in

70 CE. Eusebius writes that a succession of thirteen other bishops, "all of whom were said to have been of Hebrew descent," subsequently led the small Jewish Christian movement in Judaea.

However, the second insurrection of the Jews against Rome in 132 CE led by Simon Bar Kochba (called the Messiah by the most prominent rabbi of the period) further undermined the precarious survival of what remained of the Jerusalem Church. Its adherents may have been among the Jews expelled from Jerusalem by Emperor Hadrian after his legions stamped out the Bar Kochba uprising.

But that did not spell the end of the original Jesus movement. According to evangelical theologian Adolf Schlatter, "The Jewish church had died out only in Palestine west of the Jordan. In eastern regions, Christian communities with Jewish customs continued to exist . . . on the periphery of the Syrian desert and into Arabia [among other places], completely detached from Christianity and without fellowship with it." Small communities of Jewish Christians had already formed a diaspora of their own in the Middle East, some having existed in parts of Syria since the time Paul had scorned their forebears as "false brethren." Isolated congregations of them, sometimes called Nazarenes, clung to their Jewish identity. They considered themselves to be the true disciples of Jesus rather than the ever-greater numbers of Gentile converts to Pauline Christianity. They did not hold Jesus to have been divine, nor did they believe that Paul had been one of his true apostles. So-called Judaizers may have included Gentile converts to belief in Jesus who also chose to observe Torah law. The fundamental issue that distinguished the Jewish Christians from other Jews was their belief that Jesus was the Messiah.

Second-century Christian historian Irenaeus, testifying to their continued existence during his time, refers to them as Ebionites, who "repudiate the Apostle Paul, maintaining that he was an apostate from the Law. . . . They practice circumcision, persevere in the observance of customs which are enjoined by the Law, and are so Judaic in their style of life, that they even adore Jerusalem as if it were the house of God."

A century later Eusebius, who was Christian bishop of Caesarea as well as a historian, refers to them as heretics who regarded Jesus "as plain and ordinary, a man esteemed as righteous . . . and nothing more, the child of a normal union between a man and Mary, and they held that they must observe every detail of the Law." Theodoret, fifth-century bishop of Cyrrhus in Syria observes, "The Nazarenes are Jews. They honor Christ [only] as a righteous man and use the Gospel according to Peter."

Small isolated Ebionite communities survived in the Middle East well into the early centuries of the first millennium CE until they could no longer resist the pressures exerted by expanding Islam and Pauline Christianity. The theologian H. J. Schoeps suggests, "While Jewish Christianity was swallowed up in the Christian church, it preserved itself in Islam and some of its most powerful impulses extend down to the present day." That view was echoed by Hans Kung who maintains, "Jewish Christian communities . . . must have developed an influence which was to be of historic importance in Arabia in particular, through the Prophet Muhammad." The dietary laws of Muslims and their practice of male circumcision may provide partial evidence of that. But as a distinct entity, Jewish Christianity was swallowed into the fog of history.

Computer websites tell of the existence of present day Ebionites and messianic Jewish congregations that consider Jesus to have been the Messiah. They are the product of modern formulations rather than direct continuations of the scattered, bygone Jewish Christian communities of the Middle East that grew from the religious convictions and leadership of Jesus's brother James, Peter, and the Jerusalem Church.

# Notes

In these endnotes, the source listed as "Antiquities" refers to *Jewish Antiquities* by Josephus and the source listed as "War" refers to *The Jewish War* by Josephus.

Page

"The king of the Edomites": *Numbers*, 20.20.

2    "The Idumaeans are Nabataeans": Strabo, *Geography*, 2.34.

3    "Every man sat": *Book of the Maccabees*, 1.14.12.

11    "settled the government": *War*, 1.8.7.

19    "How long will you be quiet": *Antiquities*, 14.9.4.

20    "in a submissive manner": *ibid*.

22    "through unnatural relations": Suetonius, *The Lives of the Twelve Caesars*, Augustus, 68.

25    "a man who had distinguished himself": *Antiquities*, 14.11.4.

29    "She came sailing up": Plutarch, *Antony*, in *The Lives of Noble Greeks and Romans*.

29    "For her actual beauty": *ibid*.

33    "By biblical decree": Leviticus, 21.21.

37    "no small army": *Antiquities*, 14. 15.1.

40    "half-Jew": *ibid*., 15. 2.

41    "Their skill was that": *War*, 1.16.2.

45    "were cut to pieces": *ibid*., 18.2.

46    "This family was": *Antiquities*, 14.16.4.

46    "bend the minds of the Jews": *ibid*., 15.1.2.

48    "Do not abhor an Edomite": *Deuteronomy*, 23.7.

50    "with all possible respect": *Antiquities*, 15.2.4.

50    "Hasmonean complex": Kasher, 410.

57    "Neither political expediency": Galinsky, 174.

59    "doubtful and uncertain": Suetonius, *op. cit.*, 17.

60    "managed and dealt with": Cassius Dio, *Roman History*, 45.5.

61    "where people accustomed to servility": Craven, 23.

61    "Kings [of the lands]": Plutarch, *op. cit.*

61    "He posed with [Cleopatra]": Cassius Dio, *op. cit.*, 50:5.

62    "Were Antony serious or disposed": Plutarch, *op. cit.*

63    "make Cleopatra queen of Rome": Cassius Dio, *op. cit.*, 50:4.

64    "amorous messages": Plutarch, *op. cit.*

64    "whipped-up hysterical xenophobia": Green, Peter, *Alexander to Actium*, 678.

69    "busied in making a collection": Plutarch, *op. cit.*

69    "two Caesars were one too many": Green, *op. cit.*, 697.

70    "some legions and cohorts": Plutarch, *op. cit.*

72    "fitter [than Herod]": *War, op. cit.*, 22.1.

73    "I was made king": *ibid.*, 20.1.

76    "She's gone who shared my diadem": Lord Byron, *Herod's Lament, Hebrew Melodies.*

78    "mix among the multitude": *Antiquities*, 15.8.4.

79    "not only competent": Rocca, Samuel, *The Army of Herod the Great*, 14.

79    "At least one case is recorded": *ibid.*, 8.3.

82    "both of silver and gold": *ibid.*, 9.2.

82    "He had special attention:" *ibid.*

83    "There were neither any people": *ibid.*

83    "That which is hateful to you": *Babylonian Talmud*, Shabbath, 31a.

83    "was beloved . . . by Agrippa": *War, op. cit.*, 20.4.

85    "I have advanced the nation": *Antiquities*, 15.11.1.

85      "to correct that imperfection": *ibid.*

87      "It changed the way": McCane, Byron, *Simply Irresistible: Augustus, Herod and the Empire, Journal of Biblical Literature* 127, no. 4, 2008.

87      "money changers": *Matthew* 21.12.

87      "to enable Herod to receive": Netzer and Laureys-Chachy, 275.

87      "together in Solomon's Porch": *Acts*, 5.12.

88      "No man of another nation": Bickerman, Elias, *Jewish Quarterly Review*, April 1947, 348.

88      "a work of the greatest piety": *Antiquities, op. cit.*

88      "He who has not": *Babylonian Talmud*, Baba Batra, 4a.

88      "What wonderful stones": *Mark*, 13.1.

88      "The outward face": *War*, 5.5.6.

89      "by far the most famous city": Pliny the Elder, *Natural History*, 5.14.

90      "yet did he so fully struggle": *War*, 1.21.6.

91      "Herod's grasp of the realm": Netzer, xii.

91      "[H]is building enterprise": *ibid.*, 295.

92      "for [Herod's] beneficence": Jones, *The Herods of Judaea*, 100.

92      "originality of ideas": Netzer, 300.

92      "as famous abroad": Richardson, Peter, *Religion and Architecture: A Study of Herod's Piety, Power, Pomp and Pleasure, Bulletin* of the Canadian Society of Biblical Studies 45, 1985.

92      "It was a particular honor": *War*, 1.21.13.

93      "the dominions of Herod": *Antiquities*, 16.5.1.

96      "It is better to be Herod's pig": Macrobius, *Saturnalia*, 2.4.11.

97      "more friendly to the Greeks": *Antiquities*, 16.7.3.

98      "The craze for Hellenism": *Second Book of the Maccabees*, 4.14.

99      "pursued the wicked": *First book of the Maccabees*, 3.5.

104     "their [seeming] friends": *War*, 1.24.1.

107        "a kind brother": *ibid.*

109        "their common benefactor": *Antiquities*, 16.4.1.

113        "ready both to do": *ibid.*, 8.1.

113        "were become wild beasts": *ibid.*, 8.5.

119        "it was [Augustus's] intention": Strabo, *op. cit.*, 4.22.

119        "[Syllaeus] neither guided": *ibid.*, 23.

123        "gross wickedness": *War*, 1.26.2.

125        "did not readily make friends": Suetonius, *op. cit.*, 66.

130        "better grandfather": *War*, 1. 28.2.

134        "such a sort": *Antiquities*, 17.5.5.

137        "chief violence of his pain": *ibid.*, 6.5.

137        "Herod was very probably": Sandison, A. T., *The Last Illness of Herod the Great, Medical History*, October 1987.

138        "worms in his genitals": *New Scientist*, January 25, 2002.

138        "from a profound sense of inferiority": Kasher, 87.

141        "an insolent king": *Assumption of Moses*, 6.2.

141        "great barbarity towards all men": *Antiquities*, 17.8.1.

141        "brutality was not only normal": Wallace-Hadrill, Andrew, *The Roman Empire: The Paradox of Power*, BBC Ancient History project.

141        "just punishment": Eusebius, *The History of the Church*, 8.16.

142        "A mention of it": *Matthew*, 2.16.

143        "Oh, Miriamne": Lord Byron, *op. cit.*

143        "The preservation of order": Vickers, John, *The History of Herod*, xxiv.

143        "animated by a sincere desire": Morrison, William Douglas, *The Jews Under Roman Rule*, 77.

143        "an alien, a usurper": Jones, *The Herods of Judaea*, 154.

143        "Things are beginning": Auden, W. H., *For the Time Being: A Christmas Oratorio*.

143        "administrative vigor": Perowne, 176.

| | |
|---|---|
| 144 | "Despite a tradition that is unanimous": Sartre, 89. |
| 144 | "Thanks to [Herod]": Vermes, *Standpoint*, January/February 2011. |
| 144 | "simply [an extension] of the animosity": Sandmel, 262. |
| 144 | "sagacious and far-sighted": *History Today* 12, 1962. |
| 144 | "Herod . . . had the good": Richardson, 314. |
| 144 | "a practical and thorough man": Netzer, 306. |
| 144 | "renowned for his ruthless": McCane, *op. cit.* |
| 150 | "as though an enemy": *Antiquities*, 17.9.5. |
| 155 | "supreme power": *ibid.*, 18.1.1. |
| 161 | "for their kinship": Suetonius, *op. cit.*, Caligula, 26. |
| 162 | "to make amends": *Antiquities*, 18.8.7. |
| 163 | "he was not thought capable": Suetonius, *op. cit.*, Claudius, 2. |
| 163 | "a monster of a man": *ibid.*, 3. |
| 165 | "not to set a stranger": *Deuteronomy*, 17.15. |
| 167 | "most determined effort": Stern, M., *The World History of the Jewish People*, vol. 7, 139, editor Avi-Yonah, Michael. |
| 171 | "both horsemen and footmen": *Antiquities*, 20.8.10. |
| 171 | "This man might have been": *Acts*, 26.32. |
| 174 | "What sort of an army": *War*, 2.16.4. |
| 179 | "There were other Herodians": *Matthew*, 22.16; *Mark*, 3.6. |
| 181 | "thought as Jews": Vermes, Géza, *Christian Beginnings*, 81. |
| 181 | "Earliest Christianity was not yet seen": *Journal for the Study of the New Testament* 18, no. 5, 1983. |
| 181 | "four popular sects": Eusebius, *op. cit.*, 1.23.11. |
| 181 | "a matter of conflicting views today": see Vermes, Géza, *Christian Beginnings*; Goulder, Michael, *A Tale of Two Missions*; Wilson, Barrie, *How Jesus Became Christian*; Ehrman, Bart, *Lost Christianities*; et al. |
| 183 | "burning zeal for the law": *First Book of the Maccabees*, 2.58. |
| 183 | "Let everyone who is zealous": *ibid.*, 2. 27. |

183     "There would be no Satan": *Book of Jubilees*, 23.29.

183     "The days will come": Iranaeus, *Against Heresies*, 5.33.3.

184     "A time is coming": *Jeremiah*, 23.5.

184     "I will appoint a single shepherd": *Ezekiel*, 34.23.

184     "I am sending a messenger": *Malachi*, 3.1.

184     "a good man": *Antiquities*, 18.5.2.

185     "In the existing": Baron, Salo Wittmayer, *A Social and Religious History of the Jews*, vol. 2, 70.

186     "with one mind in the temple": *Acts*, 2.46.

186     "extremely zealous": *Galatians, 1.14.*

186     "beyond measure": *ibid.*, 13.

186     "entering house after house": *Acts*, 8.3.

187     "faith in Jesus": *Galatians*, 2.16.

187     "by God's power": *ibid.*, 8.

187     "Pretending to be believers": *Galatians*, 2.4.

188     "seemed to be [its] leaders": *ibid.*, 2.9.

188     "I opposed him in public": *ibid.*, 11–13.

188     "transformed [from] the God-centered": Vermes, *op. cit.*, 237.

188     "corrupter of the doctrines": *The Writings of Thomas Jefferson*, vol. 7, 156, editor H. A.Washington, 1854.

188     "new perspectives on Paul": see N. T. Wright, E. P. Sanders, Krister Stendahl, et al.

189     "rock" on which "I will build": *Matthew*, 16.18.

189     "disappears into legend": Goulder, Michael, *A Tale of Two Missions*, 188.

189     "chose Symeon": Eusebius, *op. cit.*, 3.11.

189     "city of Pella": *ibid.*, 3.5.

190     "all of whom were said": *ibid.*, 4.5.

190     "[T]he Jewish church had died out": Kung, Hans, *Islam: Past, Present and Future*, 42.

190     "false brethren": *Galatians*, 2.4.

190 "repudiate the Apostle Paul, Iranaeus": *op. cit.*, 1. 26.2.

190 "as plain and ordinary": Eusebius, *op. cit.*, 3.27.2.

190 "The Nazarenes are Jews": Pritz, Ray, *Nazarene Jewish Christianity*, 80.

191 "While Jewish Christianity was swallowed": Kung, Hans, *op. cit.*, 672.

191 "Jewish Christian communities . . . must have developed": *ibid.*, 42.

191 "Messianic Jewish congregations": *JewishJournal.com*, June 12, 2012.

# Select Bibliography

Avi-Yonah, Michael, ed. *The World History of the Jewish People: Ancient Times*. Vol. 7, *The Herodian Period*. London: W. H. Allen, 1975.

Brauer, Gerge C. *Judaea Weeping*. New York: Crowell, 1970.

Brodsky, Alyn. *The Kings Depart*. New York: Harper & Row, 1974.

Craven, Lucille. *Antony's Oriental Policy*. Columbia, MO: University of Missouri Press, 1920.

Eusebius. *The History of the Church*. http://rbedrosian.com.

Galinsky, Karl. *Cambridge Companion to the Age of Augustus*. Cambridge: Cambridge University Press, 2007.

Grant, Michael. *The Jews in the Roman World*. London: Weidenfeld & Nicolson, 1973.

Huzar, Eleanor Goltz. *Mark Antony*. Minneapolis: University of Minnesota Press, 1978.

Jacobson, David. *Herod and Augustus*. Leiden: Brill, 2008.

Jones, A. H. M. *Augustus*. New York: Norton, 1970.

———. *The Herods of Judaea*. Oxford: Clarendon Press, 1938.

Josephus. *Jewish Antiquities*. http://ccel.org.

———. *The Jewish War*. http://ccel.org.

Kasher, Aryeh, and Eliezer Witzum. *King Herod: A Persecuted Persecutor*. Berlin: Walter de Gruyter, 2007.

Kokkinos, Nikos. *The Herodian Dynasty*. London: Spink, 2010.

Levine, Lee. *Judaism and Hellenism in Antiquity*. Peabody, MA: Hendrickson, 1999.

Netzer, Ehud, and Rachel Laureys-Chachy. *The Architecture of Herod: The Great Builder*. Grand Rapids, MI: Baker Academic, 2008.

Perowne, Stewart. *The Life and Times of Herod the Great*. London: Arrow, 1960.

Plutarch. *The Lives of Noble Greeks and Romans*. http://plutarchpenelope.uchicago.edu.

Richardson, Peter. *Herod: King of the Jews and Friend of the Romans*. Columbia, SC: University of South Carolina Press, 1996.

Rocca, Samuel. *Herod's Judaea*. Tübingen: Mohr Siebeck, 2008.

Sandmel, Samuel. *Herod: Portrait of a Tyrant*. Philadelphia: Lippincott, 1967.

Sartre, Maurice. *The Middle East Under Rome*. Cambridge, MA: Harvard University Press, 2005.

Schuerer, Emil, Geza Vermes, and Fergus Millar. *The History of the Jewish People in the Age of Jesus Christ*. Vol. 1. Edinburgh: Clark, 1973.

Smallwood, Mary. *The Jews Under Roman Rule*. Leiden: Brill, 1976.

Stern, Menachem. *Greek and Lain Authors on Jews and Judaism*. Jerusalem: Israel Academy of Sciences & Humanities, 1976.

Suetonius. *The Lives of the Twelve Caesars*. http://suitoniuspenelope.uchicago.edu.

Zeitlin, Samuel. *Rise and Fall of the Judaean State*. Vol. 2. Philadelphia: Jewish Publication Society, 1962.

# Index

# About the Author

**Norman Gelb** is the author of a number of acclaimed books, including *Kings of the Jews: The Origins of the Jewish Nation*. He is a historian and freelance writer, who periodically contributes to publications such as *Smithsonian* magazine.